RACE, NATURE A

Anthropology, Culture and Society

Series Editors:
Professor Thomas Hylland Eriksen, University of Oslo
Dr Katy Gardner, University of Sussex
Dr Jon P. Mitchell, University of Sussex

RACE, NATURE AND CULTURE

An Anthropological Perspective

PETER WADE

Pluto Press
LONDON • STERLING, VIRGINIA

First published 2002
by PLUTO PRESS
345 Archway Road, London N6 5AA
and 22883 Quicksilver Drive,
Sterling, VA 20166–2012, USA

www.plutobooks.com

British Library Cataloguing in Publication Data
A catalogue record for this book is available from
the British Library

ISBN 0 7453 1459 7 hardback
ISBN 0 7453 1454 6 paperback

Library of Congress Cataloging in Publication Data
A catalogue record for this book is available

10   9   8   7   6   5   4   3   2   1

Designed and produced for Pluto Press by
Chase Publishing Services, Fortescue, Sidmouth EX10 9QG
Typeset from disk by Stanford DTP Services, Towcester
Printed in the European Union by Antony Rowe, Chippenham, England

CONTENTS

ACKNOWLEDGEMENTS

In writing this book, I ventured onto terrain that I was not initially very familiar with and I am grateful to many colleagues for help and suggestions about relevant reading matter, for sending me materials (some of them unpublished or still in press) and for exchanging emails and ideas about the themes I was working on. I would like to thank the following people, listed in alphabetical order: Linda Alcoff, Roberta Bivins, Susan Brems, Michael Bravo, Claudia Castañeda, William Dressler, Jeanette Edwards, Gillian Feeley-Harnik, Sarah Franklin, Sarah Green, Faye Harrison, Signe Howell, Tim Ingold, Barbara A. Koenig, Patricia A. Marshall, Kathryn Oths, Helena Ragoné, Ann Stoler, Marilyn Strathern, Elly Teman and Katharine Tyler.

My thanks are also due to Richard Wilson, who was one of the editors of this series when I began this project and first suggested that I write the book, and to the publishers at Pluto Press, Roger van Zwanenberg and Anne Beech.

I would also like to thank Laura Harrison for her sharp copy-editor's eye.

1 DEFINING RACE

Race is a topic of increasing concern to anthropologists. My contention in this book is that, although this is a welcome development, anthropologists – and other social scientists who study this subject – would benefit by focusing on a theme that hitherto has received little attention and yet that seems to be at the very centre of ideas about race. By reading across the disciplinary boundaries of the history of science, science studies, anthropological kinship studies and studies of race, I attempt to explore ideas about the nature of 'nature', that domain that seems to ground ideas about race and in relation to which scholars, either explicitly or implicitly, define a racial discourse. In a laudable, important and necessary way, scholars have tended to focus on questions of identity, politics and inequality when approaching race. In doing so, they have looked less thoroughly at ideas about human nature, 'blood', heredity, bodily substance, relatedness, biology and genes as they enter into discourses about race. Yet scholars still tend to define or recognise a racial discourse by the fact that it deploys these ideas (although this may not be the only defining criterion they use). These ideas thus tend to drop into a taken-for-granted, background position and this alone makes them ripe for a closer examination. Furthermore our understandings of identity, inequality and racism will be enhanced by a more nuanced grasp of the idioms of nature which are being used in expressing, creating and enacting these phenomena.

Social anthropology is well placed to advance such a study because it has a history of investigating ideas about nature, human relatedness, human bodily substances and what it is that makes people into people, linked (or not) to other people. Anthropology is not alone in its enquiries into human nature: historians and philosophers have also made major contributions as my use of some of their work in Chapter 3 will make apparent. Anthropology is useful in its ethnographic approach which reveals how concepts about human nature and biology are mediated through the realms of, for example, kinship. This gives a valuable insight into everyday ideas about these matters, as the material presented in Chapter 4 will show. Anthropology is also well placed for the work I want to pursue due to its inclination – shared with some other fields, including philosophy, history and feminism – to question apparently self-evident categories such as gender, nature and culture and reveal them as culturally mediated.

RACE IN ANTHROPOLOGY

Questions of race rather dropped out of post-war anthropology in Europe and the US. Prior to this anthropologists had made a mixed contribution to theories about race. On the one hand, some early anthropologists supported late-nineteenth-century and early-twentieth-century raciology or scientific racism, that is the dominant theories elaborated by scientists of the day – mostly medics and naturalists – that humans were divided into a few, distinctive racial types each with its own fairly ingrained or even immutable characteristics and all arranged in a stable moral, social and intellectual hierarchy in which white Europeans were at the top (F. Harrison, 1995, 1998; Shanklin, 1994, 1998; Smedley, 1993; Stocking, 1971, 1982). On the other hand, from the early twentieth century, anthropologists were among the most outspoken in denying a) that humans could be divided up systematically in this way, and b) that moral, social and intellectual capacities were linked in any significant way to race (as judged from appearance). The most famous among these revisionists is Franz Boas, but he was not alone in his endeavours – the black US sociologist, W.E.B. Du Bois, for example, was also a vocal opponent of racial typology (Baker, 1998; Harrison, 1992; Harrison and Harrison, 1999).

From the time of Boas onwards, scientific racism gradually weakened, although it continued to underwrite the eugenics movement – an alliance of social policy and science that aimed to restrict the breeding of 'races' seen as less 'fit' – which had its most explicit manifestation under Nazism (Kevles, 1995; Paul, 1995; Stepan, 1982). Within anthropology various views existed. Many still held that races existed as biological entities, asserting that human biodiversity could be usefully broken up into broad racial types, even though these were not very clearly bounded and had no relation to intellectual capability; in fact a number of biological and even cultural anthropologists hold such a view today (Lieberman and Reynolds, 1996). Others held that race had no biological reality at all, arguing that the history of human travel and sexual interaction has made it impossible to delineate any biological types. This is now a dominant view in social and cultural anthropology. In each argument, race is also said to exist as a purely social category or construction; even those who claim that the concept of race captures some aspect of biological reality may also concede that race can exist in popular thought as a social construction. In the social constructionist view, race is a way people think about some aspects of human difference which has no basis in biological reality, but which, interweaving with inequalities of colonialism, class and gender, generates its own very potent social reality of racism, discrimination, racial identities and so on (F. Harrison, 1995, 1998; Shanklin, 1994, 1998; Smedley, 1993).

Meanwhile, within mainstream anthropology, questions of race and racism were not major concerns. One might have thought that the issue would rear its head for European and North American anthropologists working in colonial or neocolonial contexts before 1945, but, as is well known, these researchers tended to focus on particular communities, whether within an explicitly functionalist framework or not; they did not grapple a great deal with the power politics, much less the racial politics, of colonialism. After the Second World War the notion of race faded even further from anthropology's research horizon. It was generally replaced by the notion of ethnicity which, by referring to people's ideas about cultural difference, seemed to avoid all the nasty baggage that the concept of race brought with it (Harrison, 1998). The concept of race lived on in sociology, both in the UK and the US, where the sub-discipline of 'race relations' emerged. This speciality had been around for some time in the US, based largely on the work of such sociologists as Robert Park, although anthropologists including W. Lloyd Warner and Hortense Powdermaker also made important contributions to work on race in the US while others also wrote on race in Latin America.[1] In the UK it was the post-war immigration from the ex-colonies that spurred such a concern. However, anthropologists, who still defined themselves very much as students of 'other cultures', saw little need to dabble in questions of race 'at home'.

In the 1990s race made something of a comeback in anthropology, especially in the US. The American Anthropological Association (AAA) decreed that its theme for 1997–98 would be 'Is it "Race"? Anthropology on Human Diversity' and its *Anthropology Newsletter* published over 70 articles on race in that period.[2] The AAA produced a statement on race[3] and *American Anthropologist* produced two issues focusing on race, in September 1997 (vol. 99, no. 3) and September 1998 (vol. 100, no. 3). A growing body of anthropological literature is emerging.[4] It is difficult to say why this resurgence of race has occurred in anthropology. It may be that, since it never really went away in sociology and has been a strong feature of the burgeoning field of Cultural Studies on both sides of the Atlantic, the concept of race has new appeal to European and North American anthropologists now less sure of their separation from these disciplines, partly due to their increased willingness to study 'at home'. It may also be that anthropologists feel obliged to face up to the resurgence in 'scientific' racism – which continues to make claims about links between race and IQ, for example (see Kohn, 1995; Reynolds and Lieberman, 1996) – and the continued or even increasing virulence of racism in many areas. Or it may be that the concept of race has been lent a new, more critical edge by decolonisation, the rise of post-colonial studies and the growth of social movements some of which make use of racial identifications. Whatever the exact reasons, the resurgence of race in the discipline of social anthropology invites a consideration of the concept and of whether existing approaches in anthropology might shed light on it.

WHAT IS RACE?

If the concept has persisted in many areas of social research and, in particular, has returned to the fold of anthropological ideas, then it is important to be clear about what it means. I do not want to pre-empt the argument of this book by laying all my cards on the table now, because part of my argument is that current definitions of 'race', although they seem to vary, generally reproduce some unexamined assumptions which need unpacking. But I think it will help the reader if I give a general idea of what social scientists say they are looking at when they study race – or racial identities, or racism, or racialisation, or racial formation. This in turn will indicate the direction of my concerns.

Race is generally agreed to be a social construction. Few take issue with this, but it begs the question of what kind of social construction is a *racial* one? Sometimes analysts do not address the question. Harrison, for example, in an excellent review article on race, gives no definition as such, although she implies that racial discourse builds on physical difference – specifically mentioning phenotype or physical appearance – while racism is defined as practices perpetuating oppressive power relations between populations presumed to be 'essentially different' (F. Harrison, 1995: 51, 65) or, in a later article, 'essentially and irreconcilably different' (1998: 613). The idea of 'essential difference' is left unexplored. What is an essence in human terms? How do we know an essentialist differentiation when we see one? Are all essentialist differentiations racial ones? How about gendered essentialisms, for example? If differences are said to be ingrained but not really 'irreconcilable', does that mean they are not 'racial' differences?

That aside – for the moment (see below) – Harrison's reference to phenotype is a common one, as bodily appearance is often taken to be the raw material on which concepts of race are built. I examined this assumption at some length in a previous text (Wade, 1993b), so I will not dwell long on it here. My main point in that article was that phenotype is often taken to be a neutral, objective biological fact on which social constructions build. But, as analysts such as Haraway (1989, 1991, 1997) have argued, there can be no pre-discursive encounter with biology or nature. Thus the phenotype that is taken to underlie race is, in fact, itself a social construction (see also Miles, 1989: 71; Omi and Winant, 1994: 55). After all, phenotype includes all aspects of appearance – actually it includes more even than that[5] – so why do specific aspects come to signify race: particular variations in skin colour rather than height; particular types of hair, rather than eye colour; specific facial features, rather than muscularity? The answer is that only some aspects of phenotype are worked into *racial* signifiers and they are the aspects that were originally seen to be ways of distinguishing between Europeans and those they encountered in their colonial explorations. 'Phenotype' is thus linked to a particular history.

This suggests two things, which I did not explore fully in that article. First, if phenotype is admittedly an important feature in knowing what the concept of race is, then we have to enquire into how phenotype is socially constructed in different contexts. This has attracted a fair amount of attention in comparisons between different regions of the Americas, since a person with a given racialised phenotype may be 'black' in the US and *moreno* (brown) or *mestizo* (mixed) or even *blanco* (white) in Colombia. In Brazil a person called by a given colour term in one class context may be labelled with a term denoting lighter colour – and apparently may even be perceived as such – if s/he looks wealthier. Meanwhile, in the Andes, the same person might be *indio* or *indígena* (Indian or indigenous) and *mestizo* or *ladino* (mixed, non-indigenous), depending on social context, speech, clothing and so on.[6] These facts are well known, but they have been deployed in specific, and limited, ways. For Brazil, the variability of racial labelling has generally been taken to show that 'class' is more important in defining social status than 'race' – a conclusion always drawn in comparison to the US where the opposite is said to apply. The phenomenon has been placed in a debate about the theoretical and empirical relations between race and class, rather than in a consideration of how racialised phenotypes are constructed differently in different regions. In the Andes the variation in labelling has often been taken to indicate that it is a question of 'ethnicity' not 'race', since, apparently by definition, racial identities are held to be permanent and not malleable (see Wade, 1997: 37–9). Again, this prejudges what is racial and what is not.

Outside of these American comparisons, the social construction of phenotype has been given less attention in the study of race. It is as if this apparent malleability of race is just a Latin American or Caribbean phenomenon. Often, indeed, it is said or implied that racial identifications 'fix' social classifications, since they use physical markers and refer to 'nature' and something 'innate' which are both said – I think wrongly – to necessarily imply permanence (see below). It may well be that, in particular contexts, racial identifications work to create unyielding and enduring classifications, but this would be a social process and the result of a specific history, not the automatic result of a reference to phenotype or nature. All this implies the need to include in the study of race a broad approach to embodiment which problematises the notion of phenotype. I will return to this in Chapter 6. At the least, if phenotype is not a self-evident phenomenon, it seems inadequate to use reference to it as the self-evidently diacritical feature of a *racial* social construction.

Second, the argument that phenotype became racialised in a historical process also suggests that the aspects of appearance that came to signify race had something special about them. Not only did they correlate in some perceptually intuitive way with the geographical differences that Europeans were encountering and mapping – Alcoff (1996) has an interesting point about the visual nature of both mapping places and seeing races – but they had some continuity over time and across generations. This implies that reference to phenotype is actually not the only thing that makes a social construction a racial one. Many analysts go beyond phenotype to note that racial or racist discourse refers to 'physical difference' or 'biology', without necessarily specifying which of the many aspects of these very broad categories are at issue (phenotype? genotype?); others are more specific, focusing on racial discourse's reference to descent or heritage; or they focus on reference to innateness and essence, with the implication, at least, that these are thought to be heritable.[7]

Harrison (1998: 613), for example, implies that racism exists when 'categories of human beings are subjugated or privileged because of differences purported to be fundamentally natural and/or biophysical'. A more explicit definition, which combines an appeal to phenotype with 'biology' more broadly and also notions of heritage, holds that:

> Race is one way by which the boundary is to be constructed between those who can and those who cannot belong to a particular construction of a collectivity or population. In the case of race, this is on the basis of an immutable biological or physiognomic difference which may or may not be seen to be expressed mainly in culture or life-style, but is always grounded on the separation of human populations by some notion of stock or collective heredity of traits. (Anthias and Yuval-Davis, 1992: 2)

In this view, a racial identification is one based on reference to immutable physiognomy or biology, and/or on some 'notion' of heredity. The thrust of the definition is familiar enough, but a little critical thought shows that it is not clear a) whether physiognomy (outward appearance) is an alternative to biology or some subcategory of it; b) whether both physiognomic difference and a notion of heredity have to be involved; c) whether physiognomy and biology are objective and self-evident, while heredity is a subjective 'notion'. This definition also brings in the idea of 'immutability'. It is quite common to assert that racial identifications imply fixity and permanence. (I myself made this argument some years ago; see Wade, 1985.) Often the implicit or explicit argument is that this is a result of making reference to biology, heredity and physical difference. Smedley, for example, notes that racial ideology 'imposed social meanings on physical variations among human groups' and that the ideology about the meaning of these differences is 'based on a notion of heredity and permanence' (1998: 693). Harrison's mention of essential and irreconcilable difference also has strong overtones of fixity. Goldberg (1993: 81) notes that 'race gives to social relations the veneer of fixedness', while Guillaumin (1995: 143) argues that the reference race makes to nature 'proclaims the permanence of the effects of certain social relations on dominated groups'.

It seems to me, however, wrong to assume that biology and heredity are, in themselves, fixed and permanent things and I would even question whether the discursive invocation of them necessarily entails notions of permanence. The human organism is in a constant state of change; sexual reproduction involves the random recombination of parental genetic

material, not its fixed transmission. If permanence is involved in racial identifications, perhaps we should look more to social processes – to how these
notions of permanence came about – rather than assuming it is the automatic
result of a reference to 'biology'. This in turn suggests that not all racial identifications have to connote fixity and permanence, which is precisely the case
in Latin America.

Another problem with defining race by its reference to biology is that, in
fact, this is non-specific. Shanklin (1994) spends a substantial part of her
book showing that race is a social construct, not a biological reality, and also
shows that many textbook definitions, while apparently allowing this, seem
to smuggle notions of biological reality back in (see also Shanklin, 1998).
She herself, very clear on race as a social construction, is less clear about
what kind of social construction it is and how we can distinguish it from
other folk concepts which classify people. It is perhaps not important for her
to clarify this because she wants to discard the concept and retain instead
the concept of racism, which she defines as 'a special kind of prejudice,
directed against those who are thought to possess biologically or socially
inherited characteristics that set them apart' (1994: 105). I will deal below
with the addition of the word 'socially' – what kind of prejudice would not be
racial under this definition? – but even confining things to 'biology' hardly
helps. Prejudice against women, if they were thought to have common
inherited traits, would be an example of racism.

Goldberg (1993) takes an even broader approach. For him, the notion of
race is a specifically modern one; it emerges in the early modern period and
changes over time:

Race is not a static concept with a single sedimented meaning. Its power has consisted
in its adaptive capacity to define population groups and, by extension, social agents
as self and other at various historical moments. It has thus facilitated the fixing of
characterisations of inclusion and exclusion, imparting to social relations an apparent
specificity otherwise lacking. To be capable of this, race itself must be almost, but not
quite, empty in its own connotative capacity, able to signify not so much in itself but
by adopting and extending naturalised form to prevailing conceptions of social group
formation at different times. (1993: 80)

Goldberg specifically challenges the argument that 'ideas about race are
inherently committed to claims about biological inheritance, whether of
physical or intellectual or moral characteristics' (1993: 72). Like many
others, he refers to the fact that in the post-war era, what some have labelled
'cultural racism' has emerged in which, for example, ex-colonial migrants
to the UK (Gilroy, 1987) or Maoris in New Zealand (Wetherell and Potter,
1992) are referred to by majority whites in terms of their cultural difference,
rather than supposed biological features: race is 'coded as culture' and
'stands for specific forms of cultural connectedness and solidarity' (Goldberg,
1993: 73; see also Balibar, 1991a; Stolcke, 1995). (Unlike many others,
Goldberg (1993: 70–1) recognises that this slippage between biology and

culture is not just a post-war phenomenon, but stretches back into the eighteenth century.) Shanklin's inclusion of 'socially inherited characteristics', noted above, is clearly aimed at dealing with this cultural racism. Harrison (1998: 613), although she links racism to a discourse of natural and/or biophysical difference, also states that the quality of difference can be constructed in a 'biodeterminist or culturalist idiom'. In all cases, if the (apparent) specificity of 'nature' or 'biology' is abandoned to include cultural racism, it becomes increasingly hard to see what racism is, as distinct from other forms of discrimination. Class discrimination would be classifiable as racist if 'socially inherited characteristics' or difference in a 'culturalist idiom' were the defining feature. (Anthias and Yuval-Davis, by the way, who retain a definition of race as referring specifically to physical difference alone, get around the problem of cultural racism by defining racism as prejudice or discrimination not against 'races', but against ethnic groups (1992: 12), themselves defined as 'various forms of ideological construct which divide people into different collectivities and communities' (1992: 3) – hardly a very specific definition and one which again means any form of discrimination and prejudice by one collectivity against another is racism!)

I am sympathetic to the open approach to race as a concept taken by Goldberg and others in the attempt to construct a theory of race and racism that includes cultural racism. It is very difficult to come up with a transcendental or transhistorical definition which includes all the things 'we' intuitively want to include as 'racial': the classification by Europeans of blacks, whites, 'Indians' (i.e., indigenous Americans), and Asians might seem obvious. Should we include ideas about the Jews and Irish and, if so, ideas from which historical period? How about the way Spanish Christians classified Moors and Jews after the Reconquista in fifteenth-century Spain, classifications based on notions of *limpieza de sangre* (cleanliness of the blood)? What about the way the Chinese saw white people in the nineteenth century?[8] Where do we draw the line? How do we know what is 'racial' and what not? Goldberg says: 'By "race" and "racial" I will refer throughout to the various designations of group differentiation invoked in the name of race throughout modernity' (1993: 2). But if people refer, at least publicly, to cultural or 'ethnic' rather than 'racial' difference, as he notes they do, then such references could not easily be included in the concept of race, except by the tricky tactic of arguing that such difference is 'invoked in the name of race' even though race is, precisely, not named.

In addition, then, Goldberg reverts to a notion of physical difference, but he adopts a minimalist approach – race is 'almost, but not quite empty'. Its content is 'naturalisation' which he distinguishes from biologisation: 'The minimal significance race itself bears does not concern biological but naturalised group relations' (1993: 81). This emphasis on naturalisation is adopted by others as well (see Gilroy, 1982: 281; Guillaumin, 1995: 133; Hirschfeld, 1996: 35; Yanagisako and Delaney, 1995: 20), although some people use the term nature as more or less equivalent to biology. This emphasis also helps ground the notion of cultural racism. As Wieviorka (1997: 142) says, if people refer only to 'nation, religion, traditions and, more generally, culture, with no references to nature, biology, genetic heritage or blood, it is preferable not to speak of racism'.

But what is naturalisation and how does it differ from biologisation? Goldberg (1993: 81) states that naturalisation involves establishing and rationalising 'the order of difference as a law of nature' and that the law 'may be of human and not merely biological nature', but he does not elaborate further. Now, if anthropologists know one thing, it is that conceptions of 'nature' are not self-evident. One of the reasons why so many analysts make reference to biology when defining race is probably that, from the emergence of biology as a discipline in Europe in the early 1800s, scientific and then popular opinions in the West have increasingly seen (human) nature as being coterminous with 'biology', although as biology-the-discipline changes its views on what the mechanisms of biology-as-organic-processes consist of, even this does not give us a stable view of human nature. In any event, if we recognise that notions of 'nature' are subject to historical and, doubtless, geographical variation, then it begs some pretty big questions to use 'naturalisation' as the defining feature which tells us when we are dealing with race. Furthermore one might be tempted to say that gendered constructions could equally well be seen as based on 'naturalisation'.

This has hardly been an exhaustive review of different attempts to define race, but it serves to indicate some common practices in this endeavour. On the one hand, analysts are very aware of the historical specificity and variability of the concept. Race is seen as linked to a specific European history and, within that, to have varied substantially. Many people are similar to Banton (1987) in tracing the different ways people have used and understood the term since the fourteenth century when the words *raza* (Spanish) and *razza* (Italian) appeared in Europe (see also Goldberg, 1993; Shanklin, 1994; Stepan, 1982). Briefly, Banton outlines the concept of 'race as lineage', when, from about 1500 to 1800, the term was used to refer to the descendants of a common ancestor. For example, 'the race of Abraham' would include all his descendants, whatever their appearance. In about 1800 there was a shift to 'race as type', when the concept began to assume the form it took in late-nineteenth-century scientific racism. There is dispute about when the discourse of race can properly be said to have emerged – Hirschfeld (1996: 33–4) usefully sets out the different arguments that pinpoint the pre-modern era and the sixteenth, seventeenth, eighteenth and nineteenth centuries as the crucial epochs – but all are agreed that it varies historically.

On the other hand, most analysts also want to find some underlying unity, whether for race or racism, that will allow us to know when we are confronting race or racism in any of its varied forms. As I have shown, analysts often solve this problem by seeing racial discourse as referring to such terms as phenotype, heritage, biology and naturalisation. Dikötter (1992: viii–ix) provides a good example of the tension between admitting the variability of race and wanting to ground it on some basic criterion. He says that 'a history of racial discourse can only adopt a nominalist approach: it describes how "race" has been defined and how these definitions have changed historically'. However, he has to have a means of knowing when he is looking at something 'racial', especially as he is working on Chinese thought over many centuries where there is no simple equivalent of 'race'. Therefore he adds: 'I translate by "race" ... terms that appear to stress the biological rather than the sociocultural aspects of different people.' Generally speaking, there is little attention paid to what is signified by terms such as biology, or phenotype of nature. The problem is solved only at the price of taking such terms for granted. In Dikötter's case, his apparently simple definition runs into trouble when he goes on to argue that in ancient China there was not a clear distinction between biology and culture, which must make it hard to judge whether one of these aspects is being stressed more than the other (Dikötter, 1992: 3).

This is not to say that no attention has been paid to terms such as biology and nature. Scholars such as Banton (1987), Hodgen (1964), Stepan (1982, 1991) and Stocking (1982) look in some detail at how scholars of previous centuries thought about human variation over place and time (see Chapter 3 for an extended discussion). But this does not always help us to fully grasp what they thought about human nature and what it might mean to say they were practising 'naturalisation'. For example, Banton (1987: 22) describes the work of James Prichard (1786–1848), 'the most respected writer on questions of race after [the German anatomist] Blumenbach'. Prichard was interested in 'the modifying influence of physical and moral agencies on the different tribes of the human family' – the subtitle of his five-volume *Natural History of Mankind* – without, Banton argues, positing any radical opposition between nature and culture. Prichard rejected the idea that characteristics acquired during a lifetime could be transmitted to offspring (a theory sustained by his French naturalist contemporary, Lamarck), yet he also recognised that children differed from their parents in unpredictable ways. But none of this helps us to really understand what Prichard thought human nature was or how offspring were connected to their forebears. It is clear, from Banton's account, that he saw some 'natural' connection, the mechanism of which was sexual reproduction, and that he also saw that the environment had some impact on humans, both in their physical constitution and their social organisation, but that is about as far as we get.

Banton discusses how Blumenbach also puzzled over how some traits were passed down across generations, while others were not. According to Banton, he thought that 'the genital liquid interacted with other material to produce a formative force which resulted in the normal reproduction of the animal or the plant unless it was deflected in some way', for example by climatic factors or dietary regimes (1987: 6). This is more specific stuff, and it indicates that if we want to assert that Blumenbach was thinking in a 'racial' way because he referred to 'heredity' or 'human nature' in explaining what we would now call human 'cultural' difference, we would have to tie this down to what *he* meant by human nature. It seems he did think in terms of a human essence, or genital liquid, which was passed down by sexual reproduction, but which was also influenced by the environment in the way it defined the living organism – at the least, then, he did not see human essence as immutable. But, by anthropological standards, this is a rather sketchy outline of his overall theory of human heredity and human nature. If we are going to define race in terms of a discourse that refers to nature and heredity (and phenotype), it makes sense to have a fuller picture of what these are in different historical and social contexts.

This is all the more important when we move into the twentieth century. Here, as I have shown, many analysts seem content to refer to a discourse about 'biology' as the defining feature of a racial construction. Now if among biologists it is less than clear what human nature is, biologically speaking, then it seems likely that the matter is not clear-cut for the lay public either. If, for the seventeenth century, we can pursue an analysis of the writings of medics, naturalists and other literate specialists, with less access to how the general populace thought about human nature, we have more resources at our disposal for the twentieth century. We can delve into lay understandings of race from the point of view of public understandings of human nature, sexual reproduction, heredity, genetics, 'blood', and so on. With science and associated technologies making innovative and dramatic interventions into the realm of nature with new reproductive technologies and genetic modifications, it may be that public ideas about what 'nature' is are being challenged in ways that might well have an important bearing on how the nature of race is conceived (Franklin, Lury and Stacey, 2000; Strathern, 1992b).

It seems to me that anthropology is poised to make a useful contribution here. The interface between nature and culture has long been a central concern of the discipline and this has involved delving into what these categories consist of for different peoples. As a result, anthropologists (as well as historians of ideas and science) have been important in questioning the taken-for-granted usage of Western notions of nature and culture (MacCormack and Strathern, 1980; Strathern, 1992a; Yanagisako and Delaney, 1995). Kin relations have been the bread and butter of anthropologists' understandings of social relations and this has involved them in extended investigations into how different peoples think generations are connected to each other and what makes someone into a relative ('blood' or some other type of bodily substance?, co-residence?, commensality?, nurturing?). Kinship studies have also enquired whether there is some kind of objective, 'biological' reality of kinship underlying all the cultural variations on the theme – paralleling the idea that reference to 'biology' or 'nature' underlies the varied social constructions of race (Carsten, 2000a; Franklin and McKinnon, forthcoming; Schneider, 1980, 1984; Yanagisako and Delaney, 1995). Again, anthropologists have been prominent in the study of the impact of new reproductive technologies (Edwards *et al.*, 1993; Franklin,

1997; Franklin and Ragoné, 1998; Rapp, 1999; Strathern, 1992b). Anthropologists have also been interested in the constitution of personhood and the
question of what makes a 'person'. This involves interrogating issues of the
origin and development of people in ways that are of great relevance to the
study of race, since it involves looking at where people are thought to come
from, how they become as they are and how they are connected to others
(e.g., Lambek and Strathern, 1998; Loizos and Heady, 1999).

In sum, social anthropology has a number of tools in its box which can
serve in thinking about race, nature and culture. If we want to include in
the study of race an enquiry into ideas about what human nature is and how
it is constituted (through, for example, heredity and upbringing); and into
ideas about what bodily substances (if any) are shared in racial identities and
how genealogy constructs racial identity, then anthropological accounts of
such ideas in relation to kinship, personhood and human reproduction can
be of great assistance. For example, as I discuss in Chapter 4, such accounts
illustrate that nature is a changing social construct; its significance cannot
be taken for granted. Recent studies of new reproductive technologies also
show that nature is not seen by European and American people as a simple
fixed entity, but is in constant tension with ideas of culture. These studies
also suggest that the way people live through their bodies affects the nature
of their bodies: the body is not just a natural given that a person lives 'in', it
is an ongoing process of performance. Again, then, a clear division between
nature and culture is brought into question. These seem to me important
conclusions in exploring ideas of race and probing deeper into what the naturalising discourses that race involves actually mean and how they operate.

CONCLUSION

So what *is* race? Are we now any closer to a coherent idea? How do we
resolve the dilemma of recognising the variety of things we want to class as
'racial' while defining what makes them in some sense related? I do not think
that there is a simple answer to this question and, in any case, it is not my
purpose to produce a neat, exhaustive, watertight definition of race which
would allow us to determine which of all past, present and future phenomena
can be classed as 'racial'. In fact I think such an endeavour is impossible to
accomplish. Social phenomena are not amenable to that type of Platonic
essentialist classification into mutually exclusive and exhaustive categories.
As a broad guide, I think it is right to say that racial discourse is a historically changing phenomenon that emerged in the context of European
expansion and colonialism from the fourteenth century and that built on
existing ideas about human similarity and diversity across geographical
space and over time (i.e., the continuities and changes between generations).
These ideas were in a constant state of change and were themselves
influenced by, at times almost coterminous with, racial discourse. It is these

ideas that are referred to when analysts talk about biology, descent, heredity, phenotype, blood and nature. It would be useful to historicise and unpack some of these ideas in more detail, rather than using them as a set of vague diacritical features of what a racial discourse is.

The focus must be more on history than on 'phenotype' or 'biology' per se. Of course I would be doing an injustice to all the writers mentioned so far if I implied that they were indifferent to history. As I mentioned above, analysts of race are very aware of the historically specific nature of the concept of race and the fact that it derives from a European history of colonisation and subjugation of non-European others. Smedley (1993, 1998), for example, argues persuasively that, although physical variation among humans was noted by pre-modern peoples (at least those for whom we have records), it was not accorded much social significance.[9] Smedley says that in the eighteenth century a 'new mode of structuring inequality in human societies evolved in the American colonies and spread from there' (1998: 694). This mode, developed largely by the English in North America and growing out of their peculiar ethnocentrism – itself honed by English colonisation of the 'savage' Irish – called upon 'the model of the Chain of Being, and using natural differences in physical features ... created a new form of social identity' (Smedley, 1998: 694).[10] Race 'imposed social meanings on physical variation among human groups that served as the basis for the structuring of the total society' and the 'meaning of these differences [was and is] based on a notion of heredity and permanence that was unknown in the ancient world and the Middle Ages' (Smedley, 1998: 693).

There are specific points at which I question Smedley's account. It is rather Anglocentric in attributing the development of notions of race more or less entirely to the English. The role of other European colonists – particularly the Spanish and the Portuguese – is marginalised here. It also assumes that race, or a 'racial worldview', is defined in essence by its manifestation in North America (and Europe) in the eighteenth, nineteenth and early twentieth centuries. Prior and subsequent forms of racialised thinking, and those characteristic of other regions, are implicitly judged in relation to this apogee, when race structured 'the total society' and was seen as permanent. Nevertheless the general drift of her argument is sound in linking colonialism and the emergence of the notion of race. My concern here is rather with the notion of 'physical variation', as if this were an unproblematic category onto which meanings were, or were not, imposed. The question is: what constituted 'physical variation' for different peoples at different times and in different places? Surely we need to know about this if it was the basis onto which the social meanings of race were inscribed. This involves more than asking what meanings were attributed to physical variation, because that assumes that we already know what the significant aspects of physical variation were for, say, medieval monks in Europe, or sixteenth-century Spanish colonists. If we look at Linnaeus' eighteenth-century sub-classifications of the genus *Homo*, we see that what a twentieth-century Western observer would call biophysical and cultural attributes are mixed up apparently indiscriminately in defining species of Homo (Hodgen, 1964: 425; see also Chapter 3). So what constituted physical variation for Linnaeus? Is culture being naturalised by Linnaeus, or nature culturalised?

This then has implications for Smedley's reference to a 'notion of heredity and permanence'. She raises the issue of permanence because social meanings were being ascribed to traits seen as physical and heritable. But why assume that physicality and heritability mean permanence? They might do, but it would be nice to demonstrate this for a given social context, rather than assume it as a defining feature of race. And, if the boundary between nature and culture is put in question – that is, it is unclear what is 'social meaning' and what 'physical variation' – then permanence becomes a less obvious diacritical marker of a racial situation.

Race is not subject to a final, bounded definition. This, however, does not mean we cannot investigate it in useful ways. Phenotype, naturalisation and biology are important aspects of understanding what race is. Nevertheless we should not use these as easy definitions but should interrogate what they mean in specific contexts. The analytic language we use to think about race and contest racism must itself be constantly subject to scrutiny. The modern understanding of race as a social construction bears witness to the fact that this scrutiny is an inherent, if not straightforward, part of the tradition of social science. My argument is that we should turn that scrutinising gaze onto some of the categories that – at least in the study of race – seem to have resisted it thus far, such as phenotype, nature, biology, blood and heredity.

My own partial and preliminary attempt to do this, in the central chapters of this book, reveals a long-standing tension between fixity and fixability, or between permanence and change, in ideas about human nature. Racial ideas do make reference to human biology, nature and phenotype, but these ideas do not always straightforwardly invoke fixity and permanence. This means that what may appear to be a discourse of fixity may actually allow a measure of malleability and change, but it also means that a discourse of malleability can acquire meanings of permanence. A racial discourse need not be as deterministic as it may appear, but it can also be more determinis-tic. When nature, biology and human essence are seen as not permanently fixed, while always potentially connoting fixedness, then the strategic invocation of these things by racial discourse becomes harder to pin down and more insidious. The nature–culture dichotomy is a dualist construct in which the divide between the two sides is not only subject to historical change but also to strategic manipulations that at any given period deploy ideas of naturalness and culturedness in varying ways. A key feature of a racial discourse is not simply that it naturalises, or biologises, but that it allows strategic equivocation between nature and culture. It is a discourse that, for example, allows room for culturalisation – 'Oh well', white English people might say of a woman of Afro-Caribbean parents, raised in the UK, 'she was brought up here in England, so we hardly see her as one of them' –

but also leaves open the door for re-naturalisation in particular circumstances – 'Well, after all, she *is* one of them.'

This allows us to see that the apparent shift from 'biological' to 'cultural'
racism that many scholars have noted is less straightforward than it might
appear. Both forms of racism involve the naturalisation of culture and the
culturalisation of nature: this dual dynamic makes it unclear what is being
talked of as natural and what cultural in a given context and thus provides
the possibility of seeing the natural as cultural and the cultural as natural.
People's invocations of culture are liable to summon up ideas of natural
essence and 'blood', while invocations of nature may involve ideas of change
and instability. Other scholars have noted that cultural racism may involve
a masked or coded reference to nature (Gilroy, 1987: 61; Goldberg, 1993:
81; Wieviorka 1997: 142), but they do not give us a great deal of insight
into what such a naturalising idiom involves. Enquiry into what 'nature'
(and blood, genes and biology) mean in a given context helps us to see the
flexible ways racial discourses work.

It will be apparent by now that I am placing some emphasis on the
flexibility of racial discourses and also questioning whether such discourses
automatically invoke and impose permanence and fixity. The obvious
objection to this approach is that the whole significance of dominant
discourses of race is precisely that they *do* ascribe to categories of people
certain fixed characteristics that are said to be natural and therefore
permanent. Why, then, am I apparently questioning this obvious feature of
racist formations? Racial discourses can and do create and impose fixity and
a key element in this strategy is an appeal to the realm of nature. However,
racial discourses make this appeal in subtle and changeable ways. We need
to explore what is involved in an appeal to nature and to grasp the diversity
of naturalising arguments which may go beyond genetics and biology. An
appeal to nature in this wider sense does not automatically involve a simple
idea of permanence: human nature and human essences may be seen as
changeable. But racism can also exploit precisely that flexibility to denigrate
and exclude people in varied ways. To give an example of this: people might
be seen as being racially 'contaminated' by their environment in ways that
are said to affect their nature. Here human nature is not simply seen as an
eternal unchanging essence (which may or may not be perceived as rooted
'in the genes'). Although human natures may be seen as quite ingrained,
they are also seen as changeable and flexible. Racism can exploit this
diversity of ideas about nature in ways that have not yet been explored.

2   EXISTING APPROACHES TO RACE

In the previous chapter I looked at contemporary trends in defining race, unpacking some unexamined assumptions. In this chapter I look at the way analysts of race are approaching their subject matter and suggest that advances can be made by taking a line rather different from those which are currently being pursued. One advance is in the arena of anti-racism. The reintegration of the study of race into anthropology partly obeys an anti-racist rationale. As Harrison (1998: 623) observes: 'After an extended hiatus, anthropology has again reached a moment in its history when it cannot evade the pervasive power of racism.' There is a direction for the investigation of race which anthropology is well placed to pursue and which can advance the underlying agenda of anti-racism. This involves grasping how people, in everyday practice, understand notions such as nature, 'blood', genetics, physiognomy and embodiment and how they relate these things to ideas about racial identities. This can give us a better comprehension of how racism operates, why it persists so strongly in the face of extended scientific critiques of the notion of race as a biological reality, and how it relates to more general ideas about human nature and human kinship and relatedness.

In this chapter I will examine different broad approaches to understanding race, distinguishing, for the sake of argument, between a) race and social stratification; b) race and identity; and c) race in the history of (scientific) ideas. These are, naturally, heuristic divisions and many studies involve elements of all three, with links between the first two being particularly strong.

RACE AND SOCIAL STRATIFICATION

Given the origins of ideas about race in a history of European colonialism, it is not surprising that race as a field of study has been strongly affected by theories about power, inequality, political economy, class and social stratification. It is not my intention to review and evaluate all these different theoretical approaches to race.[1] Instead I wish to indicate their general area of concern and the kinds of debates they have been engaged in.

One central debate in this field has been over the relationship between race and class, focusing on the theoretical question of the extent to which 'race' (encompassing racial ideologies and discourses, racial identifications, patterns of racism and racialised social forms such as labour and housing market structures) is determined by, or autonomous from, class structures. The major theoretical frameworks brought to bear have been Marxism, on the one hand, and liberal sociology on the other, influenced more or less by Weberian perspectives. In general, sociologists have been the main contributors to these debates. I cannot deal with the great complexities of the discussions here, but for purely illustrative purposes it might be useful to outline some varying positions.[2] A classical Marxist approach (e.g. Cox, 1948) would argue that racial ideologies and racism existed as a bourgeois ideology to a) legitimate the exploitation, via imperialism, of labour and resources in non-Western areas, and of labour within Western capitalist economies; and b) divide the working classes against themselves, so that they formed alliances and enmities along racial lines, distracting their attention from class struggle. In this view, ideas about race and racism itself are diversionary barriers to class consciousness and need to be overcome in the fight against class inequality.

Completely opposed to this 'economic reductionism' is the 'racial formation theory' of Omi and Winant which holds that race cannot be treated as 'a mere manifestation of some other, supposedly more important, social relationship' and that race must be 'understood as a fundamental dimension of social organisation and cultural meaning in the U.S.' (Omi and Winant, 1994: viii) – and, by implication, elsewhere. They examine racial formations as sets of ideas, projects and agendas about race that change over time, are contested politically and are driven by people and institutions trying to influence the way their society is structured in terms of its racial formation.

Somewhere in the middle of these two approaches is the idea of the relative autonomy of race which builds on theoretical revisions within Marxism, drawing in different ways from Althusser and from Gramsci, and proposes that 'superstructural' elements such as racial identifications have a certain degree of autonomy from 'base' economic structures. Thus racialised ideas and practices can affect economic structures and are not determined by them in a straightforward way, while not being completely divorced from them either. Some might hold to the idea that economic structures are determinate 'in the last analysis', although it is not always clear whether this means 'in the long run' or at some deep and final level of theoretical description (see Gilroy, 1982; Hall, 1980; Solomos, 1986).

A related debate concerns the value of a focus on 'race relations' as opposed to a focus on 'racism' as the key analytic term. Robert Miles, for example, rejects the race relations problematic, because it raises the purely ideological notion of race to an analytic level and thus reifies it (Miles, 1989, 1993). He contends that this reification can apply both to Marxist and to liberal sociological approaches. Taking a sophisticated Marxist approach himself, he sees the key concept as racism, because it is an ideological construct which refers to a real social process of labelling and discrimination. To understand that construct means looking at the historical political–economic processes which have shaped and changed it. Others, such as Michael Banton (1983, 1987, 1991), retain 'race' as an analytic concept on the basis that, although it is of course a social construction, it is one that has real social consequences in the world (see also Cashmore and Troyna, 1990). It therefore has to be analysed alongside other political and economic processes rather than simply be explained in terms of them.

These different positions have important theoretical and political implications, but they also tend to converge somewhat: no one denies the importance of exploring a varied set of social, economic and political factors in understanding ideas and practices about race; no one denies the importance of ideas about race in influencing economic and political ideas and practices. Most people avoid a simple reductionism that attempts to explain one set of factors in terms of one other set. In practice, analysts converge in analysing the complex interweaving of race and class, even if they continue to disagree about the precise relationships and determinations involved.

The varied approaches also tend to share some common assumptions. It is generally stated or implied that in social relations characterised by stratification and political and economic inequalities, race acts as an ideology or mechanism of exclusion (and thus also inclusion). More than this, it lends a quality of permanence and fixity to exclusion and inclusion. Miles (1989: 79) argues that, as an ideology, racism always refers to the supposed biological characteristics of a collectivity which is therefore represented as 'having a natural, unchanging origin and status' and as being 'inherently different'. Banton (1983: 135) is rather more vague, as for him 'racial and ethnic relations are not special': they are types of inter-group relations and can be studied to see how racial and ethnic boundaries are formed, change and maybe disappear, just as do other sorts of inter-group boundaries. Banton is frustratingly unclear about the difference it makes that a boundary is racial as opposed to anything else, but this is mainly because he insists on the changing meaning of race: it cannot be tied down to any one thing. However, in the end it is without doubt a reference to phenotype that marks a racial relation (Banton, 1983: 34, 77) and this is also said to create a difference between ethnic and racial boundaries: 'an ethnic-minority group member can leave to join the majority in a way that someone assigned to a racial minority cannot' (Banton, 1983: 135). This, then, is the same kind of emphasis on fixity as in Miles' formulation and that we saw in Chapter 1.

Omi and Winant (1994: 55, 71–2) take a more subtle approach by distinguishing between 'race' and 'racism'. The race concept itself refers to human bodies – specifically, aspects of phenotype – and thus invokes biology. Racism, however, invokes not just race categories, but *essentialist* categories of race which assume unchanging human essences; in addition a racist project must actively relate to structures of domination. Thus one can make racial identifications without being racist: an association of black anthropologists might be an organisation based on a racial, but non-racist, identification. There is a difference, then, between a reference that is naturalising – in this case, biologising – and one that is essentialising. This is a useful insight in that it suggests that a naturalising argument is not necessarily one that invokes fixity and permanence. However, Omi and Winant achieve this at the expense of reducing nature and biology to the superficial level of physical appearance. A racial identification is one that only refers to, say, skin colour. What is left out here is a non-essentialist reference to human essences. If people think about race as being merely 'skin-deep', then they are not racist; if they think about race as an unchanging human essence shared by all the individuals within a collectivity, then they are racist. But there is then no room to explore ideas about individual human essences which are more or less shared with some others, which are changeable and in process and which constitute the 'nature' of a person without therefore being fixed and permanent. This is an interesting and unexplored area which is worth investigation because, as I argue in subsequent chapters, such a realm between the skin-deep and the fixed, shared essence does exist and is part of the way people in the West think about themselves and others.

Questions about the relative importance of race and class continue to be important, even as, from a theoretical point of view, the upshot of many years of debate seems to be that the two are in a relationship of mutual influence, with no a priori reason to assert that one is, in principle, dominant in terms of structuring that relationship. This conclusion has led to two main developments within the field of race and social stratification. These developments are closely related and, in both, the concept of power, rather than class, is central. For the purposes of argument I will separate them out. The first, which I will look at again in the next section on race and identity, is a direct development of the recognition of the complex interweavings of race and class and it proceeds by introducing further axes of differentiation, such as nation, sexuality and gender. The second involves examining the nature, content and impact of racial discourses.

Race, Nation, Sexuality, Gender

Rather than confine the analysis to just two dimensions of unequal power relations, recent approaches have typically tended to examine the interlacing of race, class and gender. Other aspects of inequality may also be considered, such as those structured by age, sexuality and sexual orientation, ethnicity (where this is distinguished from race), nationality, region and so on. This has been a productive direction of research, revealing the imbrication and mutual influencing of the multiple dimensions of social life.

Consideration of a couple of important themes shows the significance of this theoretical trend. From about the mid 1980s, the theme of race and nation drew increasing attention. Scholars at a general level recognised that ideologies of nationalism were a central terrain on which ideas of race were developed and deployed. Generally it was noted that dominant versions of nationhood – whether these were based on whiteness, as in the British case, or mixedness, as in many Latin American nations – exclude, marginalise and devalue the status and input of some racially identified minorities. Ideas about what the nation was, or rather what it ought to be in the present or become in the future, are used by elites and by other classes who feel allied to dominant nationalist ideologies to discriminate against and belittle racialised others. Often this includes the idea that these others are ethnic or racial groups, while the dominant category (whether actually majority or not) is somehow 'normal', non-ethnic and non-racial; in a word, 'unmarked'. At the same time, however, racialised others may be included in definitions of the nation when a) this is construed as a harmonious multicultural place and/or b) when the cultural inputs of these others are valued for specific elements (music, food, sporting ability, etc.). In case (a) real inequalities and racism are often glossed over; in case (b) acceptance tends to be conditional and constrictive.[3]

Various scholars have advanced arguments about why nationalism and racism seem to have what Weber might have termed an 'elective affinity' for each other. Balibar (1991b) argues that racism intertwined with nationalism from the time that nation states tried to control population movements within a given territory and to produce 'the people' as a political and especially ethnic entity. Nationalism is intent on defining a national identity which can compete with other nation-states in the arena of modernity. Nationalism must include some who are deemed suitable participants in this progressive modern nation and exclude, or at least devalue, others deemed unsuitable. Racism is equally concerned with exclusion and inclusion, with defining who has appropriate heritage and suitable potential. Therefore racism can refigure notions of national tradition and culture into more powerful and virulent ideas of national heredity, the purity of the national/racial body, and aesthetic ideals of national men (and women). Miles (1993: ch. 2) also notes that nationalism and racism are both ideologies of inclusion and exclusion that work with purportedly natural categories, while Williams (1995) argues that these ideologies, as with ideas about kinship and caste, all involve the differentiation of an invented sameness or unity of human substance in order to create categories of relatedness which define access to shared resources and can thus form a clas- sificatory system to include and exclude people.

There are strong echoes here of Foucault's account of bio-power and the concern of the European bourgeoisie with developing healthy, fertile and vigorous nations through control and management of both national populations and the individual bodies of citizens. Foucault (1998: 148) argues that, beginning in the seventeenth century, gaining momentum in the eighteenth and consolidating in the nineteenth, there was a gradual transition in European societies from a 'symbolics of blood' to an 'analytics of sexuality'. The pre-modern emphasis on blood focused around a juridical form of power, typically held by a sovereign, which included a right to seize things, time and bodies and to dispose of them – for example, through decreeing death. The modern emphasis on sexuality relates to a form of power, bio-power, which is productive and regulating, aiming to optimise, increase and administrate the forces of life, collectively at the level of the population and species, and individually at the level of the body. Death may still be decreed, but it is now done by the representatives of peoples on behalf of those peoples for their well-being. A key focus for bio-power is sexuality, as 'sex is the means of access both to the life of the body and the life of the species' (Foucault, 1998: 146). Especially from the nineteenth century, sexuality therefore became subject to detailed examination, discussion and control. However, the symbolics of blood did not disappear: 'the preoccupation with blood and the law has for nearly two centuries haunted the administration of sexuality' (Foucault, 1998: 149). In fact in the late nineteenth century modern racism took shape and ideas about promoting the well-being and health of peoples and bodies 'received their colour and their justification from the mythical concern with protecting the purity of the blood and ensuring the triumph of the race' (Foucault, 1998: 149).

As Stoler (1995: ch. 2) points out, Foucault did not see racism as confined to the period after the late nineteenth century. He said that it emerged in embryonic form in the seventeenth century as part of a discourse about society being ridden with internal conflicts – wars of races – caused by internal enemies who threatened society and had to be dealt with by the state. This developed, through a continuous process of reinscription of meanings, into racism proper in the nineteenth century when it took on a biological discourse and had two aspects, underwriting both colonialism and the repression of so-called degenerate elements who threatened to contaminate the nation from within.

If we want to understand the connection between racism and nationalism at a general level, then we seem to be led in the direction of notions of sexuality, bodies, essences, ideas about how different bodies are connected to each other, what human nature is and how it is changed and can be altered and controlled. This implies paying particular attention to changing notions of human nature and its social constitution.

The theme of race and nation is one example of how introducing different axes of differentiation and inequality enriches the understanding of race and racism. A second example, following directly from the above, concerns the interaction of race with ideas about sexuality and gender. Again, a burgeoning literature has emerged here to show that ideas and practices about race (and nation) are mediated through sexuality and gender.[4] I will deal with one aspect of this – the politics of racial and gender identities – in the next section. Here I am more interested in the work on sexuality (which cannot, admittedly, be separated from the preceding aspect in a more than provisional way).

Stoler's work is a good illustration of the advances made in the realm of race and sexuality (Stoler, 1995). Following Foucault's lead, she focuses on 'the moral re-armament' under way in nineteenth- and early-twentieth-century Europe and connects this to the situation in Europe's colonies. European nation-states were engaged in programmes of liberal reform to inculcate ideals of civic responsibility as part of a national project. There was a great focus on propriety and respectability in matters of upbringing, schooling, sexuality and health, combined with widespread fears of (racial) degeneration (see also Mosse, 1985). Stoler shows that in France and Holland, such programmes targeted the poor and 'internal aliens' at home, but also poor whites in their colonies. There were varying degrees of concern with the native population of the colonies, colonially-born whites and the mixed race offspring of white colonials and natives. 'Proper' (and 'white') sexual morality was restrained and modest, and confined to the family. There were fears that the colonial environment would contaminate and weaken Europeans, especially the poorer men who might live in concubinage with native women. Racial divisions corresponded with sexual–moral ones, such that Asians in the Dutch Indies were seen as licentious, indulgent, sexually uncontrolled and prone to prostitution. Through sexual relations, or simply through being brought up by native servants, Europeans were at risk for themselves and even their offspring since, in Lamarckian fashion, acquired traits might be transmitted to the next generation (see Chapter 3 for a fuller discussion). Not surprisingly, the danger and permissibility of contact with the natives, sexual or otherwise, was gendered and was seen as less threatening for men than for women. Stoler's work shows how racial boundaries were also, at the same time, sexual and moral ones, with different implications for men and women – a conclusion echoed by many.[5]

I return to Stoler's work in more detail in Chapter 3, but here it is worth noting that her focus on sexuality also insistently raises the question of what a human essence is, especially in racialised terms. She shows that essences were not considered to be fixed and permanent, but were open to change – particularly to degeneration. Essence, based on natural human substances, connoted a certain ingrained, constitutive level of being, but it was also subject to alteration. Racism depended on naturalising discourses, but these did not invoke permanence in a straightforward fashion. To see exactly what was being invoked involves grasping contemporary ideas about human nature, human bodily substances and the processes by which these were transmitted across generations, creating kinship between people.

Stoler's work is also useful for thinking through the question of *why* race, sex and gender seem to be so closely interwoven. This may, at first sight, seem virtually self-evident. It may be argued that, if categories or groups of people are thought to have a given character, whether racial, ethnic or national, and the category or group and its character are thought to have some kind of continuity through time and some kind of boundedness, then the reproduction of that category or group must involve sexual reproduction, a process which clearly involves relations between the genders and implicates complex ideas about what men and women are and how they behave, particularly in the domain of sex and sexuality. Hence virtually any concern with race is bound to involve a concern with sexuality and gender.

This is temptingly obvious, but it is too simple. The reproduction of a human group or institution is not necessarily dependent on sexual reproduction, as the account just outlined assumes. A university reproduces itself through the admission and graduation of students and the initiation and termination of contracts with staff. There must be sexual reproduction in the wider society to supply new members, but the university doesn't rely on admitting the children of current members to reproduce itself; any suitably qualified children will do. As Stoler's work shows, in the French and Dutch colonies there was concern not just with sexual reproduction, but also with what one might call contagion – the transmission of moral character through living in the tropics or through co-residence with 'the natives'. To assume that sex matters because 'races' have to be reproduced through sexual reproduction therefore prejudges the issue of what is thought to constitute a 'race'. Clearly the very frequent overlap of race and sex indicates that ideas about race and ideas about sex tend to occupy a common terrain – one defined by ideas about essence, nature, heredity, etc. (see B. Williams, 1995). But we have to be careful about assuming we know what that terrain is, in particular contexts. In Stoler's colonial example, a person's 'nature' could be affected by the climate and indeed a person's nature, once altered in this way, could be passed on to offspring. 'Races' were therefore reproduced not just through sexual means but also through certain ways of living. It mattered not just who you had sex with, but also what climate you lived in and with whom you lived at close quarters.

I have introduced these two linked examples – race and nation, and race and sex – to show that recent work on race has documented the way these different dimensions intersect, forming complex imbrications. What is striking in these accounts is that we are led steadily in the direction of questions about human nature and the human body, and questions about what these things are thought to consist of in particular social and historical contexts. It is these questions that I wish to pursue in this book.

The Content of Racial Discourses

The second, closely related development in the analysis of race and social inequality is the analysis of racial ideologies as hegemonic discourses of power. This draws on a Gramscian interest in the operation of hegemony and a Foucauldian interest in the operation of discourses of truth and knowledge and the way they shape subjectivities and power relations. Equally important has been research into counter-hegemonic practices of resistance. This development is integrally related to the concerns outlined above, as it is very often through discourses that the various dimensions of differentiation mentioned in the preceding section are held to be constituted.

Thus we are not dealing here with a separate literature or set of theorists. Rather we are seeing the influence of the 'linguistic turn' in social science, the post-structuralist and post-modern interest in representation and text.

This development has been very productive in analysing the representation of racial meanings in a given context, how these meanings are reproduced through, for example, writing, the press, film, music, TV and other such cultural texts, and how hegemonic discourses are contested by those they devalue.[6] This type of analysis goes beyond the simpler notions of ideology contained in some earlier Marxist accounts which suggested a coherent, explicit construct, instrumentally created and disseminated by an elite and its allies to further their strategic aims. The image of hegemonic discourses is rather one of less cohesive, overlapping sets of notions, many of them in the realm of apparent common sense, reproduced, perhaps intentionally, but also semi- and unconsciously, by the activities of many different people engaged on widely varying projects and yet structured by some basic assumptions that tend to be taken for granted by many people.[7]

An emphasis on discourse has proved very productive and some of the debates that have characterised this trend seem to point toward the areas of research with which this book is concerned. Some critics have objected to an overriding focus on discourse itself – on text and representation. In one sense, this should not matter. A post-structuralist stance holds that subjectivity and reality (or at least the subjective perception of it) are themselves constituted through discourse so that everything – words and actions – cannot be understood outside discourse. Thus material realities are constituted through discourse and discourses themselves are material. This is fair enough. Yet a good deal of the work that takes discourse as its object has been criticised for retreating into text and semiotics and neglecting to focus on material aspects.[8] One reaction to this is to insist on keeping material realities in focus as well as symbolic meanings: to look not just at, say, representations of black peoples, but also their economic position and the material aspects of racism. This is certainly a valid response. However, an insistence on the need to look at what people do as well as what they say runs the risk of simply reproducing the dichotomy between words and action, or between mind and body, that has existed in Western thought and social science at least since the time of Descartes and that post-structuralism attempted to supersede.

Within social studies as a whole, one reaction to this has been to focus on the notion of embodiment, to look to bodily experience, enactment and performance in order to understand some of the material aspects of the discursive construction of social life.[9] 'The body' has become a hot topic in the humanities and social sciences, but this is more than academic fashion; I think it responds directly to a desire to re-ground research in materiality – even if research into the body is also subject to the same kind of disputes, in this case about the tendency of discourse-centred constructivist accounts of the body to ignore its very materiality.[10] This focus on embodiment is a welcome development, but oddly, there is very little written about the embodiment of race.[11]

In short, this strand of research on race and inequality has moved usefully from debates about race and class towards the construction of hegemonic discourses and the shaping of subjectivities, but it has yet to really move into what appears to be a productive domain, namely the investigation of the embodiment of race as one way of grounding discourse in material realities. Understanding the embodiment of race means delving into not just the daily experience of racism – which has been widely documented (e.g., Alexander, 1996; Blauner, 1989) – but into ideas people (including white people) have about how their racialised bodies come to be as they are, how they can work on their racialised bodies, what their 'racial natures' are, what it means for something to be 'in the blood' and so on.

This approach may help to undo oppositions between social constructivist and materialist approaches to the body. In a recent essay Hall notes that much recent work by black artists focuses on the (black) body and he cautions that an emphasis on the body may lead back to 'a biologically-fixed, essentialised conception of racial identity' (1996a: 21). However, there is no need to see the body as 'biologically-fixed'. In fact an emphasis on the body and a deconstruction of ideas of racialised natures might help us to untie a paradox that Hall observes but does not suggest any way of resolving. In his comments on Bhabha's reading of Fanon's work, Hall notes the 'overwhelming power of the racial binary to *fix*, and [the] argument that all binary systems of power are nevertheless, *at the same time* ... troubled and subverted by ambivalence and disavowal' (1996a: 27).[12] There is a tension here between fixity and constructedness which I believe can be approached through an appreciation of embodied racialised natures which are always in process and therefore perceived to change, but are at the same time subject to being seen as fixed, partly due to the very materiality of embodiment.

RACE AND IDENTITY

The themes considered under this heading are not separable from those in the preceding section, even if there I tended to avoid the word 'identity' and used 'subjectivity' instead. The whole drive towards grasping the multiple dimensions which structure inequality and the way hegemonic discourses of power shape subjectivities has involved an increasing shift towards identity as a key concept (Amit-Talai and Knowles, 1996; Appiah and Gates, 1995; Hall, 1992b; Hall and Du Gay, 1996; Woodward, 1997). The literature on race and identity is very rich and I do not want to review it here. A basic starting point is the idea that, because – as has long been argued (Barth, 1969; Epstein, 1978) – identity is oppositional and relational in nature; it is also multidimensional and structured by overlapping and intersecting discourses of race, class, gender and so on. Many scholars also try to understand why identity has become such an important concept.[13] In addressing this question, frequent reference is made to the roles played by a) processes of globalisation and deterritorialisation, in which identities – local, national, ethnic, etc. – act as new or reformed groundings in a world where social moorings are getting looser; b) decolonisation and other challenges to the authority of Western imperialism and knowledge (such as the emergence of a post-colonial literature and arts in non-metropolitan areas, or social constructionist approaches to science); c) the emergence of new social movements, themselves often linked to (a) and (b) and to the apparent failure of the whole notion of 'development' in many areas of the world scourged by free market capitalism and structural adjustment (see Escobar and Alvarez, 1992; Friedman, 1994; Hall, 1991; Hollinger, 1997; Wade, 1997: chs 5, 6). These three sets of factors are widely seen as contributing to a world in which personal and collective identities have become a key point of reference for many people.

The politics of identity has been part of the reason for the direction in which the concept of identity has developed. Black feminists, for example, contested both white women's representations of female identity and black male representations of black identity – I use the word representation here in its political sense of speaking for, as well as its more literary meaning of speak about.[14] Their own concerns, they felt, were not adequately catered for in either case and they felt excluded. Initiatives such as these have created continually fractioning identities as new categories of people assert some kind of community which unifies them, but makes them different from others, and which gives them a claim to certain rights (e.g., to full social equality for that community) or defines a political agenda (e.g., the creation of a 'greener' society). This type of political struggle for rights has led to a form of identity politics which some feel has become stultified and diversionary, distracting attention from more basic issues of class inequality which affect in very similar ways the various groups who insist on their difference (see Hollinger, 1997; Marable, 1995: ch. 16; Winant, 1993). There is more than a faint echo of a Marxist insistence on class here, but current critiques of identity politics tend to be more open to the importance of recognising difference and constructing a 'class agenda in racially conscious terms' (Winant, 1993: 121).

This gives a very broad background to the recent development of the concept of identity. Against this backdrop, I wish to focus on one of the central points of debate in the literature – the issue of essentialism and anti-essentialism. It is here that I think some new ground can be broken by unpacking the notion of essence.

Essentialism asserts that a person or a category of persons or indeed anything in the world has a core essence that defines its character in important respects. Anti-essentialists deny this claim, but they can do so in different ways. What I will call categorical anti-essentialism, since it operates on the level of social category, consists in arguing that no two people are alike. Thus, for example, there is no reason to assume that a white woman could speak on behalf of a black woman; or that a white homosexual man could be categorised in terms of his interests and political agenda with either other homosexuals or other white men. This is an important argument. Racism and sexism rely on essentialist definitions of racialised minorities and women: it is presumed members of each category have something in common. Contesting such arguments is necessary and important. Related to this type of anti-essentialism is a causative anti-essentialism which contests the idea that people have in them an essence which causes them to have certain characteristics – whether that essence is a genetic code or a cultural tradition handed down and imbued as a kind of blueprint. This is not necessarily a matter of arguing that people have free will, although that could be one approach; rather, it is said that people are a product of complex environments which means that they too are complex and varied and, although they might have certain things in common in certain contexts, they cannot be defined only or even principally in terms of a supposed essence which they share with others.

Another more philosophical anti-essentialism is a radical constructivism which holds that all people, and indeed all things (as they exist in a human world) are constructed through discourse and thus have no independent essence which could define them. Of course discourse could define something as having an essence, but discourses always come from somewhere and are enunciated by someone (not necessarily in the literal sense of a person actually speaking – discourse and discoursing are more broadly conceived than that). So different discourses, differently positioned, will always be constructing the same thing in different ways. There is no single essence that uniquely characterises an entity.

Critiques of anti-essentialism are varied. Some critics contend that categorical anti-essentialism leads to a fragmented and dead-end identity politics (see above). Others point out that, on the contrary, some kind of essentialism – perhaps of a provisional, strategic kind – is vitally necessary to political mobilisation and that those who seem most in favour of anti-essentialism are privileged academic elites (Cross and Keith, 1993: 23–4; hooks, 1991: 28; see also Fuss, 1989). One answer to this is that, rather than building solidarity on ideas about essential commonalities that were forged in the past, political mobilisation can be built on ideas about what people share in terms of interests that bring them together for certain purposes and to gain specific future goals (Hall, 1992a; Wade, 1995). Werbner (1997: 229) also argues that 'objectification', a positive form of collective self-identification, should be distinguished from 'reification' which is a pernicious essentialism which distorts and silences.

A broader critique of anti-essentialism is that its underlying social constructivism posits either a pre-discursive, but somehow fully formed, humanist subject who does the constructing or a passive object who is constructed by some kind of reified abstraction (society, structures) (Butler, 1993: ch. 1; see also Bourdieu, 1977). Radical constructivism may also be accused of retreating into discourse and evacuating the materiality of lived experience – for example, in relation to racist violence (Werbner, 1997: 226).

All this is interesting stuff, but one question seems to get overlooked. What is an essence? Everyone proceeds as if it were reasonably clear what constitutes the essence that is being affirmed or denied. There are hints as to what is involved – cultural blueprints, genetic codes, political agendas, even social characters. When the issue is one of racist or sexist essentialisms, it is often fairly clear that 'biology' is what the analyst has in mind. Even so, when cultural racism is under discussion, it becomes less clear what an essentialism amounts to, apart from being an assertion that a given category of people have something in common which is, in some way, ingrained. Surely it would be useful to enquire further into what people think about the essences which are the object of analysts' description and theorising.

An example might help clarify the argument so far. In the literature on racial minorities in Britain, one theme has been the idea that the children of immigrants from Asia or the Caribbean (not to mention any other group of immigrants from an area with a significantly different culture) would be 'between two cultures'.[15] They would feel allegiance to both their parental cultures and to mainstream British youth culture. Each cultural complex would make competing and often conflicting demands on them. For example, girls of Asian parents might want to wear clothes considered trendy by mainstream British youth fashion standards, and yet also conform to parental notions of modesty which conflicted with those standards. As a result, identities would be 'in crisis' (see Cashmore and Troyna, 1982).

One advance on this perspective was that the situation was different for boys and girls: for example, the morality of girls was subjected to greater control. Class position might also play a role. Race, class and gender intersected (see, e.g., Tizard and Phoenix, 1993: 38, 167). Another more challenging advance was to question the rather dramatic notion of being 'torn between two cultures'. The image invoked two homogeneous and bounded units which came into conflict and drew children in opposing directions. The notion was based on essentialist conceptions of culture. A different, less essentialist approach pointed out that very similar sorts of conflicts characterised relations between older and younger generations in Asia, in the Caribbean and among white British people. In all these areas, cultures were not simple homogeneous, static things, but were processes of hybridisation, of contestation and negotiation. 'British' culture was itself a complex and constantly changing set of processes, being strongly influenced in the post-war period precisely by Asian and Afro-Caribbean cultural practices, above all among young people (Hutnyk, 1996; Jones, 1988). Many people in many areas of the world had to deal with competing and conflicting demands deriving from processes of cultural change; what was happening to the children of Afro-Caribbean and Asian parents was not particularly new or different. It was being constructed as a 'problem' because (black and Asian) immigrants and their children were themselves being seen as 'problems' by governments, educationalists, social workers and the media (Tizard and Phoenix, 1993: ch. 3).

This debate illustrates a fairly typical anti-essentialist critique of essentialism. It is a useful critique, but it leaves certain questions unanswered. One way of advancing the debate would be not just to talk to these young people about how they feel (which is a common enough research strategy, generally employed to investigate black youths' experience of racism),[16] but to enquire more specifically into how they, and their parents, think about their 'natures', how they as embodied persons come to be as they are, what mechanisms of 'inheritance' they feel to be operating on them; to ask how they view their 'origins' and their connectedness with, and difference from, other people. This would help us to unpack a simple essentialist–anti-essentialist opposition by focusing on the taken-for-granted notion of essence. It may also be that the anti-essentialist critique glosses over the fact that some young people themselves talk in terms of being 'torn' between or 'bridging' two cultures, whether because they have absorbed a dominant discourse about culture and difference or – which amounts to much the same thing – they are thinking in 'essentialist' ways.[17] If this is so, then what are these 'essences' that are being conceived and are they the same as the 'essences' that anti-essentialists focus on – the ones that 'impute a fundamental, basic, absolutely necessary constitutive quality to a person [or] social category' (Werbner, 1997: 228) or that invoke an essence as 'existing outside or impervious to social and historical context' (Omi and Winant, 1994: 181, n. 6)? There is an interesting agenda for research here. As Stoler (1997a: 104) comments: 'I would suggest that racial essentialism is not, as we have often assumed, about a *fixed* notion of essence.' She argues that 'A notion of essence does not necessarily rest on immovable parts but on the strategic inclusion of different attributes, of a changing constellation of features and a changing weighting of them' (Stoler, 1997b: 200).

RACE AS A SCIENTIFIC IDEA

This field of study presents us with both a fruitful avenue for the investigation of the ideas I want to pursue and yet also with some of the most reactionary and racist sorties into the study of race. I will first discuss the positive aspects of the field – briefly, as I elaborate on these matters in Chapter 3. Then I will discuss some more negative interventions in the field which involve, first, racist ideas about race and IQ and, second, non-racist (?) theories about the supposed propensity of humans to think in racialising ways.

The study of race as an idea in scientific thought is fruitful because, as I noted briefly in Chapter 1, some of the work done in this field effectively helps to historicise notions of race and human nature (e.g., Banton, 1987; Hodgen,

1964; Stepan, 1982; Stocking, 1982). I don't want to elaborate on this here, since it will be the subject of the next chapter. Suffice to say, however, that historical studies of race as an idea tend to locate its origins in the fourteenth or fifteenth century, trace its encounter with natural history and biology in the eighteenth, nineteenth and early twentieth centuries and then show how scientific racism fell into disrepute, effectively severing the supposed link between biology and race (even if biologically determinist ideas persisted in the lay world and in certain corners of the scientific world). The end result has been to separate race and biology to such an extent that pairing the two has virtually become taboo, a combination that is racist almost by definition. This relies on an interpretation of biology as fixed, determinist and reduced to a genetics that is itself determinist (see Chapters 3 and 6).

So even if the historical study of race helps us historicise notions of human nature (and potentially also embodiment, although other histories have focused on this), it brakes this agenda for investigation after about 1950, since, from then, any question of investigating race and nature becomes a matter either of bad and racist science or of false, lay (and also racist) ideologies. Of course linking race and nature can be, and often is, located in exactly these camps, but it doesn't have to be. We have to look at people's understandings of their and other people's racialised human natures. This does not mean finding a 'real' link between a determinist biology and race, but it does mean allowing that racial identity might become embodied in a changing, malleable and continuously emergent human biology, and that, partly as a result of this, people might think about racial identity as linked to nature, without this necessarily meaning that they see it as fixed. We need to understand how people think of their natures, and specifically their racialised natures, in order to see how racial discourse fixes, or does not fix, or – as I believe to be the case – allows strategic equivocation between fixity and fixability.

On the negative side of discussions about how race enters into scientific discourse, I want to look at two areas: a) race and IQ; and b) racial thinking as a 'natural' human attribute. I will address the first topic very briefly and cannot here give a detailed account of the heated debates about whether or not 'race' determines IQ.[18] Rather I want to illustrate the sort of biological argument to which my approach is, resolutely and absolutely, opposed: that is, a view of human nature as a set of fixed biological attributes which determine people's character.

The persistence of arguments for and against the theory that IQ is largely determined by genetic inheritance, and also that black people are on average less intelligent than white people because of their genetic make-up, shows the constructedness of ideas about human nature, even in an age when a person's DNA can be 'fingerprinted'. As Jones says, for most of the participants in this debate 'science long ago gave way to sociology' and he complains that there is 'far too much consistency between the political and biological views of the supporters of each theory'. However, he asserts that 'science can, nevertheless, still say what is, and what is not, known about inherited differences in intellect', even though he also concedes that 'The argument about the relative importance of nature and nurture in producing racial divergence in IQ scores is unresolved and probably unresolvable' (Jones, 1997: 197, 198). Lack of resolution notwithstanding, he comes down pretty firmly on the side of nurture as the most important influence – as do a great many other commentators on the issue. He adduces, among other things, the fact that IQ scores tend to increase over time everywhere, often leaping ten points or so in a given population over one or two generations: 'not what would be expected for a character firmly wired into the genes' (Jones, 1997: 198).

In these debates the central concepts of 'nature' and 'nurture' often go unquestioned. Their relative weights are hotly debated, but less attention is paid to what they actually are as concepts. Some biologists now argue that, because of their interdependence and their relationship of mutual constitution, nature and nurture cannot really be distinguished from one another as independent determinants (see Chapter 4; see also Keller, 1995; Richards, 1998). A more fundamental argument is that both concepts are themselves cultural constructs which cannot be taken for granted (see MacCormack and Strathern, 1980). In this sense, it is important to deconstruct the notions of 'nature' and 'nurture' (or 'culture') as they are used in debates about race and IQ – on both sides of the argument. They are generally underlain by 'constructivist' theories which see nature as a pre-existing reality which is then moulded by culturally defined processes of nurture (Haraway, 1989, 1997; Ingold, 1995; Strathern, 1992a). Once this is given, the only remaining debate is a) the extent to which 'nature' has a pre-existing structure which will guide the moulding process; and b) the power of 'culture' to impose its own structure on 'nature'. Nature is seen as a fixed biological – actually, genetic – inheritance which can be overlain to a greater or lesser extent by the influence of culture. The determinist hereditarians see culture as the lesser influence, the 'nurture' camp sees it as the major influence, but there is a certain agreement about the character of the two polar concepts.

It is this idea of nature as fixed that is mistaken – not just as a representation of how many biologists think about human nature, but as a representation of what many lay people in the West think too. My point here is not to argue naively that genes do not really exist, that they are the construct of some scientists' imaginations. Of course they exist but, as historians of science such as Haraway have demonstrated, cultural assumptions about broader concepts such as 'nature' pervade and structure the way people, including scientists, think about genes and how they operate in the world (Franklin, Lury and Stacey, 2000; Haraway, 1989, 1991, 1997; see also Chapter 4). In short, the existing debate about race and IQ may or may not be unresolvable, but it does demonstrate a need to analyse the notions of human nature that are being deployed in them, not only by the new scientific racists, who see human 'nature' as strongly determinant, but also by their critics who see 'culture' as more determinant.

The second attempt to re-ground race in human nature takes a rather different tack. The basic argument is that, as a result of evolutionary processes of natural selection, it is in human nature to think and perceive racially. This is not easily defined as a racist approach in itself, as it does not discriminate against any particular category of people. Its claim is about the human species. But there is something unsettling about the argument that humans have a fixed biological propensity to think racially. There are different lines of approach within this general theme. Some are sociobiological approaches which assert that criteria of 'inclusive fitness' meant greater reproductive success for the individuals who favoured others who looked like them, since these others would share certain genes. Favouring them would mean helping to reproduce the genes such individuals carried (Van den Berghe, 1981).

A more subtle argument is put forward by Hirschfeld (1996; see also Hirschfeld, 1997). On the one hand, Hirschfeld objects to most psychological and cognitivist approaches to race and racism, because they assume that people divide up and stereotype others in terms of racial identification in a way that obeys the principles which rule all human classification processes. He argues that the way people classify *people* is different in important respects. On the other hand, Hirschfeld sees weaknesses in the major historical and sociological approaches to race. He points out the lack of agreement among scholars as to when racial thinking emerged, why it emerged and what functions it fulfilled. This lack of consensus, he says, demonstrates that racial thinking is itself very flexible and fulfils varying functions. The unifying factor behind all this flexibility, for him, is a basic process of human mentation particular to the way people think about people. People believe that 'humans can be partitioned into enduring types on the basis of highly correlated clusters of naturally grounded properties' (Hirschfeld, 1996: 38). The notion that humans are divided into natural kinds with essential characteristics that define their behaviour is what Hirschfeld calls race theory or the race concept. This basic cognitive predisposition – which Hirschfeld (1997: 75) suggests may be an 'evolved mechanism' (and it's hard to see how it could be anything else) – becomes concretised under specific historical circumstances into particular modes of 'racial thinking' or 'racial consciousness' which may vary quite widely. The ones with which we are most familiar and generally label 'racial' are those that emerged with European colonisation, slavery and so on. However, says Hirschfeld, English and US Anglo-Saxon discrimination against the Irish is equally a manifestation of racial thinking, as is discrimination against the Jews. All these forms of racial thinking are underlain by a similar race concept which categorises people in terms of presumed essential and natural differences. Rather like Goldberg (1993; see Chapter 1), he focuses on naturalisation as a key feature of the race concept, and also argues that naturalisation does not depend only on biology, as biology is one among several systems of natural causation. Unlike Goldberg, he sees the tendency to naturalise, at least when applied to humans, as itself a natural faculty of humans. Hirschfeld then attempts to support his argument by presenting the results of a number of psychological experiments carried out with samples of children of varying ages which were designed to test which kinds of observable characteristics of humans were perceived by children as most salient, most transmissible to offspring and most important in defining behaviour. The experiments show that 'racial' features such as skin colour score highly in these respects, even among pre-schoolers.

There are various problems with Hirschfeld's argument.[19] First, it seems bizarre and misleading to use the term 'race concept' to refer to the tendency to naturalise, when this is seen as a universal aspect of human mentation – why not just call it naturalisation? It might be less confusing to argue that there is a universal tendency among humans to naturalise and essentialise when classifying other humans (although this still assumes that 'naturalisation' is itself a reasonably self-evident process – which, as should now be clear, I doubt); and that notions of race are one set of specific historical examples of that tendency. In a later article, it should be noted, Hirschfeld (1997: 74–5) slightly changes his terminology to argue that a natural human process of cognition (a tendency to categorise humans in a naturalising and essentialising way) becomes a 'race concept' in 'certain environmental conditions': he clarifies that 'race is not a natural category of the mind'. However, he still argues that 'race has in itself – in its psychological core – a naturalising and essentialising potency' which makes it a good candidate for humans' natural categorising predispositions. One is left wondering, then, how 'race' can have a 'psychological core'. It is as if 'race' has some inherent characteristics that especially appeal to human cognition. Yet surely race exists only *within* human cognition. Hirschfeld is, in effect, still racialising his theory of cognition at its core (cf. Domínguez, 1997).

The nub of the second problem with Hirschfeld's account is that virtually all his experimental data come from US children; one set of data comes from French children. How, then, can he argue that the classificatory patterns he identifies are universal cognitive predispositions? These children all grew up in societies where specifically racial differences – in his terminology, forms of racial thinking – are pervasive, long-standing and of great social significance. In other words, it seems impossible to separate out, experimentally, the supposedly underlying 'race concept' from its specific manifestation as 'racial thinking'. He might argue that the fact that very young children seem to think in these ways is evidence for an underlying cognitive predisposition, but it could equally well be evidence that even very young children pick up these social classifications. Hirschfeld (1997: 87) argues that 'in view of their limited understanding of political economy and the absence of race from the power relations they do engage' children are not able to pick up such categories. But one does not need an understanding of political economy – if by this Hirschfeld means some abstract conceptual grasp – to apprehend everyday power differences and it seems to me very odd to argue that, even for young children in the US, racialised power relations are 'absent' from their everyday experience (cf. Hughes, 1997).

Like all universalist arguments – and herein lies the third problem – the thing that is argued to be universal has to be pitched at a very high level of generality in order to encompass all the empirical examples which are said to be its concrete manifestations. The universal then turns out to be virtually empty in itself; any interesting content it has is given to it by particular social and historical contexts. In Hirschfeld's case, once he generalises a tendency to 'naturalise' beyond a specifically racial form of naturalisation, the concept of naturalisation becomes so vague (and open to serious questions about what it actually means), that he is forced to reinsert that racial form into his concept of naturalisation in order to make it significant.

There are some interesting aspects to Hirschfeld's data and interpretations. For example, he argues that purely visual cues of skin colour and other such 'racial' traits do not determine young US children's ideas about racial categories of people (Hirschfeld, 1996: ch. 6). That is, the mere perception of the physical cues that mean 'race' to an adult (in the US) does not in itself lead to the development of racial categories in children. Hirschfeld (1996: 154) argues that the acquisition of racial categories occurs because children are 'speculating over the kinds of people there are in the world'. They have well-developed concepts about race – they know what the socially relevant categories are and they may express prejudice towards such categories – but they have difficulty in assigning other individual children to those categories because the perceptual cues available to them underdetermine such assignations. Hirschfeld concludes that, for young children, as for social scientists, racial categories are socially constructed in ways that are independent of, rather than determined by, physiognomic cues (1996: 157). Now this is an interesting argument (cf. Stoler, 1997a, who also notes the interest of this), but to explain the data it seems unnecessary to take the step Hirschfeld does, which is to posit a cognitive predisposition. Of course the physical cues alone can't determine the development of racial classifications. This is precisely because racial categories are socially constructed. There is no reason to suppose that such categories and their conceptual content are not learned from the surrounding environment and that the difficult skill of assigning specific individuals to such categories is learned – although never perfected – later on. There seems no particular reason to argue that the basic categories are acquired due to an innate predisposition.

The weakness of Hirschfeld's perspective is perhaps clearest when he recounts Jean-Paul Sartre's story about his encounter with a woman who hated Jews. Sartre asked her why and she replied that it was due to her bad experiences with Jewish furriers. Hirschfeld (1996: 59) comments:

Sartre astutely wonders why she chose to hate Jews rather than furriers. The answer is that it is more 'natural' to hate Jews than furriers because prejudice adheres to the kinds of people an individual recognises more easily than to the kinds of activities in which people engage.

Hirschfeld's idea that racial theory is a cognitive predisposition seems to explain everything, but actually explains very little. Everything significant about why the woman hated Jews rather than furriers relates not to an innate tendency to categorise people in naturalising and essentialist ways, but to 2,000 years of persecution of Jews and the racialisation of anti-Semitism that took place in nineteenth- and twentieth-century Europe. Nothing comparable can be adduced for furriers! Even if there were an innate tendency to categorise people in these ways, it tells us virtually nothing of interest about this woman's anti-Semitism.

In sum, it seems to me misguided and unnecessary to re-ground racial thinking – even if it is hidden into more general ideas about essentialist thinking – into human nature. Not only does it threaten to make race 'natural', but, and more relevant for my argument here, it leaves unexamined the basic notion of naturalisation on which it is based. Hirschfeld never gets further with the concept than stating that naturalisation 'involves the practice of conceptually identifying social differences with natural ones' (1996: 21) and, although he adds tantalisingly that 'to naturalise (attribute to natural causes) and to biologise (attribute to biological causes) are not the same processes, inasmuch as biology is only one of many systems of natural causation' (1996: 35), he never expands on this remark. The idea that the category 'natural' might itself be a historical construct is never broached.

CONCLUSION

My purpose in this chapter has been to review various approaches to the study of race and to suggest that, very often, they seem to point us in the direction of a relatively unexplored area of research sometimes by taking that area for granted. This area of research would focus on ideas about essences, human nature, how racialised bodies are constituted (rather than represented, perceived and experienced – aspects which have been the subject of research).

In the following chapters I pursue this agenda in an exploratory way. In Chapter 3 I look at how ideas about human nature have varied over time, focusing particularly on ideas about heredity and the uncertain relationship between things inside humans and things outside them. In Chapter 4 I look first at ideas about genetics in the twentieth century, questioning a simple trend towards an ever greater genetic essentialism in Western societies and suggesting that an uncertain and ambiguous relationship between human nature and culture still exists, not just in terms of their relative roles, but of their very constitution and separation. I also look at recent anthropological work on kinship to see how this throws light on the same uncertain relationship. In Chapter 5 I explore these themes specifically in relation to ideas about race, albeit in a preliminary way. In Chapter 6 I look at ideas about embodiment, biology and race, suggesting that biology needs to be seen as a process, rather than something fixed and that, while the process of embodiment lends itself to ideas about fixity, ideas about fixability are always in tension with notions of permanence.

3. HISTORICISING RACIALISED NATURES

If the concept of race is defined as invoking a discourse that makes appeal to such notions as nature (including human nature), heredity, biology or genetics, then it seems appropriate to explore what these notions mean in particular contexts. If a racial discourse is said to be a naturalising one, even if we admit that not all naturalising discourses are racial ones (for example, gender discourses), then we want to know what a naturalising discourse looks like and what kind of implications it has. Do we know immediately what's implied? Are the implications different at different times? Are the implications varied and perhaps contradictory even in one period? Does 'naturalising' necessarily imply 'deterministic', for example? To take a more specific claim: if a racial discourse is said to invoke notions of heredity, descent and blood, then, again, do we automatically know what is implied by this? Does heredity necessarily mean permanence, for example? If something is said to be 'in the blood', can we assume we know how it got there and what that means? If a racial discourse is said to invoke human biological difference or human genetic difference, things get more tricky: a) the domain of enquiry becomes vague (which aspect of human biology is at issue? Which aspect of genetics is at issue? Transmission genetics? Evolutionary genetics? Developmental genetics? Population genetics?); b) it is unclear whether reference is being made to particular ontological domains (human organisms, human variation and its inheritance) or to these domains only as they have come to be known by the historical disciplines of biology and genetics. In any case, we still want to ask whether it is immediately clear what an invocation of biology or genetics implies. Again, a central question is whether such an invocation necessarily means fixity and determinism.

One aspect of this exploration should be historical, particularly since terms such as 'biology' and 'genetics' have quite specific and recent histories – the first coined in 1801 by the French naturalist Lamarck (among others); the second proposed by the British zoologist William Bateson in 1906 (Jordanova, 1984: 44; Mayr, 1982: 732). In this chapter I give a brief account of how conceptions of nature and particularly human nature have varied over time and what this implies for the processes of naturalisation that are common in racial discourses and identifications. Different ways of naturalising imply different ways of thinking about supposed racial differences. I also argue that, while one can detect an overall process of 'hardening' in the way human nature is conceived – a gradual tendency to see the 'natural' part of human nature as fixed in some way, as a result of growing knowledge about the mechanisms of heredity – there is also a very long-standing interweaving of and equivocation between notions of, on the one hand, permanence and continuity and, on the other, plasticity and change. The common contention that, by naturalising, racial discourses automatically and univocally invoke fixity and permanence needs to be qualified. If naturalising discourses are never as 'fixing' as they might seem to be, however, this by no means prevents them from being racist or legitimating racism. Indeed, the idea that racism depends on ideas about natural fixity seems to me too limited. Racism does indeed make reference to human nature, but it does not therefore always deal in a currency of indelibility. Part of its force lies in the ambiguous move between ideas of indelibility and ideas of malleability.

Before presenting this historical argument in detail, I want to make two sets of remarks. First, it is important to grasp that I will be comparing ways of thinking about nature and human nature that are characteristic of the West from the early to mid twentieth century onwards with ways that were typical of earlier periods. This involves producing a skeletal outline of the recent modes of thought which, admittedly, rather oversimplifies the picture. I take it, however, that roughly from the period in which the mechanisms of heredity were outlined in a detailed way and, more importantly, integrated fully into a fairly complete picture of evolution – a period that started with the rediscovery of Mendelian genetics in about 1900, came to fruition with the 'evolutionary synthesis' which Mayr (1982: 119) dates at 1936–47, and reached a high point with the discovery of the structure of DNA in 1953 – a certain view of human nature became dominant in Western thought. This view was not without precedent and had been prefigured in earlier ideas, most notably in the nature–nurture dichotomy of late-nineteenth-century eugenic theories, but also in Hobbesian notions of the brutish, pre-social 'state of nature' and in Durkheim's theories of the relation between the individual and society. The central notion is that 'human nature' is a biological substrate of genetic material which is fixed in its characteristics. Although this nature is something that makes humans human, it is also something pre-social, instinctive and linked to non-human animals, especially the higher primates. 'Culture', in this view, is something humans then acquire (although of course they have the genetic predisposition to acquire it). It is an overlay which acts on the raw material of their natures and 'socialises' them, making them complete and fully human.[1] I will argue later on that such a view of the nature–culture divide is in fact not as simply attributable to modern Euro-Americans as it might seem and that there is a good deal of blurring of the divide between nature and culture, conceived in this way.

The second set of remarks concerns how my argument fits with existing literatures. Linking concepts of race to ideas about nature in general is not itself an original proposition. As Banton (1987: xvii) says, 'no one can understand the debates about racial difference among humans who cannot relate them to contemporary attempts to explain corresponding differences in the wider world of nature'. Many writers on the history of the idea of race – or, more widely, human diversity – take a similar approach.[2] In the same way, historians of science and natural history frequently make reference to how the ideas and practices they explore relate to ideas about race.[3] The literature on eugenics, in particular, notes how eugenicists drew parallels between the selective breeding of plants and animals and the possibility of intervening in human breeding in ways that included controlling 'races'.[4] However, I want to draw particular attention to how changing concepts of (human) nature give rise to changing discourses of naturalisation and the implications these have for racial identifications. Most of all, these implications, although they have been addressed in the historical literature, seem to have been relegated to the sidelines when it comes to post-war definitions of the field of race. The force of Banton's statement, cited above, fizzles out when he gets onto theories current from the 1930s onwards about 'race as status' and 'race as class'; questions of how people, whether scientists or lay persons, understand nature no longer seem relevant once it has been established that, in modern genetics, the notion of race has become redundant and been replaced by the concept of population (Banton, 1987: 95). For this reason, in the two chapters following this one I re-centre the implications of concepts of nature and naturalisation so that the question of the historical particularity of notions of nature, biology, genetics and heredity in their relation to ideas about race is brought into the twentieth century.

It also seems important to me to follow up the lead supplied by Williams (1995) when she locates ideas of race alongside those of kinship, noting that Schneider (1977) had rightly linked concepts of kinship and nationality in American culture, but neglected to include race. All three realms of ideas involve human relatedness and difference, mediated by theories about the continuity and division of human substance in which sexual reproduction has a central role.[5] Haraway (1997: 309, n. 1) also notes that 'Race, nature, gender, sex, and kinship must be thought together.' From this perspective, it seems relevant to look not only at the wider world of nature in general but also in particular at ideas about heredity and the transmission of substance in the formation of persons. This is also important given the significance of heredity for the concept, outlined above, of human nature since the 'evolutionary synthesis'. A good deal of the literature on the history of ideas of race focuses on the notion of diversity and why it was thought to exist in the natural world; such literature does not necessarily ignore the question of mechanisms of heredity (e.g., Banton, 1987: 6), but it gives it scant attention. On the other hand, histories of ideas about 'generation' (i.e., the generation of life) and heredity give little attention to questions of race: Mayr's 200-page section on the matter mentions race three times, so much in passing that it does not merit an entry in the index (1982: 634, 640, 688).

Stubbe (1972) and Gasking (1967) give the issue equally little attention. It is only when we get to histories of eugenics that the two issues are brought together in a more integral fashion (e.g., Kevles, 1995: 18; Paul, 1995: 41; Stepan, 1982: ch. 5; 1991).

SEX AND GENDER, NATURE AND CULTURE

Before outlining the historical material that makes up the body of this chapter, I wish to make a brief but important detour through the lessons learnt from feminist scholarship's recent approach to understanding the differences between sex and gender. These lessons indicate the importance of questioning the apparently straightforward level of natural biology and they can help us in understanding ideas about race.

In the 1960s a distinction was drawn between sex (the universal genetic biology of sex difference) and gender (the varied cultural constructions of 'man' and 'woman' built on top of this skeletal difference). The distinction was vital to feminist arguments which challenged the grounding of cultural gender characteristics in biology. The sex–gender division provided the basis for the argument that biology played a minor or even non-existent role in creating the social and cultural differences between men and women.

More recently feminists have questioned whether a straightforward distinction between sex and gender is really possible (Butler, 1990: 6–7, 1993: 1–12; Haraway, 1989: ch. 13, 1991: ch. 7; Moore, 1994b; Stolcke, 1993). It has for some time been recognised that at the level of genetic and developmental biology, there is not an absolutely clear distinction between male and female. Some individuals may have the YX chromosomes which usually facilitate development as a male – although other genetic loci also seem to be involved in sexual differentiation – but because of a particularity in the complex and multiple factors influencing this development, especially at the hormonal level, they appear to be female children and are raised as such (Fausto-Sterling, 1985: ch. 3). This raises the question of what 'sex' is. Is it a matter of genes, chromosomes, hormones or anatomy? Fausto-Sterling (1985: 81) notes further that theories about embryonic sexual differentiation tend to see female development as 'a lack' of maleness, commenting that 'such rock-bottom cultural ideas [about femaleness as absence] can intrude unnoticed even into the scientist's laboratory'. In her later book Fausto-Sterling (2000: 3) reiterates that 'a body's sex is simply too complex' to be divided neatly into either male or female, because there are actually 'shades of difference' between the two. She contends that, while we may use scientific knowledge to help us label people as male and female, 'only our beliefs about gender – not science – can define our sex' and furthermore that 'our beliefs about gender affect what kind of knowledge scientists produce about sex in the first place'.

If sex is a diffuse, complex area and if it is subject to being 'read' in particular ways, even by biologists, then its separation from the cultural dynamics of gender becomes less evident. From here, it is a short step to take up the Foucauldian contention that far from sexuality, as a set of cultural desires and bodily behaviours, being understood to derive from sex, as an underlying biological locus, the relationship is actually the other way round. In fact the notion of sex that developed during the eighteenth and nineteenth centuries in Europe and that included the idea of men and women as mutually exclusive biological categories is 'an imaginary point determined by the deployment of sexuality' (Foucault, 1998: 155). The sciences of reproduction that emerged at this time helped produce the notion of sex and construed it as a 'compulsory heterosexuality' (Butler, 1996: 67). Sex became a principle of identity which was 'always positioned within a field of two mutually exclusive and fully exhaustive identities' – male and female (Butler, 1996: 66).

In short, what counts as 'sex', that is, as 'natural' and 'biological', is itself a discursively mediated object. The boundary between sex and gender is not an obvious one. People called 'men' may generally have a Y chromosome, but it is not clear that there is a dividing line between the biological 'sexual' traits that this is said to determine and the cultural 'gender' characteristics of masculinity that are supposedly built on this substratum.

Laqueur's book *Making Sex* provides an example of the problems of distinguishing 'sex' from 'gender'. Laqueur (1990: 11) says that he has 'no interest in denying the reality of sex or of sexual dimorphism as an evolutionary process'; instead he seeks to show on the basis of historical evidence from the ancient Greeks to Freud that 'almost everything one wants to *say* about sex – however sex is understood – already has in it a claim about gender'. (It is worth noting in passing that, if one takes Laqueur at his word, then it undermines his own contention that there is something straightforwardly identifiable as 'the reality of sex'. His argument clearly implies that such a 'reality' must always be culturally mediated.) Laqueur shows that women were once thought of, in the Western 'one-sex model', as being imperfect, reversed versions of men, with the sexual organs on the inside instead of the outside. During the eighteenth century there was a shift to the 'two-sex model' in which men and women were thought of as sexual opposites, completely different from each other. Laqueur's argument is that the shift was not occasioned simply by science uncovering some more facts: these were available before that time, but were not deemed relevant. Also vitally important were the social changes occurring at the time and changing relations between men and women: 'Sex, in both the one-sex and the two-sex worlds, is situational; it is explicable only within the context of battles over gender and power' (1990: 11).

Kulick's study of *travestis*, homosexual prostitutes in Brazil who dress and live as women and have sex with men clients and boyfriends, also unsettles a clear distinction between sex and gender. Kulick shows that a person's sexual identity is given not so much by their genital anatomy as by their sexual preferences – a person who likes to be penetrated is feminine, even if 'she' has a penis:

While the anatomical differences between men and women are certainly not missed or ignored in Brazil, the possession of genitals appears to be fundamentally conflated with what they can be used for, and in the particular configuration of sexuality, gender and sex that travestis draw on, the determinative criterion in the identification of males and females is not so much the genitals as it is the role those genitals perform in sexual encounters. (Kulick, 1998: 227)

One could of course argue that this is actually a complex gender construction, built onto – and in this case 'masking' – the skeletal biological facts of chromosomes or anatomy; the travestis themselves do recognise a basic difference between a person with a penis and one with a vagina. But the point is that, in this context, the genitalia themselves and the way they are used – to penetrate or to receive – are not clearly separable in thinking about men and women. The line between sex and gender is blurred. As one travesti who had worked in Italy put it: 'I never understood whether the men in Milan were buying a women with a dick or a man with breasts' (Kulick, 1998: 191).

Kulick's material also suggests that embodiment is vitally important in constituting human nature. It implies that people's sexual natures are defined at least as much by how they use their bodies as by the anatomical 'givens' of that body. Human nature, then, is constituted at least in part by embodied performance, rather than a set of predefined biological baselines. This theme of the ongoing constitution of human nature by embodied performance is one which will recur in the rest of this chapter and also in Chapter 6.

A broader argument is that the sex–gender distinction is a version of Western nature–culture dichotomy in which nature is seen as passive and unadorned, waiting to be colonised, shaped and marked by culture. Nature is the raw material, culture the finished product. In this view, science can get, eventually, to the unvarnished facts of nature, separable from the constructions and conventions of culture. The questioning of the sex–gender distinction is part of a more general challenge to this view of nature and culture (Haraway, 1989, 1991; MacCormack and Strathern, 1980). Just as Butler (1993: 1) argues that 'Sexual difference ... is never simply a function of material differences which are not in some way both marked and formed by discursive practices', so Haraway (1991: 134) notes more generally that although '"Biology" has tended to denote the body itself', it is actually 'a social discourse open to intervention'. In short, there is no pre-discursive encounter with the facts of biology (see also Haraway, 1989). This is not the same as saying that biological facts are mere imaginative fabrications. Genes and chromosomes have material reality. But that reality is always mediated through discourse; it is woven into and shaped by interpretations and world views.

This perspective is important for considerations of race. It highlights the idea that the facts of biology, heredity and nature which a racial discourse invokes, and which make it a racial discourse according to many current definitions, are not to be taken for granted. In many approaches to race studies, it is common to adduce a realm of nature – physical appearance, biology, heredity – which acts as a basis on which the social constructions of race are built. Certain biological differences exist among humans and are themselves in reality socially meaningless in that they do not determine or even influence social differences. But people build ideas about race onto chosen perceived biological differences and the object of social analysis is these ideas. However, because the biology is irrelevant as a determinant, it is therefore also ignored in the realm of ideas about race, or it is assumed that its function there is an obvious one – it naturalises or essentialises those ideas. Little attention is given to how biology is being construed by the people espousing these ideas, or to what 'nature' or 'essence' mean to them.

The critique of the sex–gender division suggests that the realm of nature on which cultural categories are supposedly built is itself culturally mediated. The critique directs our attention to the content and constitution of that realm of nature and its historical variation. It makes us ask about how 'sex' itself is being and has been constructed, rather than assuming that we know that sex involves clear anatomical (or genetic or hormonal) distinctions between two categories called males and females. It makes us ask about how sexual natures are constituted through embodied performance. Equally, with respect to race, the critique makes us ask about how biology, blood, descent, nature, genes and phenotype are being and have been conceived, rather than assuming that we know what these concepts mean to the people using them. And it poses the question of how racialised natures are formed through embodied performance.

As I argued in Chapter 1, this unsettles the boundaries of 'race' as a field of study, since the very thing that is taken as a marker of whether to include a given phenomenon in the study of 'race' becomes itself part of the study. For example, we need to think carefully about whether we easily know when a discourse is or is not making reference to 'human nature'. With this in mind, I will review briefly some of the changing understandings of human nature and how these have interwoven with ideas about race.

CHANGING VIEWS OF NATURE AND HUMAN NATURE

As various writers have shown, the concepts of nature and human nature are extremely complex and historically changeable.[6] Various sources concur in tracing some broad changes in the concept of nature. Collingwood (1945) sees a shift from an ancient Greek view of nature as saturated by mind, through a Renaissance vision of nature as a machine, to a modern (i.e., from the late eighteenth century) view of nature as analogous to society itself, that is, as an entity in process (and, often, progress), with evolution as the key idea. Greene (1959) describes a shift from a 'traditional' view of the world as a static system, divinely ordained and ordered, through a Newtonian and Cartesian concept of nature as a mechanical law-bound system of matter in motion, to an evolutionary notion of process and progress which, from the eighteenth century onwards, has lived in tension with notions of mechanism (see also Greene, 1989: 406). Williams (1988: 219–24) traces a change from a view of nature as a monarch or goddess, through an eighteenth- and nineteenth-century notion of nature as a 'constitutional lawyer' who defined a set of operational laws governing the universe and discoverable by science, to, from the late nineteenth century, the idea of nature as a selective breeder, constantly on the move.

In the confines of this book I cannot provide a comprehensive review of these changes in ideas of nature, nor of those relating to 'human nature', nor even of the material that relates very directly to ideas of race. I am not a historian and have not gone back to the primary sources in what follows. My account is necessarily abbreviated and selective. The overall purpose is to illustrate that in different historical periods, ideas about human nature have always shown a degree of uncertainty about what was fixed and what changeable in human nature and have often seen internal human nature as in some measure participating in and constituted by the external world of human experience. Let me elaborate on this.

Permanence and Change in Human Nature

I will start by outlining what seem to me two fundamental problems underlying ideas about human nature and its relation to nature. The first is that, in the Western tradition going back to the ancient Greeks, humans are both part of nature, subsumable within it, and yet also somehow beyond and above it. The position can be appreciated in the form of a paradox: it is human nature to supersede nature. Thus human nature can be conceived as something that humans have in common with animals, and in common with each other as a result of our animal origins (see Ingold, 1990), but it can also be conceived as including the ability to be cultural, that is, to go beyond purely natural responses and constraints. If something is within human nature then it might be seen as fixed and immovable; on the other hand, if it is the nature of humans to go beyond nature, including their own, then whatever is fixed must also be alterable. There seems to be a fundamental and paradoxical ambiguity around notions of permanence and change.

This is reinforced in a second related problem area, that of the relation between humans and the external natural environment. There are two related strands here. First, it has been widely held in the Western tradition of thought, again at least since the ancient Greeks, that humans are affected by their environment, that external conditions mould people in important ways. The nature of humans is seen as moulded by the environment, creating fairly fixed dispositions which are ingrained, as colour becomes ingrained into dyed wool. But if these ingrained attributes were formed through a process of change, of becoming, then logically they must themselves be subject to change, if the environment changes – just as a dyed wool will be 'permanently' dyed until such time as it is re-dyed with another colour or bleached. This ambiguous relation between permanence and change can be partially resolved by invoking time: changes produced over the *longue durée* are not easily changeable over the shorter term. But how long does the term have to be to create permanence? How old is the dog that cannot learn new tricks?

The second strand is ambiguity about what constitutes the environment. Is this the purely 'natural' environment or does it include the 'social' environment too? If it is in the nature of humans to be cultural, then it seems logical to include the social environment. As humans interact continuously with the natural environment, altering it all the time (as do all animals), then it is by no means clear that the two things can be separated out in any straightforward way. This again relates to questions of stability and change. If humans change their environments, then they change the very thing that acts to ingrain characteristics into them.

This tension between permanence and change does not seem to me resolvable in itself; it is part of the human, or even cosmic, condition. Every state of being is, from another point of view, a process of becoming. From the perspective of ideas about race, this is significant insofar as racial discourse is often held to invoke permanent, ingrained characteristics; it does this by referring to nature or biology, or possibly, in cultural racism, by associating certain cultural features with a given phenotype and/or making a coded reference to nature such that 'culture [is] almost biologised by its proximity to "race"' (Gilroy, 1987: 61). I will argue that, in the rather different historical understandings of nature, human nature (and racial nature) that I will survey, there is always a sense in which this tension between permanence and change makes itself felt.

The Ancient Greeks

I do not start with the Greeks from a simple desire to be comprehensive. I wish to show what a naturalising argument might look like in a context distant from that of the classic period of racial theorizing – the nineteenth century. However, it is also the case that distant as they may be in time, some of the basic theories of the ancients about nature and human nature had currency for over 2,000 years, strongly influencing the whole medieval period and appearing, for example, in Darwin's ideas about the mechanisms of heredity (even if Darwin himself was not aware of the connection). In what follows, I must of course be highly selective in my account.

According to Collingwood (1945), the ancient Greeks saw nature as saturated by a rational mind which gave it order. Aristotle conceived of a teleological purposiveness to the universe, although the purpose was not that of a conscious mind but rather a drive immanent in nature as a vital force within all living things. The purpose was directed towards harmony, rational order and a certain economy and tidiness of housekeeping. Although nature operated according to the so-called principle of plenitude – nature would fill up all available spaces with things – there was also a principle of neatness and order at work; nature did not make things unnecessarily (Glacken, 1967: 46–9). Humans were part of this overall order, even if there was a recognised distinction between *nomos*, the product of human artifice, custom or law, and *physis*, naturally determined things (Soper, 1995: 37; for an account of the meanings of physis, see Lovejoy and Boas, 1965: 447–51). Strong analogies were drawn between cosmic, earthly and human orders and, as these orders were linked into an overall unity, astrology occupied an important place as a form of 'cosmic environmentalism' (Glacken, 1967: 15).

For Plato and Aristotle, human nature was characterised fundamentally by its rationality, seen as morally virtuous. But humans could also go against their true nature and obey more animal emotions and urges (Trigg, 1988: chs 1, 2). It is worth noting that a divide between human reason and human animality did not parallel the divide between nomos and physis. Even though one meaning of physis was that which was spontaneous and instinctive in humans, as opposed to that which was learned, it was natural for people to be both rational and animal. This was not a view in which a natural, animalistic, irrational substratum in people had to be tamed by a cultural overlay.

Human diversity was recognised, including variation in skin colour, although dark skin was not seen as a mark of inferiority (Snowden, 1983), and accounts of such diversity included various monstrous beings (Hodgen, 1964: 20–9). The causes of such variation were not the subject of a great deal of theorising, but both the historian Herodotus and the physician Hippocrates considered that environmental influences were at work, although environment included both the physical and the social environment (Glacken, 1967: 7, 82–91). Just as the natural world was made up of four basic elements (water, air, fire and earth), so the human body was made up of four corresponding humours (respectively, phlegm, blood, yellow bile or choler and black bile or melancholy). Climatic influences impinged on the humours and could affect not only individual well-being but also the character of entire peoples (Glacken, 1967: 10–12, 88). However, according to Hippocrates, social institutions could influence the traits established by the physical environment. Polybius, a historian writing in the second century BC, reinforced this. He said, 'To our climate all of us become adapted by necessity', but he noted that the Arcadians, living in a tough climate, had introduced music and other measures 'to tame and soften the hardness of the soul through education' (cited in Glacken, 1967: 95).

There was a variety of theories about mechanisms of heredity, but a guiding principle was that, as Aristotle put it, 'in nature, like produces like' (cited in Huet, 1993: 13; see also Stubbe, 1972: ch. 2, on which much of what follows is based). This principle of continuity, which carries strong connotations of stability and permanence, was made operational in animals and humans by the fact that male semen (and female semen according to theorists such as Hippocrates) derived from all parts of the body. This theory is commonly known as pangenesis (after a similar theory proposed independently by Darwin over 2,000 years later). However, a host of other factors influenced the process of heredity, producing deviations from pure continuity. For example, according to Aristotle, male semen embodied the active, immaterial principle that gave form to the passive material contributed by the female by way of her menstrual blood (Aristotle rejected the idea that females produced semen). Thus children should resemble their father. Yet menstrual blood also influenced the embryo in its development and could suppress to some extent the formative action of the sperm. Therefore some children could also resemble their mother. More distant relatives – e.g., grandparents – also affected embryonic development, as indeed did the genus as a whole. That is, human children came out generically human as well as similar to their immediate relatives. Similarity was not confined to physical characteristics: 'the concept of heredity ... included the totality of physical and mental characters and features' (Stubbe, 1972: 12). As Pindar wrote: 'The noble spirit of the father/ Shines forth in the nature of his son' (cited in Stubbe, 1972: 15).

Meanwhile diet and climate affected the constitution of the body and thus the 'vital heat' of the male and his semen; this in turn affected the embryo. According to Aristotle, if the water, which was contained in all foods, was hard and cold, a man was more likely to produce female offspring. A belief in the impact of the environment was widespread and has lasted through the millennia. For the Greeks, however, such 'environmental factors' could, for some thinkers, include the experiences of the mother during pregnancy: a fright, for example, might affect the embryo's development. Such a belief can also be found in Genesis, chapter 30, where Jacob is said to have affected pregnant ewes by showing them spotted tree bark, resulting in spotted lambs (Stubbe, 1972: 10). This notion developed particularly in the Renaissance (Huet, 1993) and persisted into the nineteenth century, particularly in lay circles (Ritvo, 1997: 112–13). Traces of the belief exist today in ideas – often recounted as 'old wives' tales' – about influencing the gender of a baby by doing or eating certain things (see also Pearson, 1972).

Furthermore both Hippocrates and Aristotle believed in the inheritance of acquired characteristics. This idea, which again remained current into the early twentieth century, held that traits acquired during the lifetime of a person, usually through habit, could be transmitted to his or her offspring. The idea, as Mayr says (1982: 636), is intimately linked to the theory of pangenesis in the sense that this theory provides the mechanism by which such inheritance occurs: if the seed material that forms the next generation comes from all over the body then it can reflect the body's acquired characteristics.

What does all this add up to in terms of the themes of this chapter? The central issue is: What would a naturalising argument be in ancient Greek terms? This is not directly related to ideas about race, but it helps us to think more broadly about what naturalising discourses are and the forms they take.

For a start, we can see that, given the broad encompassing view of nature, a naturalising argument about humans did not by any means refer only to some organic substratum of biology. People's natural dispositions could be influenced by the planets (a belief still credible for some today): a naturalising argument could be an astrological argument. Second, although there was a distinction between physis and nomos, there was also a blurring of what Westerners would now call nature and culture: for example, a person's moral qualities would be transmitted, along with his/her physical qualities, in the natural process of sexual reproduction. Third, we can detect a tension between ideas of continuity and permanence, on the one hand, and change and instability, on the other. Nature, including human nature, had the connotation of something intrinsic and permanent (Lovejoy and Boas, 1965: 448), and this was expressed in concepts of heredity which held that like produced like. Yet this was in some sense an ideal – one could say a Platonic ideal, an essentialist concept which Mayr (1982: 87) argues has never been able to deal with the world of living organisms – and in fact human nature was subject to all kinds of alterations and changes in the process of its development. (It is worth noting that, for the pre-Socratic physiologists to whom the word physis meant intrinsic permanent qualities, it also, 'according to certain interpreters', meant 'becoming' (Lovejoy and Boas, 1965: 448).) The environment affected the humours in ways that conditioned the constitution of whole geographical aggregates of people in an ingrained way, yet it also had very specific effects on the changing constitutions of individuals as reflected in their well-being.

The Late Eighteenth Century

To shift suddenly to a period many hundreds of years later may seem to be taking liberties, but I repeat that this chapter is not by way of a comprehensive review. These snapshots are only illustrative. I choose this period because, by this time, views of nature and human nature had several features which are very familiar to Western readers today (although the views of the Greeks, as outlined above, perhaps do not seem so foreign either).

Ideas of change and progress of an evolutionary kind existed by this time. Such change was not a Darwinian process of evolution, driven by natural selection, but was driven by a cosmic teleology, ultimately divinely ordained, which had produced newer, more complex, 'higher' forms from older, simpler, 'lower' ones and which had also underlain human 'progress' from simple hunting societies through pastoral and agriculture stages to higher civilisations, of which European societies were the prime exemplar (Meek, 1976). The role of God was variable. For British scientists, 'natural theology', with its roots in the Christian Middle Ages, retained its power into the nineteenth century; God's presence in the natural world was quite immediate. For German and French scientists, a 'deist' perspective, in which God was a much more distant overseeing figure, was more attractive (Mayr, 1982: 103–7; see also Spary, 1996: 181–4).

Old theories were still current. The notion of a Great Chain of Being, dating from the ancient Greeks, still commanded respect and indeed attained its widest diffusion and acceptance at this time (Lovejoy, 1964: 183). According to this, every being was arranged in a *scala naturae* or unitary natural hierarchy of perfection, designed by God, with God and the angels at the top and the simplest forms at the bottom. This basically static idea was taking on a developmentalist form (Hodgen, 1964: ch. 10; Lovejoy, 1964: ch. 9), but the corollary idea of analogous relationships between different levels (cosmic, earthly, human, individual) was still strong (Jordanova, 1986b: 29). The scala naturae was also increasingly in conflict with other ways of classifying the natural world: it posited a hierarchy of infinite gradations and intermediate forms, yet work in the classification of plants, for example, seemed to show that they could not be arranged into a single chain (Mayr, 1982: 201–2).

Older views of nature as a machine, with roots in the work of Bacon, Newton and Descartes, also still held sway in the sense that nature, while understood as something in progress (and thus unlike a machine), was also seen as a rational, regular, law-governed entity. Its structures and functions, while ultimately given by God, were open to discovery. For the Swedish naturalist Linnaeus, for example, a truly 'natural' classification system would reflect the divinely created diversity of the natural world (Mayr, 1982: 199–200). The natural order could, in principle, be broken down into constituent parts and, while such mechanistic materialism was arguably a dominant force, it lived in tension with more vitalistic perspectives, expressed especially later on in nineteenth-century German *naturphilosophie*, linked with the Romantic movement, according to which the world of nature was moved by immanent vital forces, in themselves more or less inexplicable (Gasking, 1967: 96; Jardine, 1996; Larson, 1979; Mayr, 1982: 105–6). In any case, nature was open to intervention and improving nature through empirical experimentation and careful management was part and parcel of improving the human situation (Spary, 1996).

From a moral and aesthetic point of view, ideas about nature were ambivalent (Lovejoy, 1948: 69–77). On the one hand, neo-classical values held that universal aesthetic standards were natural: they related to simplicity, balance, symmetry and regularity of form. On the other hand, 'nature' also began to have more pronounced Romantic meanings associated with getting to the heart of the particularity of individual places, cultures and epochs, all part of a diversity which evolved and expanded. French writers of the period, for example, sometimes saw nature as an ethical norm in its justness and harmony, and also questioned such a view, portraying nature as blindly amoral (Pilkington, 1986).

Human nature was seen in rather varied ways during the Enlightenment period. Philosophers such as David Hume and Adam Ferguson posited a basic universal constancy in human nature which 'still remains the same in its principles and operations' (Hume, cited in Jahoda, 1992: 34). As Ferguson said: 'Nature ... having given to every animal its mode of existence, its disposition and manners of life, has dealt equally with those of the human race' (cited in Jahoda, 1992: 38). Hume saw human nature as consisting of a set of fixed wants, mainly selfish, but which could include sympathy for others. Reason helped people to achieve their ends and the social order developed to serve their aims (Trigg, 1988: ch. 5). Rousseau thought, however, that humans were less subject to the dictates of nature and that 'man participates in his [functioning] as a free agent' (cited in Jahoda, 1992: 64). For him, as for the German philosopher Herder, human nature was a less fixed entity. In any event, a division between nature and culture which is familiar to – if not exactly the same as that of – today's Western world was clearly apparent. Central to the epoch were debates about the relation between 'nature' and 'custom' or 'art' (broadly meaning artifice or the product of human design) and, in affairs of human art and custom, it was seen as morally good to follow the dictates of nature in a specifically human way: 'the proper exercise of choice respected nature while going beyond it' (Strathern, 1992a: 96).

Yet the familiarity of eighteenth-century concepts to today's readers is deceptive. There was in fact a rather blurred division between 'nature', if this is seen as a more or less fixed underlying biological substrate, and 'culture', if this is seen as a socialising and civilising overlay. To start with, let us look briefly at the doctrine of environmental influences which was the principal means of explaining human diversity at this time: 'Climatic causality flourished in previous centuries, but never so independently as it did in the eighteenth' (Glacken, 1967: 620). Although a minority of thinkers, such as Voltaire, were proponents of polygenesis – the idea that different 'races' of humans had different origins and were fundamentally different, even constituting different species – most believed that all 'races' or 'varieties' of humans formed a single species and had a single origin – the doctrine of monogenesis (Greene, 1959: 221). Therefore differences among humans were generally explained by the action of the environment.

Of course the very reliance on the environment as a major explanatory factor, in principle at least, would appear to go against a notion of an inherited biological substrate, but in fact this is not necessarily so. Environment can be adduced as effecting very slow change (just as, in the theory of natural selection, environmental pressures influence the overall distribution of genetic material and cause species to emerge, change and disappear), so that in the shorter term it produces more or less permanent characteristics. This argument was certainly implied in eighteenth-century accounts, allowing for the possibility of a fairly clear distinction between a permanent underlying nature and more flexible overlying culture, but this possibility was not fully taken and the distinction was ambiguous. On the one hand, it was common currency in much Enlightenment thought that humans shared a universal, constant nature; on the other hand, the environment caused differences amongst humans. The ambiguity lay in whether those differences affected 'human nature'. How permanent were they? How deep did they go? Referring to the period 1755–83 in North America, Jordan says that human nature was not seen as malleable; it was seen instead as an 'unstable constant' in that people held the potential for both barbarism and civilisation, depending precisely on their surroundings (1977: 288). Jordan does not really explain how malleability and instability differ (the former may be more controllable than the latter, but they both necessitate change), nor how something can be both constant and unstable. This captures neatly the paradoxical tension between permanence and change.

Comte de Buffon, one of the century's leading natural historians, put considerable weight on environmental influences, rejecting ideas of evolutionary change (Glacken, 1967: 587–91; Mayr, 1982: 335). For example, he stated that 'the differences in [human skin] colour depend much, though not entirely, upon the climates. There are many other causes ... The nature of food is one of the principal causes ... Manners, or the mode of living, may also have considerable effects' (cited in Todorov, 1993: 102). At the same time, for Buffon 'moeurs [manners] depend on both climate and food' (Glacken, 1967: 591). There is a general correlation in the animal world between climate and types of physique and temperament, but also within each species one finds 'the climate made by manners and manners by the climate' (cited in Sloan, 1973: 304, my translation). We see here a complex interaction between environment and culture or, as Todorov (1993: 103) suggests, a fusion of the physical and the moral. Jahoda (1992: 24) reiterates that no clear distinction was made at the time between ecological and cultural aspects of the environment, although David Hume did separate physical from moral causes of human variation. He thought that climate was responsible for causing differences in major geographical groupings of humans, but that moral factors also operated at a smaller scale, such as within Europe where national differences could be influenced by variations in wealth, work regimes and government (Jahoda, 1992: 39–40).

The importance attached to food by Buffon was related to his ideas about the mechanisms of generation and heredity. He thought that species did not evolve from one to another, but formed spontaneously from the chemical combination of organic molecules. The first exemplar of a species was a prototype which defined a *moule intérieur* or internal mould which every member of the species had within it as an immanent archetype, guaranteeing species permanence. Food ingested by an individual supplied organic molecules and these were formed by the mould which, as a kind of force itself, organised the operation of Newtonian-type forces acting on the molecules. The continuity produced by the mould was continually in tension with change produced by circumstances which created variation within the species: 'sometimes these organic molecules are not perfectly assimilated to the interior mould' due to variations in food intake (cited in Sloan, 1973: 305, my translation). The rather abstract notion of species form was allied to a theory of pangenesis in which all parts of the body supplied living particles, derived from ingested food, that made up male and female seminal fluids which mixed in the womb to form a small structured body (Gasking, 1967: 87–90; Mayr, 1982: 333; Sloan, 1973: 300–2; Spary, 1996: 185; Stubbe, 1972: 80).[7] This is very close to Aristotle's ideas about a general underlying species form and more immediate parental influences. The point is that a person's physical nature was formed in very direct, constitutional ways by environmental influences such as food intake. Although the idea of climatic influence on skin colour suggests a level of permanence and fixity, the allied idea that food intake and even mode of living could have important effects suggests a much more flexible process. The permanence of the internal mould was balanced by the forces of changing circumstances, as the mould was dependent on the intake of food which supplied the human substance for reproduction. Indeed, in discussing domestic animals, Buffon suggested that the internal mould itself was subject to gradual modification through the influence of food and the 'quality of the humours' in the milieu (cited in Sloan, 1973: 303).

Sloan (1973: 309–10) argues that Buffon's theories allowed his avowed monogenism – the doctrine that all human beings originated from the same source and therefore shared an underlying nature – to carry within it the latent seeds of polygenism – the idea that different sorts, or 'races', of humans had separate origins and might therefore be radically distinct, even different species – a doctrine that was to be become increasingly popular in the nineteenth century. As Buffon posited a mechanism by which the environment could create long-term difference within a species – and Buffon considered all humans to be one species – this could underwrite notions of significant and stable differences between kinds of humans, that is, between 'races'. The wider context for Sloan's argument is that, whatever Buffon's precise theories, he concurred with most of his contemporaries in the view that blacks and other non-Europeans were inferior to whites (see also Todorov, 1993: 102). Nevertheless there is clearly a tension between stability and change in Buffon's thought and this is typical of the difficulty of reconciling the two: what can be seen as introducing flexibility (the action of the environment on the expression of the internal mould and even its very form), can also be seen as suggesting stability (the changes introduced are then fixed for practical purposes).

Some thinkers did make a more radical disjunction than did Buffon between permanent nature and more transient characteristics. The German philosopher Johann Gottfried Herder thought that 'the Negro form is transmitted in hereditary succession and it may be changed only by genetic means' such as miscegenation with a European. Environmental moulding of human forms was a slow process: 'regions alter them [the shapes and forms of nations] very slowly'. Change and variation entered this picture of permanence and stability mainly by means of sexual reproduction which blended parental 'souls' to produce new forms; however, the 'forms of long-departed ancestors' could also return to later generations and Herder further believed that the 'bodily and mental affections of the [pregnant] mother' could influence the unborn child (cited in Stubbe, 1972: 91–2).

Many scientists and thinkers, however, saw a more intimate and interactive relation between continuity over generations and processes of change. Lamarck – who I include here despite the fact that he published mostly after 1800, when he was already over 50 years old – was a proponent of the doctrine of inheritance of acquired characteristics, an ancient and widely accepted theory (Jordanova, 1984: ch. 5; Mayr, 1982: 353–6). He held that the use and disuse of organs in everyday life affected their development. For him, the structure of an organ and its function developed together and he rejected the Cartesian idea of the body as a mechanism made up of a set of fixed structures with predetermined functions. The notion of habit was central: habits were adaptations to the environment and the way an organism satisfied its needs; habits materially affected physiological development. Usage influenced the movement and behaviour of 'subtle fluids' in the body and these fluids, though not open to direct observation, were the underlying forces behind all organic processes and such observable forces as magnetism, heat and electricity. The physical changes acquired during one generation could be transmitted through the mechanisms of heredity to offspring – which remained unspecified by Lamarck, although he did say the changes had to have occurred in both parents. Jordanova (1984: 56, 60) says that it was not clear whether the inheritance of acquired characteristics over the individual life cycle was a mechanism by which changes occurred at the larger scale over longer periods, or simply an analogy for these changes. (This of course is connected to the ambiguity of the time factor when it mediates the paradox of characters being fixed in nature by the action of the environment and the same characters being changed by the environment: it is always unclear how long a time period is at issue.)

In another work Jordanova reinforces this idea of the imbrication of nature and culture in the late eighteenth century, in this case, in relation to sexuality and the family and the ways these were represented in literary and medical texts (Jordanova, 1986c; see also Jordanova, 1987: ch. 2). Female physiology was increasingly a focus of medical concern, especially in the domain of sexual reproductive functions. This was part of the general increase in scientific attention to and intervention in the human body, but it was also related to a growing concern with managing national economies and moralities. In this process the family was sacralised and naturalised as the proper place for sexual and social reproduction and also, in the context of the increasing commodification of social relations, as a non-commodified domain. According to prevailing views of human nature, female physiology was not seen simply as a biological substrate, separable from culture. At this time, 'life was commonly associated with activity and plasticity, with the adaptive powers of the organism and with organisation, that is the structural complexity of a living being'. This view

sustained an approach to sexuality which stressed not the reproductive organs or genitals, but the sex of the entire organism. Every fibre of a female carried femininity within it – a femininity which was acquired by custom and habit ... A rigid demarcation between mind and body thus made no sense, since the organism was one integrated whole. Hence, clearly, the moral and the social emerged out of the natural organisation of living matter ... Organisms interacted with their surroundings, giving sexuality a behavioural dimension, in that females became full women by doing womanly things, like breast-feeding their children. (Jordanova, 1986c: 106–7)

Spary (1996: 190–2) also notes how explicit connections were made between the anatomical structures and the moral qualities of both animals and humans. This was done partly through the 'language of sensibility' – in which sensibility was construed as a property of animal bodies under control of the will, as opposed to 'irritability' which was the simple reflexive reaction of the muscles. Sensibility was controlled by the will, yet it too 'resided in the fabric of the animal body'.

In all this, the social was naturalised by seeing social behaviour as constitutive of human nature and physical constitution. This was reinforced by seeing humans as shaped by and shaping themselves within an 'environment' which included both social and non-social elements (Jordanova, 1987: 25). This is rather different from attributing particular observable human traits to an underlying biology or genetic code. Above all, it gives people a significant element of agency in their own constitution as a natural person.

In sum, in the late eighteenth century we find a view of human nature which is recognisable in many ways with views current today in the West, but which also had significant differences. Nature and culture, although distinguished from each other, were not distinguished in the way with which we are familiar in the West today. When in 1758 Linnaeus characterised the American variety of *Homo sapiens* as 'copper-coloured, choleric, erect', with 'hair black, straight and thick; nostrils wide; face harsh, beard scanty', as 'obstinate, content, free' and as a person who 'paints himself with fine red lines' and is 'regulated by customs', he was adducing elements which we would normally see as natural and cultural as together constituting the nature of these people (cited in Popkin, 1973: 248). In this fusion of nature and culture, people's behaviour helped constitute their natures, as Jordanova shows. Buffon's environmentalism and his ideas about the mechanisms of heredity were also affected by this conception. Such were the manifestations of an underlying tension between permanence and instability in ideas about human nature.

What were the implications of these ways of thinking for notions of race? Ideas that non-Europeans were inferior to Europeans were very widespread in the West at the time. Notions about the fusion, imbrication or mutual constitution of nature and culture did not ameliorate this (see Barker, 1978; Jordan, 1977; Popkin, 1973; Todorov, 1993: ch. 2). Indeed, Todorov's contention that at this time 'there is no reason as yet to speak of racialism: we are operating within a classification of cultures not bodies' (1993: 101) seems a little weak, given the ambiguous boundary between culture and body.[8] In fact this ambiguity was one of the characteristics of ideas about racial hierarchy: non-Europeans were seen as inferior in both nature and culture in a way that, precisely, did not distinguish very clearly between them. This allowed culture to be naturalised, just as it also opened the possibility of culturalising nature.

The importance of environmentalism, albeit beset by logical paradoxes about the relative roles of permanence and change, allowed debates in which human equality could be asserted and human differences explained by environmental factors amenable to change. Thus the Reverend Samuel Stanhope Smith proposed that blacks in North America were getting whiter (which presumably seemed to him a good thing) due to the influence of the environment and the inheritance of acquired characteristics; he was also a fervent believer in the basic equality of humans (Jordan, 1977: 486–7, 513–15). In this sense, American Revolutionary ideologies of equality sat well with doctrines of environmentalism. On the other hand, believers in the inferiority of blacks could use the very same environmentalist arguments to assert that the African environment had ingrained certain traits into black people so deeply as to be 'natural' to them (Jordan, 1977: 287–94, 305). Views of the kind I have described above did provide certain possibilities: social behaviour could be seen as creating aspects of the physical and heritable constitution and this avoided a biological determinism of the genetic kind familiar today, putting greater responsibility onto the individual and his or her surroundings. However, environmentalism could also be used to adduce fixity in a domain of nature which was expanded to include larger realms of the human constitution.

Jefferson and the Distinctions of 'Nature'

As a way of rounding off the argument above, we can look at a quotation that Banton takes from the writings of Thomas Jefferson, the second President of the US. Discussing Jefferson's view of black people, Banton notes that he advocated the abolition of slavery, but that he believed blacks to be different from – in fact inferior to – whites and found environmentalist explanations of the difference unconvincing. Jefferson wrote: 'It is not their [the blacks'] condition, then, but nature, which has produced the distinction.' Banton comments that although Jefferson was 'uncertain whether blacks were "originally a distinct race, or made distinct by time and circumstance" the difference between them and the whites was equated with the difference between species' (Banton, 1987: 13).

One could quibble with the last assertion, noting that Jordan – whom Banton is using as his source here – actually observes that Jefferson was very evasive on the question of species difference (Jordan, 1977: 489). However, I am interested in the appearance of the word 'nature' and how this is understood by readers whether in 1987, when Banton was writing, or now. It is easy enough to assume that we know what Jefferson meant but, in the absence of a consideration by Banton of how 'nature' was conceived by Jefferson and his contemporaries, we are likely to be misled. Like many other thinkers and naturalists of his era, Jefferson believed that nature was an orderly system, the basic character of which had been divinely ordained and designed. In the simplest terms, then, for a difference to be natural meant it had been designed by God, in the beginning, and was immutable. Differences could, however, also be caused by the environment, which included ways of living, not just the 'natural' environment. For example, in explaining the situation of indigenous Americans, Jefferson availed himself of environmentalist explanations (Jordan, 1977: 478–80; see also Greene, 1984: 321–2). This was partly because he admired these people more than he did blacks and partly because he was engaged in disputes with such Europeans as Buffon who, in his attempt to glorify Europe, held that the New World environment produced weakness and degeneration – Jefferson went so far as to ship the bones and hide of an American moose to Buffon in order to convince him of its huge size (Glacken, 1967: 682). Jefferson was concerned to defend the American environment and the people it had produced.

Jefferson was caught in a contradiction between his belief that all humans had been created equal by God and his belief that blacks were – by nature and therefore by God's design – inferior. He partly resolved this contradiction by holding that, 'whatever be their [blacks'] degree of talent it is no measure of their rights' (cited in Jordan, 1977: 454), meaning that even if blacks were inferior intellectually they still had a natural and equal right to freedom. He also avoided the contradiction by equivocation: were the differences between blacks and whites really 'natural' and permanent or rather caused by 'time and circumstance' and thus in principle reversible? Jordan shows that Jefferson hedged his bets on this question time and again (1977: 429–90). In sum, the matter is not quite as straightforward as it appears, either in Banton's representation of it or in likely understandings of his account by today's readers. Jefferson both rejected and used environmentalism; the environment could encompass ways of living as well as climate and such like; there was uncertainty about the permanence of nature and Jefferson hovered between a conviction that blacks could not be improved by a change in their circumstances and the possibility that they could.

Jefferson's conception of what comprised the natural difference between blacks and whites is also instructive. He focused above all on intellectual capacity which he thought to be part of human nature (whether or not that nature could be altered). Moral capacities – conscience, for example – were the same for blacks and whites. But this did not mean morality was a 'social' thing while intellect was 'physical'. On the contrary, 'moral sense, or conscience' was 'as much part of man as his arm or his leg' and was 'a part of his physical constitution' (cited in Jordan, 1977: 439). In his writings the American physician Benjamin Rush listed under the heading of 'Physiology' the various human faculties of instinct, memory, imagination, understanding, will, passions and emotions, faith and moral sense (Jordan, 1977: 441). Jordan argues that Jefferson separated moral sense from intellect as distinct faculties, so that he could argue that blacks were equal to whites on one level but inferior on the other. However, they were both seen as part of human physiology in a way that is familiar from the writings of Spary and Jordanova, discussed above.

To summarise, racial differences were naturalised by Jefferson and others of his contemporaries. Looking at this from today's perspective, we may assume that we know what such naturalisation consisted of – for example, assigning biological causes to things – but the account given above shows that things were a good deal more complex than this. This did not prevent such naturalisations being racist. On the contrary, the idea that a person's morality was part of their physiology – not because biology simply dictated culture, but because habit became imbued in physical constitution – could easily be deployed to racist effect. It is just as racist – perhaps more so – to say that people who live poor lives become 'naturally' inferior, as it is to say that people who are 'biologically' inferior are destined to live poor lives. In seeking to understanding racisms and how they operate, it is important to grasp the complexities of the naturalisations on which they rely.

The Late Nineteenth Century

The nineteenth century has received much attention from scholars working on the understandings of and debates about both race and nature. This was the period during which the British physician Robert Knox wrote in his book *The Races of Men* (1850) that 'race is everything ... civilisation depends on it'; the idea of race came to assume a huge explanatory significance. This was also the period in which the ideas of Darwin, among others, set the scene for modern understandings of the operation of the natural world. It is not my purpose to attempt a neat synthesis of this entire period and the literature produced about it. As before, my account has to be selective.

Approaches to nature are not easy to characterise. Mayr (1982: 113) writes that, in the biological sciences at least, it is very hard to sketch successive paradigms of thought; too many conflicting ideas existed contemporaneously. Nevertheless by the late nineteenth century the idea that nature was an evolving system, as opposed to a static one, was well established. The mechanism driving it was not entirely clear, but notions of, first, adaptation and, second, natural selection were gaining ground. In addition – and in some ways despite this, as a machine is not an evolving entity – mechanistic understandings of nature were also dominant. Vitalism lost ground during this period and the workings of nature were generally seen as amenable to reductionist scientific explanations. Natural theology also weakened during the nineteenth century, even in Britain where it had been strongest, and God became a more distant figure in explanations of natural processes.

There were contradictory elements at work. For example, Darwin established that the concept of species was ultimately an arbitrary designation: as a constantly evolving system, nature could not be divided up into definite species, except for purposes of classificatory convenience. Yet the concept of species continued to have a powerful hold, as if it represented a substantive and permanent reality (Mayr, 1982: 269–70; Ritvo, 1997: 86). As usual, the different time scales involved caused different views: nature might be continually on the move, but that movement seemed to be so slow and gradual as to be imperceptible in the shorter term, such that nature appeared to be divisible into real categories.

Perspectives on human nature were also varied in ways that had much in common with the late eighteenth century. Marx might have been writing that 'the real nature of man is the totality of social relations' (cited in Stevenson, 1987: 61), but more common was a view, derived from the Enlightenment, that human nature was a set of biological needs and wants and that human nature, although unique and perhaps God-given, was also linked to the non-human animals with which humans were connected through common descent. That there might be links between apes and humans was not a new idea: it was a connotation of the idea of the Great Chain of Being which, with its infinite scale of gradations, had always opened up the theologically dangerous possibility of intermediate steps between humans and animals (Jordan, 1977: 228–34). Now, however, that connotation was a more widely accepted fact.

As in the eighteenth century, there was a basic distinction between nature and culture, but ideas about the way continuity and variation operated in sexual reproduction still made the distinction rather different from that which would dominate the twentieth century. It is true that important developments had laid the seeds of the later form of this distinction. Mayr (1982: 695–8) argues that ideas about 'soft inheritance' were in decline this time, while mechanisms of 'hard inheritance' were being suggested (see also Paul, 1995: ch. 3). Soft inheritance is based largely on the inheritance of acquired characteristics, a notion that, as we have seen, goes back to the ancient Greeks. This is connected to the theory of pangenesis which states that reproductive seed material derives from all parts of the body. More generally, soft inheritance is the idea that the environment can affect the reproductive seed material that is passed from parents to offspring, whether or not this occurs by way of acquired alterations to the parents' external physique. Hard inheritance, in contrast, implies that the genetic material a parent passes on is constant and is not affected by the environment and experiences of the parent. This is the view established most incontrovertibly after the 1953 discovery of the structure of DNA which made it clear that the genetic material consists of a code which each parent passes on and which is not itself altered by environmental influences (with the exception of environmentally-induced mutations), although the way the coded instructions, or genotype, influence the development of the physical organism, or phenotype, certainly is affected by the environment.

Ideas of soft inheritance continued to be the norm throughout the nineteenth century. Various people challenged the idea of the inheritance of acquired characteristics and the associated influence of the environment. The naturalist James Prichard did so early on, at least in the first 1813 edition of his work *Researches into the Physical History of Mankind*; in later editions he changed his views to a more environmentalist position (Mayr, 1982: 688, 695; Stepan, 1982: 43; see also Stocking, 1971). The German biologist August Weismann did so in a much more detailed way, based on laboratory experiments which led him in the 1880s to postulate the existence of 'germ plasm' which was the reproductive material that controlled heredity but was separate from and unaffected by the organism's bodily development. (Even Weismann, however, suggested that parental experiences over several generations could lead to hereditary abnormality; see Lubinsky, 1993: 82.) Darwin's cousin, Francis Galton, trained as a medic but with wider scientific interests and best known as the founder of the eugenics movement which was to flower from 1900 to 1930, also proposed in 1875 a hard theory of inheritance based on the concept of a 'stirp', similar to Weismann's germ plasm (Cowan, 1985; Kevles, 1995: 18; Mayr, 1982: 695–704; Stubbe, 1972: ch. 8). Despite these developments, the theory of soft inheritance held sway during the nineteenth century – characterising Darwin's ideas, for example, and having particular force in France where neo-Lamarckism was popular – and retained some hold in scientific and medical circles until the 1930s (Jordanova, 1984: 108; Lubinsky, 1993; Mayr, 1982: 793; Paul, 1995: ch. 3).

Ideas of soft inheritance were evident in the widespread belief in telegony, the notion that a male who reproduced with a given female could influence the offspring the female had by subsequent mates. Although the precise mechanism by which this occurred seems to have been vague – as were in fact most ideas concerning heredity at the time – the male's form somehow shaped the female's reproductive capacity in a long-term fashion, perhaps because the sperm impacted directly on the female's store of unfertilised eggs or because paternal germs cells spread, via the embryo, throughout the mother's body (Pearson, 1972: 9). Animal breeders thought that a pedigree female who had 'crossed' once (especially if it was her first mating) might thereafter produce hybrids (Ritvo, 1997: 107–10). Pearson (1972) observes that in lay circles the belief persisted into the 1970s with respect to sexual relations between white women and black men (see below; see also Banton, 1987: 27).

All this meant that while human nature was seen as a biological substrate, it was not easily separable from culture. This is not the same as saying that the final character of an individual was a mixture of 'nature and nurture' – although it is significant that this dichotomy was used by Galton, one of the few who proposed a theory of hard inheritance.[9] The point is that 'nurture' affected the very constitution of 'nature' rather than just its manifestation.

How did this affect ideas about race? The nineteenth century has been characterised as the period during which ideas about racial diversity hardened into scientific racism and racial typologising. In an essay on French anthropology in 1800, Stocking (1982: 21–30) compares two advisers to the Société des Observateurs de l'Homme: the philosopher and intellectual descendant of the Enlightenment *encyclopédistes*, Citizen Degérando, and the renowned naturalist Georges Cuvier. The first represented a monogenist view in which race was not an important concept in understanding and categorising human diversity. The second represented and 'indeed might even be said to have promulgated the point of view which largely dominated biology in the first half of the [nineteenth] century: the essentially static, non-evolutionary tradition of comparative anatomy' (Stocking, 1982: 29). Although the static nature of the perspective would change, Cuvier established the emphasis on the measuring of skulls and bones that was to play such a large part in racial typologising.

Stepan, following other work by Stocking, describes how, in the first half of the nineteenth century, British racial science was generally environmentalist and monogenist, shaped largely by James Prichard. But doubts about environmentalism already existed in the late eighteenth century and by the 1820s many scientists were expressing their dissatisfaction with the idea. After about 1850, polygenism began to win through, with its theory that different 'races' had different origins, that environmental influences could not alter racial type and that racial type was innate and immutable (Stepan, 1982: 38–9, 43–4; see also Stocking, 1971). Jordan (1977: 533) also notes that in discussions about the causes of skin colour in the US, 'environmentalism showed signs everywhere of giving way during the early years of the nineteenth century'. Banton (1987) traces a shift from the pre-1800 view of race as lineage, in which all the descendants of a given set of ancestors were members of a common stock, to the nineteenth-century concept of race as type, in which humans were divided into a limited number of permanent racial types, often seen as having distinct origins.[10]

Such authors note how the growth of evolutionary thought, despite its monogenism and its emphasis on continuous change and adaptation, which all fundamentally challenged the basic concept of polygenetic, static and permanent racial types, nevertheless failed to undermine these ideas about race (Banton, 1987: 73; Stepan, 1982: chs 3, 4; Stocking, 1982: ch. 3). In fact ideas about competition and the survival of the fittest were seen as substantiating ideas about the superiority of Europeans, who could be seen as a 'race' favoured by natural selection. The square peg of polygenism was made to fit into the round hole of monogenism by affirming that, although humans all had a common origin at some remote point in time (and the great antiquity of the earth was by then commonly accepted), they had separated out into distinct types at some less remote but still very distant time and had remained distinct ever since. Indeed, both the founders of the theory of evolution by natural selection, Charles Darwin and A.R. Wallace, subscribed to such views themselves (Stocking, 1982: 46).

Polygenenist theories implied that 'races' were, or were virtually, species. By the usual criterion – that of the ability of members of the same species to produce offspring which could themselves produce offspring – humans seemed self-evidently to be of the same species. But many theorists held that the human racial 'hybrids' were in fact infertile or, at the least, were weak, inferior and doomed to extinction. Such apparently contradictory thinking was not unusual. Animal breeders were very concerned about the 'purity' of their pedigree stock and avoided 'mongrelisation' with care. Yet it was also obvious that some pedigrees had mixed origins or indeed had originally sprung from an intentional cross-breeding; the 'purity' that was maintained over generations was also subject to dispute and wild strains were sometimes purposely introduced to improve domestic breeds. None of this, however, dispelled the basic notion of pedigree nor the concern with avoiding *unwanted* mixture (Ritvo, 1997: ch. 3). These overarching conceptual values – pedigree, purity – provided the perspective from which the evidence could be viewed with relative ease.

In short, ideas about race had taken a decisive turn. Monogenism did not disappear nor did environmentalist explanations, but the notion of race as type was dominant. Yet even in the midst of such thinking, the tension between permanence and change was not entirely resolved. For a start, the theory of the inheritance of acquired characteristics and other ideas of soft inheritance persisted and this inevitably introduced possibilities of short-term variation through environmental influence. Mayr (1982: 688) notes that this seems to have involved contradictions:

The acceptance of an unchanging essence, the basic credo of the essentialists, would seem to necessitate a belief in hard inheritance. It puzzles me therefore how universally the essentialists at the period were able to reconcile soft inheritance with the concept of an unchanging essence.

(For Mayr, the essentialists were not just the racial typologists – he refers only in passing to racial theory – but naturalists and biologists of all periods who held to Platonic ways of thinking about natural kinds, assuming that there were definite, separable kinds, each with a common underlying essence which represented its true character.) Mayr (1982: 688) continues: 'They escaped the dilemma by defining all characters subject to soft inheritance as "accidental", their variation not affecting the essence.' This is an important point. Stepan (1982: 93) also notes that the notion of racial type was explicitly understood as something not directly observable. It was precisely an underlying essence, subject to all kinds of variation in its observable manifestations. As an example of this kind of thinking, Stepan (1982) and Stocking (1982: 61–5) both use the writings of the US sociologist William Z. Ripley who, in his book *Races of Europe* (1899), summarised the results of European research into physical anthropology. Ripley used maps of trait distributions to infer underlying racial types. These types, three originally, had been confused over time by 'chance, variation, migration, intermixture and changing environments' (Ripley, cited in Stepan, 1982: 94). It was the job of the analyst to get behind these confusions and establish the underlying type. (Interestingly Ripley used the sort of statistical methods that are characteristic of what Mayr (1982: 45) calls populational thinking. Mayr sees populational thinking as completely opposed to essentialist thinking by virtue of its emphasis on shifting populations made up of unique individuals, describable as aggregates only in statistical, stochastic terms and changing in both time and space. Yet Ripley used these techniques to think in essentialist ways.) Ripley had, in the end, to be both an environmentalist and a racial typologist; he believed in permanent, hereditary racial types, but also in the shaping influence of the environment and in the inheritance of acquired characteristics. Ripley was not alone in making these combinations. Louis Agassiz, the well-known US anti-evolutionist who believed that differences between 'races' were like species differences, claimed that it was part of the potential of the essence to respond to the environment (Banton, 1987: 40; Mayr, 1982: 688). Todorov notes how the French historian Hipployte Taine considered races to be innate and immutable: 'There is one [fixed element], a character and a spirit proper to the race, transmitted from generation to generation, remaining the same through cultural change' (Taine, cited in Todorov, 1993: 155). Yet he also held that the same fixed element was an adaptation to the environment. Todorov (1993: 155) comments: 'The inside that was supposed to be opposed to the outside is only a slightly older outside.' We are back to the usual paradox: the changing environment creates 'fixed' qualities – but fixed over what time period? Robert J. Young (1995: 27) has also noted this point:

The question is whether the old essentialising categories of cultural identity, or race, were really so essentialised, or have been retrospectively constructed as more fixed than they were. When we look at the texts of racial theory, we find that they are in fact contradictory, disruptive and already deconstructed.

The difficult balance between permanence and change existed not just in debates between polygenists and monogenists but also within the thinking of the polygenists themselves. It is also apparent when we look at contexts beyond the confines of scientific and literary thought. This brings up difficult questions of the relationship between lay and expert knowledge, but I do not wish to tackle these directly. Suffice to say that I assume that there is a complex series of interactive relationships linking scientists, popularisers of science working through books and other media, educationalists and different sets of lay people who have more or less formal education and interest in scientific knowledge. In the account of a particular historical context that I refer to below, it is unclear exactly what impact contemporary scientific debates were having. What is evident is that the same tension existed between the permanence of a racialised human nature and its protean qualities; in this case, it caused anxiety for colonial administrators.

I am referring to Stoler's excellent studies of the Dutch and French colonies in south-east Asia in the late nineteenth century (see, e.g., Stoler, 1992, 1995, 1997b). I am particularly interested in some specific details of the historical material she presents, but some of her wider concerns are also relevant. She draws on Foucault's idea that a new form of knowing emerged in the nineteenth century which sought 'great hidden forces' in order to group and know things by means of what was hidden 'down below' (Foucault, cited in Stoler, 1995: 205). This is in line with Foucault's ideas, outlined in Chapter 2, about the predominance of bio-power in nineteenth-century European nations and the consequent interest in the hidden natural forces of life, including human sexuality. The thematic of blood and race was intertwined with ideas about nations and bodies, so Stoler (1995: 205) wishes to interrogate 'the epistemic principles, the ways of knowing' on which racisms rely. She contends that 'racism is not only a "visual ideology" where the visible and the somatic confirm the "truth" of the self' and that 'folk and scientific theories of race have rarely, if ever, been about somatics alone'. Instead 'Euro-American racial thinking related the visual markers of race to the protean hidden properties of different human kinds.' Stoler's general concern with ways of knowing certainly fits well with my own concern to understand ways of naturalising and the notion of hidden forces ties nicely to the nineteenth-century concept of underlying racial type, not necessarily easily visible on the body. What is of specific interest is the idea that human kinds had properties that were not only hidden but also protean. In the midst of nineteenth-century theories about fixed racial types and permanent, innate racial differences, people in the colonies were anxious about the subtle changes being wrought on and in human bodies and temperaments which might alter their racial status in problematic ways. Stoler's is a rather different way of dealing with the contradiction noted by Mayr, above, between Platonic essentialist thought and the doctrine of the inheritance of acquired characteristics. Instead of relegating 'soft' changes to the unessential, Stoler contends that essences were themselves seen as malleable: 'A notion of essence does not necessarily rest on immovable parts but on the strategic inclusion of different attributes, of a changing constellation of features and a changing weighting of them' (Stoler, 1997b: 200). This notion of strategic naturalisation is one to which I return in Chapter 4.

Stoler shows how Dutch colonials of bourgeois background were concerned on several counts. A central preoccupation was with mixture and the offspring of mixed Dutch–Asian unions. However, 'mixture' was not just a question of sexual reproduction, but also of cultural attributions; not just a matter of phenotype and ancestry, but also of morality, behaviour and psychological disposition. Moreover there does not seem to have been a clear division operating between 'biology' and 'culture' here. Stoler (1992: 522) argues that cultural attributions were the means for calculating the relation between an invisible essence and visible appearance. Further still, that invisible essence was in some sense formed by cultural behaviours rather than simply being manifested through them.

One Dutch writer, addressing a European audience in 1856, challenged the idea that a 'European is a European and will remain so wherever he finds himself'. On the contrary, the influence of living in the Indies could be such that 'he no longer can be considered as a European, at least for the duration of his stay in the Indies' (cited in Stoler, 1995: 104). This writer was referring explicitly to morals, customs and habits, but with Lamarckian theories of soft inheritance in common currency, there was not necessarily a clear boundary between 'culture' and 'nature'. In any case, the point was that Europeanness was not a fixed racial identity; it was a malleable racial identity. A Dutch doctor writing in 1907 shared these fears: he thought that Europeans born and bred in the Indies 'could easily ... metamorphize [sic] into Javanese' (cited in Stoler, 1995: 105). This seems to have been more than a case of a basic European racial biology being overlain by a changing – and, in this view, corrupting – cultural overlay. The entire nature of the person was changing, and this was manifested in his or her morality – for example, in sexual behaviour.

The anxiety of the colonial middle classes focused not only on those who had been born in the colonies, but also on the poorer whites who lived there and were assumed to be particularly open to contaminating influences and to be affected by concubinage with native women. Neo-Lamarckian notions of the environment affecting a person's nature and essence raised fears about such people and the moral degeneration thought to afflict them. Concern also centred on white children being brought up by native servants who might corrupt them (Stoler, 1992: 536). Ideas from previous centuries that the breast milk of a nursemaid could influence a baby's nature were also still current (Stoler, 1995: 145). When, as was often the case in Dutch–Asian concubinage, the nurse and the mother were the same native woman, fears for the child's morals were redoubled (Stoler, 1995: 159). Stoler (1997a: 105) summarises the variable character of essence in this context:

> What went into determining European and 'white' in the Indies in 1834 was not the same criteria as that used 100 years later. At both moments, there was some 'essence' at issue, some 'essence' of what it was to be European. But the content of that designation was subject to a changing set of power relations, to changes in perception and policy about who should be eligible for membership and who should not.

This attention to milieu and the mutability of people's racialised natures can be seen in a Latin American context, in Nancy Stepan's book, *'The Hour of Eugenics': Race, Gender and Nation in Latin America* (1991). Stepan assesses the impact of eugenics as a movement on various Latin American countries from the turn of the century through until the 1930s. Although her book focuses more on the twentieth than the nineteenth century, eugenics is certainly a child of nineteenth-century racial theorising: the idea of attempting to intervene in collective human sexual reproduction with a view to 'improving the stock', as breeders did with animals and plants, was put forward as 'eugenics' by Francis Galton in 1883. He defined it as 'the study of the agencies under social control that may improve or impair the racial qualities of future generations either physically or mentally' (Galton, cited in Stepan, 1982: 111). It was not until the turn of the century that eugenics emerged as a social movement, seeking to influence public policy with regard to the control of human sexual reproduction. Its adherents in Britain and the US were mainly the progressive middle class, often more concerned with the 'lack of fitness' or 'feeblemindedness' of the working classes than with racial minorities. Its impact on public policy – as opposed to public opinion – was rather minor. In the US, however, where eugenicists were most influential, they succeeded in getting sterilisation laws into some state statute books and Kevles estimates some 9,000 people were sterilised under these laws between 1907 and 1928 (1995: 106).

Of particular interest to me is the way eugenics was received in Latin America. Stepan argues that Anglo-Saxon versions of eugenics, pioneered in Britain and developed in the US, took a relatively hard, innatist line: lack of fitness or feeblemindedness could only be corrected by sterilisation. French versions of eugenics took a softer, more Lamarckian line. Improvements in 'the race' could be effected by 'social hygiene' measures which ameliorated the environment, leading to a permanent improvement in the 'racial stock'. This more environmentalist approach was popular in Latin America, due in part to strong links with the French intellectual milieu and also to the power of physicians in the Latin American context who wished to see an effective role for themselves as social reformers. The Church took a predictably pronatalist stance. Also important was the mixed nature of most Latin American national populations. Such hybridisation of the European 'race' with black and indigenous peoples was generally deemed degenerative by European scientists and many Latin American intellectuals and nation-builders agreed with them. But to agree totally, especially with a hard-line, innatist eugenics, would be to condemn national populations to permanent inferiority. Although many elite commentators certainly envisaged European immigration as a highly desirable corrective measure, they often combined this with an environmentalist perspective that, assuming the inheritance of acquired characteristics, held forth the prospect of moral and physical improvement within the existing population.

In fact, within the eugenics movement in the US, a similar blurring of nature and nurture occurred. Condit (1999a: 43) states:

> Eugenics was ... a discourse about heredity, but it was not strictly about genetics. It incorporated both family environment and biological inheritance in its purview. Indeed, this was precisely the component of American eugenics that the biologists (especially the British geneticists) disdained as they sought to create a biological science of genetics.

Eugenicists in the US – generally not scientists – wanted to improve child raising techniques, family health and education as well as simply sterilise the 'feebleminded'. A child's 'inheritance' was thus both biological and social. Eugenics seemed at odds with Lamarckism, but in public versions of eugenics they actually combined and Lamarckian theories of the inheritance of acquired characteristics were being publicly touted in 1919 (Condit, 1999a: 50).

CONCLUSION

In this chapter I have looked at different ways of conceiving of human nature in the natural world. This has given some insight into what a naturalising discourse involves. To say that something – typically, a human behaviour or characteristic – has been naturalised does not automatically reveal all the meanings of that act. The meaning might be that the stars are controlling a behaviour or trait in a given person; it might be that some underlying substance, transmitted from two parents via sexual reproduction, is controlling the trait; it might be that the person was affected permanently during embryonic development by a shock the mother experienced during pregnancy; it might be that the environment has shaped the nature of the person in enduring ways, even ways s/he might transmit to the next generation through sexual reproduction; it might be that the behaviour of the person in the environment, the habits of use and disuse that s/he practises, have moulded his or her basic constitution as a person. All these are, or have been seen as, natural processes.

What was thought to constitute a natural human essence has also changed over time. In the late eighteenth century feminine nature was constituted in part by acting and deploying the body in a feminine way. By the late nineteenth century some theories saw human natural essence as much more fixed and less subject to a performative becoming, especially with reference to racial type. It may be possible to see some of these historical shifts in terms of Foucault's history of sexuality, outlined briefly in Chapter 2, in which, by the late eighteenth century, an analytics of sexuality was already emerging which focused on the calculated management of the productive forces of life at the level of the individual body and of whole populations. This created a growing concern with sexuality. This interest in controlling bodies, life forces and the reproduction of vigorous populations had, by the late ninteenth century, flowered and intensified. It had also harnessed notions of blood, genealogy, descent and race which, more dominant prior to the late eighteenth century, had never disappeared – far from it in fact, as my discussion of the late eighteenth century shows (see also Stoler, 1995) – but had become interwoven with an analytics of sexuality. The fusion of these two thematics, in what Foucault (1998: 149) describes as racism in its 'modern "biologizing," statist form', may be linked to the fixity and permanence ascribed to human, racialised natures at that time.

However, I have also argued that there has been a long-standing and underlying tension between ideas of permanence and change and this was apparent even in the late nineteenth century. To naturalise is often seen as implying permanence and, while this is clearly a strong possibility, from the Greeks to at least the early twentieth century, there has also been the possibility that human natures can change and be plastic. This means not just that the expression of an underlying fixed human nature can be altered by the way it is affected by nurture or the environment, but that human nature itself is formed through an embodied process of becoming. Allied to this were a set of theories, vague and lacking in detail, about how heredity worked that retained a remarkable continuity over this entire time span. As more detailed theories about the mechanisms of heredity have emerged, from the late-nineteenth-century account of August Weismann to the discovery of the structure of DNA in 1953, ideas about a fixed biological substrate of genetic coding have also grown and become dominant. But certainly well into the twentieth century, ideas of plasticity in human nature existed alongside ideas of permanence.

In terms of analysing racial thinking, this indicates that the meaning of the naturalisation that is often associated with such thinking should not be taken for granted. Stoler's material shows that the naturalisation of racial difference in nineteenth-century European colonies also meant seeing human nature as shaped by the milieu. This was not some random product of European racist paranoia about the tropics depleting European mettle, but fitted in with current theories about human nature and procreation. One can detect, however, certain similarities with other contexts: just as in

Kulick's study of Brazilian travestis, sexual nature is defined in great part by how the body is used in sexual encounters (Kulick, 1998), so in Stoler's work, racial nature is defined in part by how the body is deployed in a given physical and social environment.

Admitting plasticity did not necessarily undermine racism in the context Stoler describes: in fact it made it all the more pervasive by raising the spectre of racial 'contamination' from the human and physical surroundings and reaffirming hierarchies of essential purity that had to be controlled through strictly regulated behaviour, as behaviour could affect essence. More generally, my argument that naturalising idioms can admit of plasticity is not an argument that racism can be less pernicious than it appears at first sight. As for Stoler's material, the admission of plasticity in human nature actually gives racism greater potential scope for making pernicious judgements and discriminations.

The key point emerging from all this material is that we need to be alive to the way that naturalising arguments work, rather than assuming we already know what is involved. Once we start to nuance the notion of naturalisation, other questions emerge. One consequence of pursuing this avenue of enquiry is that new insights can be gained on the widely cited post-1950s shift from 'biological' to 'cultural' racism. The biological racism often linked to nineteenth-century racial typologising and racial science was not as straightforwardly 'biological' as it seems, not only in the practical world of the colonies, but also in strictly theoretical thinking. In fact when the basis for a truly hard theory of inheritance emerged with the discovery of the structure of DNA – which suggested that genes are a type of code or blueprint, unchanged by somatic processes – this was also the time when ideas about race were publicly divorced from biological theory (at least among the majority of scientists and public commentators); before that the conceptual divide between nature and culture had been less clear. On the other hand, cultural racism also involves important processes of naturalisation. This has been noted before (see the discussion in Chapter 1), but less attention has been paid to what these processes are and what they imply. Recent patterns of cultural racism, then, can be seen as one more variant on long-standing and complex ideas about the interweaving of human nature and the environment, and about permanence and change in human nature. This is a theme I return to in Chapter 5. In the next chapter I move into the twentieth century and, exploring ideas about genetics and the constitution of persons in kinship, challenge whether, even in the wake of advances in genetic science, there is a neat, clear divide in everyday thought between 'nature' and 'nurture'.

4. GENETICS AND KINSHIP: THE INTERPENETRATION OF NATURE AND CULTURE

The last chapter ventured, in chronological terms, into the twentieth century, but the eugenic movement I considered briefly there had very strong continuities with nineteenth-century science, even if the issues it raised – determinism, perfectability, inequality, human rights – have proved to be equally relevant to the twentieth century and after. In this chapter and the next I focus on developments in the twentieth century. Two things stand out here. On the one hand, this period is often said to be one of a general increase in genetic determinism, both in science and in popular thought (although most commentators allow that, from the 1980s, molecular biological science started to become less genetically determinist). On the other hand, it is also said that, dating from the Second World War, a biological discourse about race – whether it referred to scientific concepts such as genes or more vague lay concepts such as blood – was publicly discredited and replaced by a culturalist discourse of race (Balibar, 1991a; Barker, 1981; Gilroy, 1987; Lury, 2000; Stolcke, 1993, 1995). 'Race' itself often disappeared as a term, being replaced by the apparently more neutral term 'ethnicity'. (This is all despite the continuing focus on a genetic basis for 'racial' difference by the small but significant group of scholars, mainly psychologists, briefly mentioned in Chapter 2.) There seems, then, to be an underlying contradiction here. Just as genetic determinism was taking hold in many areas of life – particularly in relation to notions of well-being and illness, but also in relation to ideas about gender and sexuality and other vaguer 'dispositions' such as criminality – so determinism was, for the most part, being evacuated from ideas about race. (In the next chapter, however, I show that there have been recent fears that public discourse about race is adopting a more overtly genetic idiom.)

It may be that this contradiction is more apparent than real. After all, the increase in genetic determinism has hardly gone unchallenged by those – usually social scientists – who insist on the predominant role of 'the environment' or 'culture'. It could be that ideas about race have simply been channelled more effectively into an environmentalist or culturalist view than ideas about illness or gender, perhaps as part of the overall reaction against Nazism. Also biologists themselves have been instrumental in demonstrating that 'races' do not exist as biological entities. (Against this, it should be recalled that Lieberman and Reynolds (1996: 158) found in a 1985 survey that 70 per cent of biologists specialising in animal behaviour and 50 per cent of biological anthropologists believed that biological races existed in the human species; these were the highest percentages among scholars from four different disciplines.)

However, I think there is more to this than meets the eye. My first hunch, developed in this chapter, is that the increase in genetic determinism is not as straightforward as it looks, especially if one looks at lay beliefs, rather than scientific discourse or popular representations of science in the media. Some of these beliefs can be approached through Western ideas about kinship insofar as this domain involves ideas about the constitution of people through both biology and culture. My second hunch, developed in the next chapter, is that the simple shift from biological to culturalist discourses of race is not as straightforward as it looks either – even if apparent recent trends back towards a genetic idiom are taken into account. Again this is especially so if the focus is on everyday, lay discourse, rather than the public, 'politically correct' domain. I argue that lay views of race, as well as referring to culture, continue to make reference to ideas about 'blood', biology and perhaps genes. This, however, should not necessarily be seen as some kind of throwback to versions of scientific raciology current a century ago. Just as these older versions actually contained within them an ambiguous divide between the unchanging (biological) and the changing (environmental/cultural), so post-war lay discourse on race contains reworked renderings of the same ambiguity.

The key to this is a theme that I elaborated on in the preceding chapter: a shifting tension between ideas of permanence/continuity and change/instability. In twentieth-century Western ideas about people, how they come to be as they are and how they are related to others, there is a vague and shifting line between elements seen as relatively fixed, which may also be handed down unchanged from previous generations and shared with some people but not others, and those seen as malleable and changing. The shifting line means that it is not clear what is permanent and what is not; it also means that the two realms interact and become mutually constitutive. It is not just a question of dividing elements into two categories of 'nature' and 'nurture': nurture can constitute (human) nature. In everyday talk people may use the shorthand dichotomy of 'nature *versus* nurture' to talk about these things, but the underlying model actually undoes the dichotomy (in ways that harmonise surprisingly both with scholarly post-modern theorising about the performative nature of identity and with post-1980s biological theorising about the interactive nature of the relationship between DNA and the rest of the organism).

This is a particular case of Latour's broader argument about nature–culture dichotomies in societies labelled as 'modern'. Latour (1993: 10–12) contends that modern people try to keep nature and culture apart as pure categories and also separate this practice of 'purification' from the practice of 'translation' which produces hybrids of nature and culture. Being modern means keeping these separations intact and thus maintaining a coherent nature–culture dichotomy in the face of hybridisations. But, in fact, purification has never been clearly divided from hybridisation during the modern period; this lack of separation has become more visible recently, but it was always there. This is the sense in which 'we have never been modern'. Strathern (1996: 522) glosses Latour:

> Moderns divide society from technology, culture from nature, human from nonhuman, except that they do not – Euro-American moderns are like anyone else in the hybrids they make, even though they are rarely as explicit ... The divides of modern people's thinking do not correspond to the methods they deploy.

I argue that people's use of nature and nurture when thinking about human natures and the constitution of persons is also like this.

In sustaining this argument, I will mostly present examples from anthropological studies of kinship and new reproductive technologies. The reason for this is that, above all in the realm of discourse about race, there is little ethnographic evidence to go on. There are not many studies about how lay people in their everyday lives perceive and experience racial identity in relation to concepts of 'blood', 'genes', or 'the environment'; about how they think they came to be as they are, what they owe to their parents in terms of 'inheritance' (however that is construed) and how they are connected to others perceived as 'like' and 'different'. Even going beyond the domain of race, there is not a great deal on lay concepts of inheritance, blood, genes and so on. While there is a burgeoning literature on the representation of genetics in 'popular culture', this is usually restricted to the media, films and books in ways consonant with the non-anthropological restriction of 'culture' to expressive media and the symbolic realm (cf. Wade, 1999b). Not many researchers ask people outside these spheres about what they think and do.

Luckily anthropological studies of kinship and reproduction provide a good area in which to explore these themes and in this chapter I rely extensively on such studies. Even then, however, studies that challenge the taken-for-grantedness of the nature–nurture divide have only recently begun to appear. Many studies of English, Euro-American or Western kinship assume that Westerners use a straightforward model that divides clearly between biological and social aspects of kinship. Such studies may emphasise that anthropologists have in the past been taken in by such a model and unwisely imported it wholesale into their analytical models; such studies may also emphasise that new reproductive technologies have recently begun to challenge such a simple divide. But the divide itself is often seen as an integral part of twentieth-century Euro-American kinship.

What follows in this and the next chapter is not a sustained ethnographic elaboration of the argument sketched above: it is rather a series of suggestions and possibilities elaborated from a reading of some of the literature on genetics, kinship and race in the twentieth-century Western world. In this chapter I barely mention race. I make no apologies for this as I believe that reading across from studies of genetics and kinship to race can help to understand the latter.

GENETICS AND GENETIC DETERMINISM

Keller observes that 'Historians of biology routinely note that for nineteenth-century biologists, the term *heredity* referred to both the "transmission of potentialities during reproduction *and* [the] development of these potentialities into specific adult traits"' (Keller, 1995: 3–4, references removed). This refers us back to the idea I developed in the last chapter that human nature was seen to be constituted by behaviour as well as by substances passed between generations by sexual reproduction. In the first decades of the twentieth century such a notion had to be abandoned in biological circles. Theories of hard inheritance became completely dominant as it became irrefutably clear that acquired characteristics could not be inherited (previous experimental proofs of this had not scotched the basic doctrine). In 1909 the distinction between 'genotype' and 'phenotype' was coined by Danish geneticist Wilhelm Johannsen, who also coined the term 'gene' (Mayr, 1982: 736, 782). Although his definitions of the terms were not quite those used today, he did lay the basis for a clear distinction between the genetic component of an organism, which was passed on, unchanged in itself, through sexual reproduction, and the physical expression of that genetic component in the material body of the organism. Keller (1995: 4) notes that this distinction effectively made 'heredity' into a mechanism of biological transmission alone, to be studied within the new discipline of genetics, while development remained the province of embryology.

The nature of the gene was not fully understood at the time and indeed it remained a hypothetical particle. Yet already there was a strongly determinist view of its operation. Keller (1995: 7) cites the geneticist Brink who wrote in 1927 that 'the Mendelian theory postulates discrete, self-perpetuating, stable bodies – the genes – resident in the chromosomes, as the hereditary materials. This means, of course, that the genes are the primary internal agents controlling development.' This view, which Keller calls 'the discourse of gene action', attributed agency, autonomy and causal primacy to the genes in a way which has 'become so familiar as to seem obvious, even self-evident' (Keller, 1995: 8–9). Geneticists and indeed embryologists were concerned with 'how genes produced their effects' on the developing organism, operating with a one-way, linear causal model (although Keller notes that German biologists adhered less to this discourse of gene action).

The discovery of DNA in 1953 heralded a new era in genetics, but it also confirmed some existing ideas, such as the radical genotype–phenotype distinction. DNA was talked of primarily as a code, a programme of instructions which controlled the organism's development into a phenotype, but which was itself unchanged by that development; it could also replicate itself exactly and be passed on in sperm and ovum. Mayr – who, it should be noted, writes from within the discourse of gene action – calls DNA the 'unmoved mover' – a term, interestingly, that usually refers to God – and its discovery meant 'the last nail could be hammered into the coffin of the theory of the inheritance of acquired characteristics' (Mayr, 1982: 824).

The nature–nurture dichotomy preceded these developments. As I mentioned in the previous chapter, the eugenicist Francis Galton was already talking in these terms in the 1870s. But I also showed how other ideas blurred such a distinction and how, even in the early decades of the twentieth century, eugenic discourse itself made the distinction less than watertight by emphasising the role of family environment as well as family heredity in projects to mould human nature. The new developments in genetics now gave a stronger basis for the dichotomy and several anthropologists note that the dominant model for the person in mid-twentieth-century Western views posited a given, inherited, 'natural', biological substrate onto which was built an overlay of cultural/social characteristics, acquired through processes of 'nurture' or, more broadly, from 'the environment'; such a view is still dominant today in many domains (Edwards, 2000: 27–30; Ingold, 1986: 160–1, 358; 1990; 2000a: ch. 21; Richards, 1998; Schneider, 1980, 1984; Strathern, 1992a, 1992b; Toren, 1993).

Celeste Michelle Condit, in her book *The Meanings of the Gene*, notes that most observers of genetics as a popular discourse argue that there has been a progressive shift towards genetic determinism since the early twentieth century (Condit, 1999a: 6, 166; see also Condit, 1999b). For example, Nelkin and Lindee (1995a) see a move towards 'genetic essentialism' in images and narratives of the gene in popular culture: 'Genetic essentialism reduces the self to a molecular entity, equating human beings, in all their social, historical, and moral complexity, with their genes' (cited in Condit, 1999a: 6). The same authors argue that, 'Increasingly in the 1990s, differences between men and women and between racial groups are appearing in popular culture as genetically driven' (Nelkin and Lindee, 1995b: 387). Van Dijck also argues that popular notions of genes as controlling agents retain a 'tenacious' hold (1998: 126), while Richards (1998: 136) believes that a 'new innatism' has being promoted over the preceding two or three decades and, although he is not very clear about the domain in which this promotion is occurring, he links it to the way in which new developments in molecular genetics are being talked about.[1] Haraway (1997: 142–8) talks of the emergence of 'gene fetishism', linking it to genetic essentialism, while Rapp (1999: 215) notes that, in popular consciousness, there is a growth of 'geneticisation' or an ideology 'linking individual attributes and social problems as if they could be effectively reshaped or eliminated only in the realm of biomedicine now reduced to genetic diagnosis'.

Now most authors admit that, at the level of the science of molecular biology, the idea of genes as 'unmoved movers' began to lose currency in the 1980s. Keller (1995: 26) identifies a gradual and uneven shift from the 'discourse of gene action' to one of 'gene activation' in which genes are no longer seen as simple determinants in a one-way linear model. Instead 'the expression state of each gene [is] determined by the dynamic interaction of regulatory proteins present in the cell at any given time' (David Baltimore, cited in Keller, 1995: 27). The locus of control shifts from 'the genes themselves to the complex biochemical dynamics ... of cells in constant communication with each other' (Keller, 1995: 28). Similarly Van Dijck (1998: 148) cites one authority who states that

> DNA acts in the dual capacity of program and data, and the cellular machinery likewise acts as both passive interpreter and program. The genotype and phenotype are intertwined, both acting responsively to each other, both contributing to the process and the result. (Thomas Foyle, cited in Van Dijck, 1998: 150)

Keller (1995: ch. 3) argues that, from the 1980s, molecular biology was forced to move towards metaphors of networked computing and complex cybernetic systems in understanding how DNA and cell cytoplasm[2] interact, thus moving away from earlier telegraphic images of the one-way delivery of information between sender (the genotype; the DNA contained in the cell nucleus) and receiver (the phenotype; the cytoplasm). Condit (1999a: 162) also notes the shift to more systemic, developmental and interactive ways of thinking about genetics and Richards (1998) argues that the recent developments in molecular genetics that are linked to the 'new innatism' actually point in entirely the opposite direction – that is, towards developmentalist models in which genotype and phenotype are in constant, developing interaction (see also Fausto-Sterling, 1985: ch. 3).

Despite these changes at the level of 'science', many commentators see increasing genetic determinism at the 'popular' level – by which they mean the mass media, such as the press, popular fiction and film. Condit takes issue with this overall approach, arguing that critics have read the images purveyed in the press too narrowly, overemphasising the determinism in them; she backs her argument with a systematic and quantitative analysis of press articles over the whole of the twentieth century. Her historical account of shifts in discourse about genes converges in many ways with those of Keller (1995), Turney (1998) and Van Dijck (1998), but she argues that images of genes were always more ambiguous and flexible than other accounts assume.

Condit (1999a: ch. 1) begins with the period of classical eugenics (1900–35) when the dominant metaphor for talking about human heredity was that of stockbreeding in which there were clearly the breeders and the bred. As I mentioned in the last chapter, although there was a strongly determinist conception of the 'germ-plasm' – a term which remained current in the press, despite growing scientific knowledge about genes – the family environment was also seen as important: biological and social heredity were conflated to some extent. Condit's next epoch is that of 'family genetics' (1940–54) when advances in biological science gave rise to the metaphor of gene as an atom, or a bead on a string: a fixed, solid, bounded entity. Attention was on medical intervention in family reproduction to ensure normal children. At this time, a sharp divide was evident between genes and 'the environment' – the latter passive term tending to replace the more active notion of 'nurture', while the relatively passive 'nature' was displaced by the more active image of 'gene'. Heredity came to mean genetic inheritance alone and genes were seen as quite strongly determinist. Genes fixed heredity at conception and their determinations worked in quite a direct and constant way throughout a person's life. However, most press articles also attributed a significant role to the environment in shaping humans. Genes set immovable limits within which environmental influences could operate (Condit, 1999a: 82–9). This was a temporal image (the genes are given first, environmental influences come later) and a spatial image (the genetic boundaries are set, environment works within them) (Condit, 1999a: 163).

Condit then moves on to the era of 'genetic experimentation' (1956–76) which followed the discovery of the structure of DNA. At this time, the metaphor of code became dominant (although it had first been suggested by the quantum mechanics theorist Erwin Schroedinger in his 1944 book, *What is Life?* (see Keller, 1995: ch. 3)). DNA and the genes, which were generally visualised as discrete segments of DNA, were seen as similar to texts, books of instructions or the computer programs which were being popularised with contemporary advances in information technology. As before, a majority of press articles assigned significant influences to both genes and environment, but the metaphor of code, so Condit argues, allowed more flexible views of the genes. A text could be rewritten and journalists speculated about genetically altering (i.e., 'improving') humans and other organisms and the attendant risks involved (cf. Turney, 1998). In another spatio-temporal metaphor genes were often seen as a starting point which environmental influences could effectively move beyond (Condit, 1999a: 100–11). Keller (1995: ch. 3) also notes the use of the code metaphor, but says the genetic science of this period employed it to convey a rather simple, one-way process of data transmission; in contrast, contemporary information sciences, which had inspired the metaphor, were fast moving towards complex, cybernetic systems models. Van Dijck (1998: ch. 2) recognises the emergence of the code metaphor, but sets it alongside the image of the gene as 'foreman' in a factory, evoking a one-way, mechanical process with the gene as commander.

Finally, Condit deals with the period of 'genetic medicine' (1980–95) when recombinant DNA techniques allowed the manipulation of genes, giving rise to the commercialisation of genetic material which in turn encouraged a consumerist attitude to genetic medicine among the public. During this period, Condit argues, the main metaphor for genes became that of 'blueprint' and the focus shifted from the individual's genotype to the entire genomes of species. She contends that the blueprint metaphor develops still further the notion of genes as 'starting points', plans which are actualised through the activities of a host of other agencies which progressively constitute the end result. She links this to developments in molecular biology itself which, as I mentioned above, began to adopt more developmentalist, interactive perspectives. Her argument, though, is that the popular press was also able to take on board these more flexible ideas and did not descend monolithically into ever greater genetic essentialism (Condit, 1999a: 161–7). She admits that journalists might have made big claims for the power of genes or use shorthand expressions – 'the gene for breast cancer' – that could be read as highly determinist, but she maintains that such claims and shorthand were generally vague, leaving unclear exactly what degree of determinism was being claimed.

Van Dijck (1998: ch. 5) takes a different view. She also observes a change in the 1990s towards the genome as a whole and recognises the metaphor of the blueprint. For her, images of code, program, library, database and CD-ROM are equally prevalent in popular ideas about genes. The major metaphors are the book and the map, in 'their digital manifestations' (1998: 148). The 'computerisation of genetics' (1998: 121) links with a shift in molecular biology towards seeing genes as involved in complex cybernetic systems, but in the popular realm this digitalisation of genetics has not had progressive consequences, translating instead into images of flattened maps of sequenced genes on which particular genes for particular traits can be definitively located by scientists who are portrayed as engaged in heroic voyages of discovery (see also Haraway, 1997: ch. 4).

Clearly the representation of genetics in the popular realm is open to different readings. The value of Condit's approach lies in its openness to the variety of ways in which genetics appears in the popular media. She tellingly notes that the critics who see the metaphor of genes as code as monosemic and determinist are themselves engaging in a monosemic and determinist reading of those metaphors (1999a: 287, n. 2). She is also one of the few who goes beyond the mass media sources and asks lay people what they think. In 1995 she and a colleague conducted a questionnaire survey of university students in the southern US, quizzing them with closed and open questions about their understanding of genetics – and especially the 'blueprint' metaphor which has been described as reductionist and determinist by various critics. She found that, in the majority,

audience members saw the blueprint metaphor as relatively open and non-determin-istic because they interpreted the blueprint as probabilistic rather than absolute, as partial rather than totalistic, and as malleable rather then fixed. Rather than seeing the blueprint as isomorphic with human outcomes, in the fashion that critics have read it, these audience members seem to have been more alive to the nuances of the metaphor – the fact that blueprints are simply outlines and plans, and that the particular features of brick and mortar can not only change a plan, but can also make a substantive difference in the reality of the finished structure itself. (Condit, 1999b: 172–3)

Some respondents said a person with 'flawed genes' could nevertheless develop normally, that all people had some 'bad genes' but varied according to whether these became manifest, and that the 'blueprint' allowed for variation in eventual outcome. Some of those questioned referred to the new possibilities offered by gene therapy for altering the blueprint, making it malleable; others, however, saw the blueprint as just a general starting point which did not determine eventual outcomes. Condit admits that some respondents did have a deterministic view – one type of determinism was religious, rather than purely materialist, in holding that God defined one's genetic blueprint – but these were not in the majority. Condit also admits that her sample is specific – university students are not representative of society as a whole. But they might well be taken to be fairly representative of the readership of the 'popular' press that many of the studies of the discourse of genetics actually investigate (which tends towards such periodicals as *Time*, *Newsweek*, *Reader's Digest*, *Science* and *New York Times*).

In sum, Condit argues that both the press and at least certain segments of 'the public' do not swallow in a straightforward way the idea of genetic essentialism and have not done so throughout this century. The metaphors for thinking about genetics have changed, indicating different ways of thinking about the role of genes, but there is no clear move towards greater genetic determinism. In genetic science the move is certainly away from such determinism – notwithstanding the influence of such scholars as Richard Dawkins and his 1976 book *The Selfish Gene* which popularised the image of gene as controller.[3] In terms of my argument in this book, Condit's material shows that there has been a constant debate about determinism and indeterminacy, or continuity and change, in the development of individual human natures.

Some authors see the new genetic technologies, which allow the direct manipulation of genetic materials and structures, as heralding a new era of flexibility and fluidity in imagining human natures. Franklin (2000: 190), for example, notes that the recent idea of genetics as information and code – a notion that Condit, Keller and Van Dijck observe actually dates back to the 1940s – introduces the possibility of rewriting that code, reducing its determinism. She also observes that recent changes in the concept of nature have made it more like recent notions of culture, that is, based more on doing than being (see also Rabinow, 1992). Van Dijck (1998: 194) similarly points out that new genetic technologies implode and mix categorical distinctions between the technical and the organic, the technical and the natural and the technical and the textual (see also Strathern, 1992b: 1–30). However, both Franklin and Van Dijck also note that established categories and distinctions are not erased: they are instead 'vigorously reinstated', according to Van Dijck (1998: 194), while Franklin (2000: 217) sees new technologies as both drawing on and displacing pre-existing beliefs about nature. In fact Van Dijck (1998: 194) states:

> The paradox of postmodern hybridisation [i.e. the mixing of these categories] ... is that it can apparently function only through a constant insistence on the distinction between science and nature, science and representation and science and society. New concepts of flexibility and fluidity cannot exist without prior notions of fixity.

She goes on to argue that notions of the fixity of genes are now complemented by the notion of the fixability of genes.

It is undoubtedly the case that new concepts depend on older ones for their salience and impact and that new concepts rarely simply displace old ones; I would also agree that new genetic technologies have made a substantial impact on the public imagination. However, Condit's material – and my argument in this and the previous chapter – suggest that flexibility and fixity have long been in a complex and ambiguous relationship and that notions of fixity have not simply been recently complemented or overtaken by notions of flexibility. Late-twentieth-century versions of the relationship are, of course, particular – it is not a case of *plus ça change, plus c'est la même chose*; genetic technologies realise imaginative possibilities that before were only science fiction. Yet, as I have shown, the notion that (human) nature is based on doing as well as being has some resonances with ideas about human nature spanning the eighteenth and nineteenth centuries.

From the early twentieth century, the relationship between fixity and fixability in human nature has generally been phrased in terms of the relative roles of 'nature' and 'nurture' or, with increasing currency from about the 1940s, of 'genes' and 'the environment', suggesting that there is a fairly clear conceptual distinction between the two, whatever the ambiguities of their relative contributions. This seems to be particularly characteristic of the twentieth century. The ideas that I described for earlier periods suggested that there was not a radical, or at least there was a rather vague, distinction between an underlying biological nature and an overlying cultural personality; it seemed a person's nature was conceived in less dualistic terms and behaviour could help constitute it, partly due to theories of soft inheritance and the inheritance of acquired characteristics. Now advances in molecular biology appear to point us back in that direction: although there is a clear distinction between DNA and cell cytoplasm, the complexities of their cybernetic intertwining mean that, as a writer for *Scientific American* put it in 1991, 'organisms control most of their genes' (Beardsley, cited in Keller, 1995: 28).

However, there are also certain indications that, even from the mid twentieth century, the distinction between nature and nurture has not been ironclad and that lay beliefs not only see both domains as operating in the constitution of a person, but also understand 'human nature' in terms wider than simple biology or genes and see 'human nature' as itself constituted by social experience. My evidence for this comes mainly from the study of kinship.

THE PERFORMATIVE CONSTITUTION OF KINSHIP

In 1968 David Schneider outlined the beliefs about kinship held by ordinary people in the US (Schneider, 1980). He said that people held ideas about shared 'blood', understood as 'biogenetic material'. They assumed that their ideas about the nature of this material were derived from whatever science knew about biogenetics at any given moment (Schneider, 1980: 23–4). These ideas were thought by Americans to be the 'facts of nature'. Schneider (1980: 114–15) clarified what the phrase 'facts of nature' meant by distinguishing between three levels. First came the 'biological facts' which simply existed as part of the world. Second were cultural constructs about these facts which organised and studied them; one such system of constructs was the academic discipline of biology; another system was 'informal ethnoscience' or lay knowledge of the biological facts. Third, there was a symbolic level of cultural notions which were symbolised by cultural constructs about biological facts, or things taken to be biological facts. It was at this level of symbolism, said Schneider, that notions of shared blood or biogenetic substance operated. Blood was shared through the central institution of sexual intercourse and shared blood constituted a relation of kinship:

The fundamental element which [for people in the US] defines a relative by blood is, of course blood, a substance, a material thing. Its constitution is whatever it is that really is in nature. It is a natural entity. It endures. It cannot be terminated. (Schneider, 1980: 25)

The cultural constructs about blood links symbolised, at the third level, 'diffuse, enduring solidarity' in interpersonal relations and 'a special kind of trust which is not contingent and which does not depend on reciprocity' (Schneider, 1980: 116).

As well as the consanguineous relation of blood, there was a code of conduct which defined how to behave towards a relative. Relatives by marriage were related only in terms of this 'order of law'; relatives by blood were related both in terms of the 'order of nature' and the order of law (Schneider, 1980: 26–7). Schneider's description of the US kinship system rested on this fundamental distinction between what is effectively nature and culture.

It is important to appreciate that Schneider was very clear that this was a lay American model, not an analytical one. Indeed in his later book, *A Critique of the Study of Kinship* (1984), Schneider argued that many anthropologists had mistakenly assumed the underlying existence of a US-type biological model of kinship in all kinship systems in the world. They assumed that a basic kinship system simply existed everywhere by virtue of biological relatedness, as understood by Westerners, and that different cultures then carved up this natural reality in different ways. As Strathern (1992a: 3) put it, kinship was generally seen as 'the social construction of natural facts'; first came nature, then came the various social constructions of it. Schneider said that anthropologists needed to grasp the nature of relatedness in a given society and understand it on its own terms – which would include asking whether or not these terms included such concepts as relatedness by 'blood' in the first place.

Underlining this critique, Williams reviews some kinship studies of the late 1970s which indicate that 'nature' is produced socially and that kinship can be produced by nurture (see also Carsten, 2000a). As she puts it for the Trukese of Micronesia, as analysed by Marshall, there is an interpenetration of 'biology and biography'; in fact, for the Trukese 'blood can be culturally, rather than biologically, *made* and thickened by shared adversity' (Williams, 1995: 206, 208–9). More generally, 'the meanings and implications of the "facts" of consanguinity are culturally constructed, rather than biologically given in a western-derived sense'. This is different from saying that 'natural facts are socially constructed' because this wrongly assumes that 'the processes by which we socialise nature have no impact on the content of nature' and this is a 'fiction' (Williams, 1995: 206, 209).

The idea that 'nature' is itself a social construction has become widely accepted in most social science circles, although Franklin (1997: 20–1) notes that 'the legacy of the distinction between "natural facts" and "social facts" remains a powerful epistemic tradition which is not easily displaced'. Meanwhile it is generally agreed that English or Euro-American or Western ideas of kinship are based on a clear and foundational divide between natural connections of blood, understood as simple facts of life, and social connections arising from experience. Introducing a recent collection that aims to interrogate the role of biology in kinship and relatedness, Carsten (2000a: 3) notes that research on non-Western kinship shows that 'the boundaries between the biological and the social which ... have been so crucial in the study of kinship are in many cases distinctly blurred, if they are visible at all'. However, in the West, biology has 'a foundational function' and 'we can say quite definitely ... that a contrast between the biological and the social is central to ... indigenous northern European discourses and practices of relatedness' (Carsten, 2000a: 3, 27).

It is true that scholars have recently become interested in the way that new reproductive technologies, such as surrogacy, artificial insemination and cloning, have challenged a straightforward divide between biology and culture by complicating and disturbing notions of what constitutes a 'natural' link in kinship and what 'natural' links mean (Edwards *et al.*, 1993; Edwards, 2000; Franklin, 1997; Franklin and McKinnon, forthcoming; Franklin and Ragoné, 1998; Hartouni, 1997; Ragoné, 1994, 1996; Ragoné and Twine, 2000; Strathern, 1992a, 1992b).[4] Recent studies of kinship in gay and lesbian families also explore how these arrangements question the role of natural procreation in constituting notions of kinship (Hayden, 1995; Weston, 1991).[5]

Such challenges form part of what Strathern describes as 'the increasing discourse on the role of "social" construction in the conjoining of natural and social relations – of the artificiality of the human enterprise'. Yet this, rather than dissolving a simple nature–nurture distinction, 'has given a different visibility to natural relations'. Even greater emphasis is now put on biology and specifically on genetics: there is an 'exaggerated attention to biological idiom' and 'genetic relations have come to stand for the naturalness of biological kinship' (Strathern, 1992a: 52–3). In this sense, challenges to the clarity of the nature–nurture divide in Western kinship are seen to be recent and even to reinforce the dominance of a biological idiom. Some of the material discussed below, while it does not dispute that a conceptual distinction between the biological and the social is present and important, also suggests that the distinction is vague, contextual and shifting and that in English kinship there is a blurring of the boundaries which is not just a recent development.

Some evidence for this proposition is provided by Jeanette Edwards in her book, *Born and Bred: Idioms of Kinship and New Reproductive Technologies in England*. Here she puts forward a model of 'Born and Bred kinship' (Edwards, 2000: 28) to characterise people's ideas about kinship in Bacup, a town in the north of England. She contests Schneider's basic premise that there is a clear, underlying divide between blood and social relatedness in Western ideas about kinship. In England, as well as in Micronesia, kinship links of substance can be made; in Williams' terms, blood can be made and thickened through social relatedness. Edwards agrees that 'relatedness between persons is traced and symbolised in ways that might be described as belonging to the realm of the biological and the realm of the social; there are both given and forged elements in kin relations'. But, she goes on, 'one (the biological) is not the substratum on which the other (the social) is constructed'. Thus,

> being biologically related to a person does not axiomatically make them kin. A claim of belonging (to persons and places) can be made through upbringing as much as birth. The juxtaposition of being born and bred allows for kinship to be conceptualised through both or either. (Edwards, 2000: 28)

Before I go onto a more detailed consideration of Edwards' data, it is worth making two critical comments about Schneider's account of American kinship. First, there is at least a hint from his own data that things are not quite as straightforward as he makes out. There is rather little in the way of verbatim interview material in the book, but one example occurs when Schneider is discussing how 'substance' and 'code for conduct' are separable ideas. The anthropologist is quizzing a respondent about close and distant relatives and what it takes for a person to be 'a relation'. The exchange goes like this (Schneider, 1980: 64):

Anthropologist: Can you give me any kind of rule for the person who is related to you?
Informant: Well, they got to be sociable with you or they're not related.
A: All right, but some of the people you named [earlier on in the interview] are related to you by blood, right?
I: Yeah, you get them by accident. You can't do anything about them – and grand-children are the bloodiest!
A: Then you have relatives by accident. Your father's sister had children, right?
I: Yeah.
A: So they are related to you by blood.
I: No, they are not related. They'd have to be social. They were at one time, but they aren't now.
A: Do any of your female first cousins have husbands?
I: Yes.
A: Are they your cousins?
I: I never see them.
A: Are their children related to you?
I: No, because I never saw them.

This, it seems to me, does not easily confirm Schneider's basic thesis. The respondent here categorically denies that people who do share biogenetic substance with her are relatives of hers. Without the social link, they are not relatives. There is some hint of confirmation of Schneider's argument in the idea that relatives can be got 'by accident': because of the blood link, they are relatives whether one likes it or not. But this is at least as strongly denied in what follows which suggests quite clearly that blood alone is not enough, that a blood link does not necessarily 'endure' and that it can 'be terminated'.[6] This relates to a more general ambiguity which is that, in Schneider's account, the blood link itself symbolises a code for conduct: it expresses 'diffuse, enduring solidarity' and 'a special kind of trust' (Schneider, 1980: 116). The order of nature, then, is not easily separated from the order of law, where law means 'custom', 'code for conduct' or 'pattern for behaviour' (Schneider, 1980: 27).[7]

A second problem with Schneider's book is the rather limited account he gives of how ordinary Americans think about 'blood' or 'biogenetic substance'. We don't even know if his respondents actually used terms such as 'biogenetic material'. This relates to Schneider's view of the relationship between scientific and lay knowledge which assumes that non-specialists more or less absorb approximate versions of the scientific facts and certainly think they're working with the scientific facts, even if this is not true (Schneider, 1980: 24, n. 3). As a shorthand model for a complex relationship this may not be wildly astray, but it remains rather thin.

A study by Richards (1997) on people undergoing genetic counselling in the UK looks at how they think about heredity. It indicates that most of these people have little grasp of basic Mendelian genetics and that, although they generally think that the mother and father contribute equally to a child's genetic make-up, this belief varies when it comes to the inheritance of a predisposition to breast cancer which is often seen as passing down the maternal line alone. Richards (1997: 190) concludes that 'lay accounts do not seem to specify how inherited features are passed on'. Terms such as 'gene', 'DNA' and 'chromosome' are employed frequently, but people use them to refer to 'the general concept of the biological transmission of characteristics between generations'. In that sense, these concepts are of a piece with the older concept of 'blood'. People know that conception occurs through the fusion of egg and sperm and that 'blood' as such is not involved in the process, but Richards argues that in people's minds 'there are separate domains concerned with sexual intercourse and conception on the one hand, and with the transmission of inherited characteristics on the other'.

The lack of data on ordinary Americans' ideas about 'blood' in Schneider's book and the indications in Richards' study that these ideas are complex and not self-evident (even if Richards himself tends to see lay knowledge as deficient and in need of improvement) together show that it is dangerous to make assumptions about the relative status and separability of biology and culture in kinship until more detailed information is gathered about what 'biology' means in the local context.

Born and Bred Kinship in Bacup

Edwards' work on Bacup interrogates in detail the complexities of how people see their kinship links, what constitutes them and what is passed down through generations. She focuses on the trope used by some Bacup people who say they are 'Bacup born and bred'. This gives her a starting point to examine what people think about being born (in a particular place, of particular people) and being bred (in a particular place, by particular people). Interestingly Edwards does not interrogate the semantics of the trope itself. The word 'bred' has various connotations, the ambiguities of which actually strengthen her case. Edwards is taking the word to mean 'brought up' or 'raised' and this, when the term is juxtaposed to 'born', seems to be its primary meaning. However, the word also has strong connotations of producing, generating or bearing offspring – indeed this is its first meaning in several dictionaries. A 'breed' is a strain, variety or even 'race' (*Chambers English Dictionary*, 1990). 'Breeding' can mean education or good manners, but it is also the activity of producing as well as raising offspring, as in 'cattle-breeding'. So when people say they are 'born and bred', ambiguous images are evoked: either they are first born and subsequently raised in a particular place; and/or they are not only born and raised in a place, but also of a genealogical line or family that is rooted in that place. Being 'bred' therefore seems to equivocate between images of environmental influence and blood lines – which is precisely the equivocation that Edwards is interested in.

The notion of place is very important in Edwards' study. Being born and bred happens in relation to a specific place – or rather a complex moral topography of places – as well as in relation to specific people. Edwards establishes that becoming attached to a place, and – even more important – being seen by others as legitimately attached to the place, can happen through various means: being born there, being raised there, living there long term or contributing something to the place. 'Bacup is said to exert an influence – moulding people who live in the place – and, while not born in the town, incomers can be socialised into its customs and expectations. Bacup grows persons.' Although this formulation suggests a process in which persons are rather passive, Edwards sees people as actively making themselves as well: 'Neighbours do not come preformed and ready made, instead they are made into neighbours as much as they make themselves neighbourly' (Edwards, 2000: 134).

I mention Edwards' treatment of place, because it parallels in some ways her analysis of the domain that concerns me most – that of kinship. Much of her data and analysis are similar to Schneider's basic model. People in Bacup do distinguish between 'blood relatives' and in-laws and step relatives. They also say that 'blood is thicker than water' indicating the strength and permanency of blood connections that Schneider also emphasises – although Edwards (2000: 216) goes on to note that 'there are as many exceptions to this edict as there are examples'. Bacupians' views of inheritance are also similar to those studied by Davison (1997) and Richards (1997). For example, inheritance is seen as having both a biological and a social aspect.

Davison (1997: 171) contends that, for the Welsh people he worked with, these two aspects are seen as 'quite distinct' conceptually, 'relating to a contrast between nature and nurture'. Physical inheritance is seen as relating to the realm of nature in which substance is reproduced; tropes such as 'she is a chip off the old block' are used to evoke similarities between mother and daughter. Social inheritance is seen as relating to the realm of nurture in which experience is reproduced; tropes such as 'she is following in her father's footsteps' are used to evoke similarities between generations. The things that can be inherited include attributes of physique (e.g., eye colour, build, specific ailments), 'constitution' (e.g., toughness, sickliness, longevity) and personality (e.g., sunny or anxious disposition, sweet tooth, facial expressions). However, Davison does not give any evidence of how people divide these various traits into biological and social realms and indeed the only extended example he does give makes one wonder how such a conceptual distinction would work. People might deploy the distinction clearly when asked in abstract terms, but in practice there could be ambiguity. Davison (1997: 172) refers to a 30-year-old woman who was recognised by her friends and family as having a build and a gait similar to that of her grandmother at the same age. She had also just acquired a habit of flicking her hair from her eyes and of missing sections of conversations and interjecting inappropriate opinions that was so exactly like her mother that it was a cause of merriment. Such parallels caused relatives to worry that she would also suffer from arthritis later in life, as her mother and grandmother had done, and might also suffer from periodic depression, as her mother had done. Davison does not reveal how all these traits were divided up in a 'quite distinct' fashion between the biological and the social, but it would have been interesting to know if there really was such unanimous clarity. Richards (1997: 189) also notes in passing that inheritance has this dual meaning for the people he worked with. He is prompted to this conclusion by the fact that 'it is possible to find examples where it seems that a kinship link that does not involve a biological link (such as a step-parent) is seen to have led to inheritance of a characteristic'. This suggests that there may not be such a 'distinct' divide between the social and the biological as Davison thinks.

Edwards takes the issue a little further. She notes examples in which people puzzled openly about what was biological and what social in a given individual's make-up. There is a conceptual distinction of some kind between biology and society still operating here, but in practice this becomes blurred when people are unsure how to deploy this distinction. Edwards (2000: 217) records a conversation in which she asked two women what a 'blood line' was. One replied that it was a 'purely biological thing', but the other, reflecting on the intense and physical empathy between her two sons – one got ill when the other did, for example – was not so sure: was it because they'd been 'brought up close' or because they were biologically related? She concluded: 'It's hard to tell, isn't it? what's been made and what's in their make-up.' Edwards (2000: 216) observes: 'Not only are there inherited items passed on "in the blood" or "in the genes" and said to be immutable and given, but also characteristics imbued through example.' So far there is little new. But she goes on:

There is not, however, a measurement of each in each person, but different elements of inheritance are congealed (purified) for different purposes. Different aspects of a person's make-up are made up (put together as in a prescription) according to the question being asked and the reasons for asking it.

Reflecting on the conversation mentioned above, she adds that, in thinking about the biological and/or social origins of a person:

Either or both are possible: the question of which, or in what combination, is again not a question which requires a definitive answer. It is another version of a culturally significant and perennial opposition, sometimes couched in terms of nature and nurture, that has no resolution: each is implicated in the other. (Edwards, 2000: 217)

There are suggestions here of what Thompson (forthcoming) calls 'strategic naturalisation' (see below), but with the added element that what counted as 'natural' in the first place was also open to strategic considerations.

Rapp (1999) reinforces this picture in her detailed ethnographic study of amniocentesis in the US. Her study included many interviews with women undergoing the test and the genetic counselling that went with it. Her interviewees often discussed issues of heredity and relatedness between generations, usually in the context of health 'problems'. She found that lay people's ideas about heredity were often at odds with those of the genetic counsellors. Babies could be badly affected by their mothers' anger during pregnancy, causing death or mental retardation (Rapp, 1999: 85). Women were seen as much more responsible than men for an unborn baby's welfare. This went beyond standard medical ideas about the need to avoid smoking and to eat well: Rapp (1999: 87) found that women from many backgrounds 'believe that the behaviour they define as healthy or unhealthy is responsible for a pregnancy's outcome, and they do not distinguish genetic health from any other cause or manifestation'. Rapp (1999: 162) also observed a 'melding of the biological and social' in people's accounts of why they and their families suffered from a variety of problems. Although she was inter-viewing women who were undergoing amniocentesis and related genetic counselling that focused on a very specific genetic condition of the foetus, the risk of which was known to increase with the age of the mother, she found that many women spontaneously volunteered information about family health in general and that African American women in particular might say that problems such as alcoholism, childhood seizures and diabetes 'ran in families'. The emphasis was thus sometimes shifted from individual genetics to collective social influences. In sum, Rapp's material indicates a certain vagueness in the way people thought about the dividing line between genetic and social influences.

Returning to Bacup, it is significant that Edwards framed many of her enquiries into kinship in the context of discussions about new reproductive technologies (NRTs). The way NRTs separate gametes from their producers – for example, in egg and sperm donation and in surrogacy – challenges ideas about connection, blood, relationship and kinship, in the same way that new genetic technologies and techno-science in general challenge ideas about the limits and relationships of nature and culture. Gamete transfer, Edwards argues, renders visible features of Born and Bred kinship. For example: 'Gametes are both discrete entities *and* contain and transfer past relation-ships which make up a person' (Edwards, 2000: 230). This is rather different from Schneider's formulation in which a blood relative is related 'first by common biogenetic heredity, a *natural substance*, and second, by a *relation-ship*, a pattern for behaviour or a code for conduct' (Schneider, 1980: 26). Where Schneider separates the gamete from the social relationship, Edwards sees them as interpenetrating – although she recognises that people fear that NRTs might cause the separation of the two, so that 'children born with the aid of NRTs are disconnected from those relationships which root them in places and pasts' (Edwards, 2000: 230), a fear which indicates some level of conceptual separation between gamete and social relationship, even if in practice the two are indecipherably intertwined.

This ambivalent coexistence of a basic conceptual distinction separating the biological from the social with ideas about their interpenetration appears again in issues around adoption and step-parenting. Edwards notes how some step-parents in Bacup reject the term 'step' and insist on a full kin term: father, mother, son, daughter. In some sense, this actually reinforces the difference between 'step' and 'real' kin, but these examples 'suggest a resistance to the privileging of biological connection while reaffirming biological connection ... In order to emphasise shared substance, often couched in idioms of "biology", an alternative, such as shared sentiment, is needed' (Edwards, 2000: 232). One adoptive mother insisted that the 'real' mother was the one who cared for and raised the children, while also acknowledging that adopted children might want to know where they 'actually' came from. 'Both the origins of the adoptees and the parent who looks after them are "real" together, and there is no difficulty holding these two "reals" together' (Edwards, 2000: 243). This again betokens the highly ambiguous way in which the distinction between the biological and the social is recognised at the very same moment that it is impenetrably blurred.

In an article Edwards co-authored with Strathern the same argument emerges. They refer to the 'impasse set up by imagining kinship as divided between social and biological manifestations of itself' and instead explore the 'interdigitation of diverse kinds of linkages' and 'the division and combination of social and biological facts' that are used in English kinship to reckon relatedness (Edwards and Strathern, 2000: 150, 158, 159). They find that the 'amount of blood' that is thought to connect people 'may *or may not* be relevant to the strength of the connection' and also note that birthplace and mother tongue are seen as 'immutables not open to choice' which 'echo the definitive transmission of substance at conception' (Edwards and Strathern, 2000: 160, 161).[8]

Given Edwards' focus on adoption and NRTs, it is worth looking, albeit briefly, at some other studies in these areas to see if they support her approach.

Adoption

Other studies of adoption tend to emphasise the dominance of a biological idiom in reckoning kinship. In her study of adoption in the US, Modell says that, from the late nineteenth century onwards, adoption has been primarily based on the 'as-if' principle (Modell, 1994: 3, 225): adoption seeks to emulate biological family models perceived as the norm; adoptive connections are seen 'as if' they were biological ones. The 'fictive kinship' that adoption involves, while it masks the absence of 'blood' ties, serves to reinforce their basic significance: 'a social relationship makes no sense without a reference to a genealogical relationship' (Modell, 1994: 227; cf. Schneider, 1972: 36, who makes the same point). In her view, adoptive parents strive to make their family as much like a biological one as possible; birth parents who have relinquished their children see the bond of 'blood' as enduring and unbreakable and so, generally, do adoptive children. Adoption in this mode is characterised by tensions and paradoxes which arise from the fact that fictive kinship strives to be just like genealogical kinship, but can never totally obscure the fact that it is based on a paper contract. This, to most Americans, makes it a less 'real' form of kinship. Modell then argues that a better mode for adoption would be a totally open system in which birth parents and adoptive parents would be parallel sets of kin, without one being more or less real than the other. Such a practice would, she admits, go against the grain of American views of kinship (Modell, 1994: 230–2).

There are various things in Modell's account that run counter to the very definitive emphasis on the primacy of biological kinship evident in her concluding chapter. To begin with, she describes at some length how, since about the 1960s, there has been a gradual move towards slightly more open adoption practices in which adoptive children know about their origins and some contact may be maintained between birth parents and the adoptive family (Modell, 1994: chs 7, 8, 9). This greater openness, she suggests, has not come from social workers and legislators, but from people involved in adoptive families, from the children who have sought out birth parents and vice versa: 'people choose to transact parenthood that way' says Modell (1994: 237). They have had to fight against the hegemony established by the courts, the social work departments and the legislatures and these institutions have been obliged to follow suit. But surely this 'counterhegemonic' struggle (Modell, 1994: 235) suggests that the dominance of the biological view was not quite as neatly and uniformly established as Modell says it was. Admittedly the struggle mostly involved people trying to regain the biological links that had been denied them, but this very search also forced them to reckon with the significance of the links established through caring.

Second, while much of Modell's material clearly shows that blood links were considered very important by all parties involved – hence the extended searches for blood relatives, the tremendous emotion surrounding reunions, the eagerness of adoptive parents to erase the birth parents from the scene – she also shows how important nurturing was. 'That was the dichotomy that adoption created: a mother who was real because she gave birth to the child and another mother who was *equally real* because she raised the child' (Modell, 1994: 196, emphasis added). As one birth parent put it: 'There is a special bond [between birth parent and child] but it can *never wipe out* what they [the adoptive parents] gave them' (Modell, 1994: 196, emphasis added). This link of nurturance is strongly reminiscent of Schneider's unbreakable bond of blood and it suggests a model in which blood and nurture are equal principles intertwining, and perhaps competing, with each other on a level footing, rather than blood forming the permanent foundation on which more fragile social connections are constructed. As Modell herself said in an earlier article (Modell, 1986: 649): 'The choice between blood and law is not an obvious one; the significance of an "order of law" is more problematic than Schneider allows.' Modell (1994: 197–8, 199) adds further to the significance of performance in creating kinship: 'Reunions between blood kin

showed the importance of cultivated parent–child ties: of *doing* something';
this was because 'birthparents worked at not just *being* but *acting like*
parents'. This suggests rather the reverse of the idea that the 'fictive' tie
recalls the genealogical one: it seems that when separated blood kin were
finally reunited, the single-stranded and one-dimensional nature of the
genealogical link made evident the richness and power of the sociality
created between parents and children who actually lived together.

Howell's work on transnational adoption in Norway also reveals the
symbolic importance of the 'normal' family based on genealogical links of
blood for the way adoptive parents try to build their families (Howell,
forthcoming). For example, the whole process of being approved as adopters
and getting a child from abroad, culminating in the final arrival at the airport
in Norway is likened by both adoption agencies and adopters as pregnancy,
ending in a successful 'delivery'. However, although the 'shadow of biology
always looms' over this 'self-conscious kinship' – Howell rejects Modell's term
'fictive kinship' as misleading – Howell notes that, in adoption, people
'negotiate a fine balancing act between biological and social accounts' which
enables them to 'engage in seemingly contradictory understandings of the
process'. While such contradictions might be problematic for the analyst,
they are much less so for people living, rather than studying, kinship.

Thus adoptive parents start with a decidedly biologistic turn of mind, in
which adoption is seen as very much second best; after learning more about
adoption, they take a more culturalist angle and, once engaged in adoption,
they conclude that it is not second best. They use a birthing idiom to connect
the still unknown child to them (i.e., the adoption process is likened to
pregnancy), while recognising some essential link between the child and
his/her culture of origin. After adoption, kin work, or 'kinning' as Howell
calls it, builds the child into existing family networks; birth links are marginalised. New kin-like networks are created with other adoptive families
who shared the same process or whose children came from the same
countries. As the child grows, his/her 'original culture' is re-emphasised,
often in slightly 'superficial' ways – for example, children are dressed in the
national costume of their country of origin for parties to which they take
typical national foods. Children's 'biological origins' are recognised at the
same time as adoptive parents are 'sensitive to any hint that the child is not
their real child'. Howell concludes that, in thinking about adoption,
'sometimes biological and sometimes cultural models are foregrounded' in
people's discourse. This recalls the 'interdigitation' of the social and biological
of which Edwards and Strathern (2000) speak.

This juggling of different elements of discourse is given another twist in
work by Gailey on US adoption. Again, she emphasises what she calls a
'dominant' ideology according to which biological kinship is seen as
preferable, stronger and more real: in the US adoption scene it is believed
that 'attachment through care-giving cannot substitute for the connection
created in giving birth' (Gailey, 2000: 18). Although it is not very clear,

Gailey seems to derive her dominant ideology both from talking to people directly involved in adoption and from representations of adoption in the media, schools and the 'state ideological apparatus' (Gailey, 2000: 20). She then nuances this picture by seeing how people of varying race, class and marital status situate themselves with respect to the dominant ideology. For example, she found that single mother adopters were very conscious that kinship was built through care and attachment, that motherhood was 'learned, not natural' (Gailey, 2000: 34). Less affluent adopters working through public agencies saw kinship as a 'process of claiming and fitting in' (Gailey, 2000: 41), while more middle-class adopters tended to be keen to break all birth ties and were also more genetically determinist in their views of their children's development. Gailey's work suggests that the way the tensions between permanence and change, between being and doing, between nature and nurture, are worked out depends on social context and social location.

Finally, Carsten's work on adoption reunion narratives explicitly questions a neat biology–society dichotomy. She found that British adults adopted as children who had sought out birth parents were very conscious of the powerful bonds that linked them to their adoptive parents, by virtue of the nurture and love they had given. While seeking birth parents clearly underlined 'the primacy of birth ties', in other ways, these adopted people also disturbed that primacy. She found that birth alone did not imply 'certainty or endurance or solidarity'. In fact 'time itself [had] a key role in producing new meanings for kinship' (Carsten, 2000b: 691). Carsten (2000b: 693) concludes that her 'overwhelming impression is that this distinction [between 'biological' and 'social'] is rather more muddled than any simple model would lead us to expect'. She states that we cannot perceive 'a very sharp or consistent distinction between what "travels in the blood" and what is absorbed from the environment'. Citing Weston's work on gay and lesbian families, Carsten argues that the adoption material also shows not only that non-biological kinship can be 'really real', but that it questions 'the taken-for-granted link between permanence and biology' (Carsten, 2000b: 695; Weston, 1995).

New Reproductive Technologies

So far I have been trying to show that, while a nature–nurture division certainly exists in Euro-American thought – specifically, in thinking about kinship – it is not as clear as is often supposed and does not necessarily fall into a 'vertical' model, in which nature underlies nurture, but instead may take on aspects of a 'horizontal' model, in which nature and nurture compete as equal principles and it is not clear where the boundary between them lies. This is also evident in some of the literature about the new reproductive technologies. As I mentioned above, much of this literature stresses that NRTs challenge existing ideas about human nature and human biology: in surrogacy, for example, 'motherhood' can be split into three elements – the woman supplying the ovum and thus the genetic material; the woman gestating the embryo; and the woman involved in caring for the child from birth. People involved in this process thus confront issues about what makes a 'mother' in ways even more complex than for adopters. As with the adoption literature, many researchers suggest that this has put increasing emphasis on biological and indeed genetic idioms: there is an 'exaggerated attention to biological idiom' and 'genetic relations have come to stand for the naturalness of biological kinship' (Strathern, 1992a: 52–3); 'nature becomes biology becomes genetics', says Franklin (2000: 190). Now, it may be true that NRTs and other genetic technologies highlight biology and genetics as constitutive elements in human nature, but some evidence indicates that, as with Born and Bred kinship in Bacup and with adoption, many different elements are brought into play in reckoning relationship, and biology or genetics are not always simply the dominant idioms. Of course, in dealing with NRTs we are dealing with discourses and practices of relatively recent origin, so these may not tell us much about more established ideas of kinship and human nature. But reactions to NRTs do not come out of nowhere; they build on previous notions just as they change them. As Haraway (1997: 134, 265) notes, while blood ties may belong to a different, older 'regime of nature' than the 'streams of information' that genetics evokes, it is also the case that the 'blood [is] recast in the coin of genes and information'.

In her study of surrogacy in the US, Ragoné contends that 'although the means of achieving relatedness may have changed, the rigorous emphasis on the family and on the biogenetic basis of American kinship remains' (Ragoné, 1994: 109). For example, people prefer the increasingly successful option of gestational surrogacy (in which the surrogate gestates an embryo formed from the gametes of the couple who commission her services) to the option of artificial insemination (AI) surrogacy in which, typically, the commissioning father's sperm is used to fertilise a surrogate who then gestates the baby, thus contributing her ovum and her womb to the process (Ragoné, 1994: 198, n. 11; see also Ragoné, 1998: 120). The former method creates a 'normal' genetic link between the commissioning couple and their child, while the AI method creates a genetic link between surrogate and child and may even suggest a sexual and adulterous relation between surrogate and commissioning father (Ragoné, 1996: 359). In gestational surrogacy the surrogate typically emphasises the genetic link, thus marginalising her contribution to that of mere 'vehicle'. In AI surrogacy, however, the surrogate does exactly the opposite, downplaying the genetic link, sometimes to the point of denying it. Ragoné (1994: 76) cites one AI surrogate who said, 'I never think of the child as mine. ... I couldn't relate that *it had any part of me*' (emphasis added). This puts in a different light Schneider's idea of an enduring link created by shared biogenetic substance and indeed slightly questions Ragoné's own conclusions about a 'rigorous emphasis' on biogenetics in American kinship. AI surrogates emphasise the overriding importance of caring in constituting motherhood; biology becomes practically irrelevant. Of course, the very denial of it in some sense reaffirms its importance – as Modell argued for adoption – but while it is true that the nature–nurture split is made pretty well as evident as it could be in these reproductive arrangements, it also seems to me that it is being fudged, that nurture is seen as, in some contexts, blurring into nature. This is also evident from the interesting fact that nearly all couples in AI surrogacy arrangements do not bother with the offered paternity test on the child. (The surrogate's husband or partner, if she has one, promises to abstain from sexual intercourse with her until she is pregnant by the commissioning father's sperm, but such promises are not necessarily cast iron.) They simply say that they 'knew' at once the child was theirs, or that it didn't matter anyway – the child was theirs (Ragoné, 1994: 132). Biology became irrelevant in this context, despite the fact that these couples had paid a lot of money to have a child by these means, rather than adoption. Having the child was as good as giving birth to her. But biology could resurface later: some couples engaged the services of the same surrogate to have a second child, explicitly so as to give their first child a 'full' sibling (Ragoné, 1994: 130).

This contextual and situational way of selectively emphasising genetics and caring, which I noted above for adoption and which I argue effectively blurs the boundaries between them, is described in detail by Thompson in her work on NRTs. She argues that people involved in these processes do constantly make distinctions between natural and social facts, but that there is an indeterminate relationship between 'the biological facts taken to be relevant to kinship' and 'socially meaningful kinship categories' and that people use 'a mixed bag of surprisingly everyday strategies for naturalising and socialising particular traits, substances, precedents and behaviours' (Thompson, forthcoming). She examines a number of case studies to show the strategic ways people naturalised and socialised. As in Ragoné's study, gestational surrogates downplayed the link established through gestating a child. By contrast, one woman carrying a baby formed from her own husband's sperm and a friend's egg focused strongly on the powerful (indeed biological, though not genetic) link established through gestation in which substances other than DNA but including 'blood' are shared between mother and child. This experience established her motherhood. Hartouni (1997: ch. 5) reinforces the importance of gestation by arguing that in the US 'both abortion and infertility discourse constitute "maternal nature" in and through gestation; indeed, gestation is regarded as precisely what activates or brings fully into play woman's essential maternal core'. This again nuances the idea of a 'blood' link. The fact that this link is now separable into genetic and non-genetic biological components means that both components can intertwine in the constitution of kinship: not only genetics can create a natural biological bond.[9]

Thompson (forthcoming) also discusses an African American woman undergoing a donor egg procedure who likened using an egg from her sister or a friend to the extended parenting arrangements she saw as typical of African American communities in which women might act as mothers or 'second mothers' to relatives' children. This effectively socialised the genetic component, assimilating it to a particular sort of sociality. This and the previous case are examples of socialising (even if the first case is really more one of de-geneticising and re-biologising, than it is of socialising) and they were outnumbered by cases in which people focused on genetic linkages. Thompson shows, however, that people still traced rather particular genetic linkages in ways that suited how they wanted to understand their relatedness. One woman, for example, using the eggs of her daughter by a first marriage to conceive a pregnancy late in life with a second husband, mentally erased the genetic contribution that her first husband was making via her daughter's eggs. In contrast, another woman, also using her daughter's eggs, saw these as a version of her own eggs because of the genetic relation between them. In short, what was thought to constitute a natural link was rather indeterminate and socially mediated.

CONCLUSION

My argument in this chapter has been that lay belief in Europe and the US is not necessarily characterised by a clear and simple divide between nature and nurture, between the biological and the social, between genes and the environment.[10] While a conceptual distinction is recognised between the elements of these three pairs, it is a distinction that is continuously blurred. As a result, notions of what constitute 'human nature' are not easily restricted to the biological alone. There are things seen as relatively fixed that are handed down through 'the blood' or 'in the genes', but the material discussed above indicates that people also mix and match such elements with other elements, which may also be perceived as durable, but which are seen as developed through upbringing, through non-genetic biological links and through 'doing' or performance. People mix and match in changeable and contextual ways. They see both sets of elements as 'real'. They move between the biological and the social, the given and the developing, the permanent and the changeable, in ways that blur the boundary between them and, although it is clear that both have a role to play in constituting a person's 'nature', it is not clear what these relative roles are.

As I have noted, various authors argue that, in denying biological kinship or replacing it with kinship built through performance, people are simply reinforcing the underlying primacy of biology. This is an attractive argument partly because it draws strength from a fundamental premise of structuralist and post-structuralist theory – that in naming one thing, its other is automatically evoked (albeit in masked form); that is, meaning is established relationally. This is true, but it is also true that the semantic content of the other is not established in the process of naming; although there is a relationship of alterity, this is not necessarily a relationship of diametric opposition. Thus sociality may be established in relation to naturalness, but the meaning of sociality cannot necessarily be limited to everything that naturalness is not. This implies that while the two domains are mutually referential, they do not necessarily mark out exclusive territories on the same terrain. Instead they may overlap and interpenetrate.

How does the argument of this chapter fit into the concern of this book with ideas about race? My initial contention was that ideas about such apparently diacritical features of the domain of race as biology, heredity and nature were not being interrogated sufficiently. One assumption commonly made was that the natural and physical invocations made by racial discourse automatically implied fixity and permanence. I have tried to suggest, by looking at a different but related area of social relatedness, kinship, that modern Western ideas about nature are more flexible than is generally assumed, mainly because the dividing line between 'nature' and 'culture' is by no means clear and is subject to ambiguity and strategic manipulation. Further, it seems that culture is capable of producing human character and human relatedness that, rather than being an overlay onto nature, competes on a level playing field with it. That is, nature can move away from fixity towards a kind of cultural malleability, just as culture can assume a natural engrainedness. This has implications for the way we understand ideas and practices about race and it is these implications that I develop in the next chapter.

Telegony, a Case Study

By way of a bridge between this chapter, which considers ideas about inheritance and blood connections generally, and the next, which moves on to questions of race in particular, I present here a very brief account of a small study done some 30 years ago in Bristol on the lay beliefs in telegony (see Pearson, 1972). Telegony is the theory, mentioned in Chapter 3, according to which a male who reproduced with a given female could influence the offspring the female had by subsequent mates.[11] The male's sperm or germ cells were assumed to leave some permanent impression on the female's eggs, womb or body such that all her subsequent offspring would bear faint marks of this male, above all if he was her first mate. This theory was current in the nineteenth century in scientific circles and especially among animal breeders. According to Pearson, the Kennel Club's rules for registering pedigree puppies still revealed the presence of this theory in the 1970s (Pearson, 1972: Introduction). The study done in Bristol is of interest not only because it explores the persistence of this idea in late-twentieth-century lay circles, but also because it considers this belief in the context of sexual relations between blacks and whites: that is, the idea that if a white woman had intercourse with a black man, she would thereafter be likely to bear children 'tinged' with blackness, even if the father was white.

Pearson worked with old women, assuming older people would be more likely to retain outmoded beliefs. One group of women was of working-class origin with no secondary education, another group consisted of retired school teachers. She found that, outside a specific belief in telegony as such, there was a strong emotional and symbolic importance attached to blood as a substance. For example, she asked how they would feel about receiving a transfusion of blood that had come from 'a coloured person': 'The thought of having a black man's [sic] blood coursing through their veins was often totally repellent to these old ladies' (Pearson, 1972: 22).[12] The fear of contamination evoked by the prospect of blood transfusion attached equally to the idea of sexual intercourse with a black man (hence perhaps Pearson's reference to the blood of 'a black man', when her questionnaire specified 'a coloured person'). Another relevant finding was that many women believed that a mother's experiences during pregnancy would have a direct impact on the form of the embryo. This sounds similar to accepted medical opinion about, say, the deleterious effects on embryonic development of a mother's excessive consumption of alcohol or tobacco, but these women were not considering how a mother's behaviour might alter the developmental environment and growth processes of the embryo. Their beliefs were of the kind noted in Chapter 3, going back to antiquity, according to which events experienced by the mother would leave a direct and permanent impression on the embryo (see Huet, 1993; Ritvo, 1997: 112–13). In the Bristol study the case of a woman who gave birth to a baby with two heads was mentioned: this was said to be due to the fright caused when she unexpectedly came across a hanged man during her pregnancy. A pregnant woman who had been in the habit of strolling in her garden, overlooked by a synagogue, gave birth to a son with very 'Jewish' features. A mother broke her wrist during pregnancy and gave birth to a child with a deformed wrist.

Both ideas about contamination and about the susceptibility of the child to the mother's experiences and emotions formed the background to ideas about telegony. Twenty-one of the 50 women interviewed had heard of this belief and only 14 believed it might occur when a black man had intercourse with a white woman; ten of these were in the less educated group of women. According to Pearson (1972: 26), typical comments on the matter were: 'blackness goes into the system and clots in the blood'; 'a woman's blood would become infected'; 'the womb is polluted in some way'. The resulting impact on subsequent children might be very mild – perhaps no more than a slight coloration of the fingernails.

Banton (1987: 27) interprets Pearson's findings as evidence of the persistence of outmoded and cock-eyed theories and as showing us that beliefs about race need to be taken in the context of other beliefs about the mechanisms of inheritance. Pearson's own conclusions are similar, although she adds that the social context of race relations in 1970s Bristol – especially in St Pauls, an area with a substantial black population which was where most of the working-class sample lived – created a fertile milieu for whites' fears of being overwhelmed and contaminated. Such beliefs are also part of a more widespread and not so obviously outmoded or cock-eyed set of ideas about the intertwining and interpenetrating of 'nature' and 'nurture' in constituting a person's nature. Although ideas about telegony and the direct impact of maternal experiences on the embryo are perhaps extreme examples, they do suggest a very contingent and ambiguous boundary between biology and culture, or genes and environment. Notions of blood, although apparently notions only about biology, are actually semantically charged with a complex set of ideas which cannot easily be separated into those about biology and those about culture.

5. RACE, NATURE AND CULTURE

Where does the preceding discussion lead us in terms of understanding race? It may seem that I have wandered very far from the central theme. But the central theme concerns the fact that a racial and/or racist discourse is often said to be one that refers to human nature, generally conceived in essentialist terms and often grounded specifically on human biology or, more specifically still, on human genetics. The typical Western model of human nature depicts this nature as a biological substrate defined largely – indeed increasingly, according to some of the kinship theorists cited above – in terms of genes. On top of, or chronologically after, this essential base is constructed the overlay of culture, more or less influenced by the structure of the base. The material adduced in the previous chapter indicates that such a model is not quite so clearly adhered to by many people in Western societies as is generally thought (with or without the advent of NRTs). It reinforces the point made in Chapter 3 that a naturalising discourse is not only a biologising discourse and *a fortiori* not only a geneticising discourse. It also suggests that notions of essence need to be unpacked in order to examine the extent to which they rely on biologisation and ideas of fixity. In short, if racial discourse is to be characterised as an essentialising, naturalising discourse – to use an open definition – we need to look at what such a discourse might include in the context of racialising naturalisations.

My argument in this chapter will be, first, that ideas about 'blood' and human nature – whether expressed in terms of genes or not – continue to have an important part to play in much everyday thinking about race (exactly what part must of course depend on a host of factors). This suggests that the shift from biological to cultural discourses about race which is generally agreed to have taken place in Euro-American contexts after about 1950 – despite the persistence of a minority of psychologists who insist on a racial link between genetics and IQ – is not a simple one. It is not new to suggest that a culturalist discourse about race retains important elements of naturalisation. While some scholars may refer easily to 'the shift from race to culture' (Wetherell and Potter, 1992: 128), others note that cultural racism still involves some reference to the realm of 'nature, biology, genetic heritage or blood' (Wieviorka, 1997: 142). However, less attention has been paid to what this reference implies. Second, therefore, I argue that, while such naturalising idioms are probably quite common in discourse about race, we need to examine these to see what they consist of. We should be careful about a) assuming they automatically refer to genetics or even, more broadly, to biology; and b) assuming that they are automatically deterministic and evoking of permanent essences and fixity. In passing, I critique a couple of recent treatments which take a different angle on the idea of a shift from biological to cultural idioms of race by arguing that the new ubiquity of a genetic discourse is re-biologising race into a specifically genetic idiom. It is too limited to see racial discourse in general as characterised by a growing genetic essentialism. Third, I go on to discuss some empirical material which I suggest shows that, in talk about race, a biological idiom can be employed in a variety of ways, not all of them genetic and not all of them highly deterministic. We need a more flexible approach to racial discourse, one which does not automatically seek reference to biology and genetics, or if these are present, does not automatically assume such reference to invoke fixity and permanence.

RACE, BLOOD AND GENETICS

In this section I explore, albeit tentatively, how ideas about race intersect with those about biology – genes, blood, human nature – in everyday discourse about these things. The term 'everyday' is admittedly a loose one – *whose* 'everyday' is at issue? – but I will retain it here simply to indicate that I want to look beyond the specialist discourse of psychologists or the interpretations of texts and representations. The texts and images that form the subject matter of many investigations are, of course, very much in the public realm; they are everyday. But what is missing is a broader ethnographic account that explores how a wide range of people think about the role that blood, genes and nature play in racial identity, in relation to culture, the environment and nurture.

Surprisingly – and frustratingly for me – there seems to be rather little material on this theme. This must be either because it is a theme which is of little interest to most people to whom anthropologists and sociologists talk about race or because researchers do not make such matters the focus of their enquiries. But the preceding section on kinship makes it clear that people are very concerned, in some areas of their lives, with questions of biology, blood and genes. This makes it seem unlikely that such concerns are not also refracted through ideas about race when, as several scholars have noted, race also concerns notions about relatedness through bodily substance and intersects powerfully with ideas about sex, sexual reproduction and family (see Chapter 3). My guess is therefore that future ethnographic work may reveal much more along these lines. In the meantime, existing work does contain some valuable material.

One study that is suggestive in this respect is Wetherell and Potter's work on New Zealand. Their overall argument is one which I find too simple. They maintain that a general shift is observable from a biological discourse of race, similar to that found in the Victorian period, towards a culturalist one (e.g., Wetherell and Potter, 1992: 128). I would agree that Victorian ideas are not necessarily evident in 1990s New Zealand, but, this does not exhaust the realm of discourse about biology. I am interested in the fact that many of their white respondents used a strongly biological idiom when talking about the Maoris. One says, for example, that the Maoris' 'gang team work comes from a hereditary factor within their own communities'. Another talks of the Maoris' 'innate shyness', while someone else says: 'They are people of the land really and therefore it's probably come through their make-up, or their genetic make-up that that [sic] studying is a bit foreign to them' (Wetherell and Potter, 1992: 121). The authors state that fully two-thirds of their sample used this type of discourse, even though 'very few developed sustained arguments based on race discourse alone' ('race discourse', for Wetherell and Potter, includes references to biology, genes and so on). However, they see this discourse 'mainly as a kind of residual sediment' (Wetherell and Potter, 1992: 123) because, in their argument, such ideas are being displaced by an emphasis on culture. However widespread these notions may be, the narrative structure of the argument means they have to be classed as a residue. I wonder, however, whether such notions are not a fairly common part of everyday discourse, not as a residual sediment, an anachronistic hangover from the past, but as a way of thinking about human beings that overlaps with more general ideas about kinship, relatedness and human nature. This does not make such notions any less subject to being harnessed to racist ends, but it does relocate them as part of people's everyday conceptual tool kit rather than a simple residue.

More evidence – and a better interpretative framework – comes from Frankenberg's study of white women in the US and their discourses about race, including whiteness. She outlines three discursive repertoires which women used to talk about these matters: essentialist racism, based on biological notions of difference between people identified racially; colour- and power-evasion, which seeks to avoid recognising difference, inequality and racism, asserting that everyone is the same 'under the skin'; and race-cognisance, which recognises and celebrates racial difference seen as a historical and social construction. In one sense, these discourses can be 'considered as the first, second and third phases in U.S. race discourse in the sense that they originated in that order'. However, they cannot be 'conceptualised as unfolding chronologically in any simple sense'. Instead, in different contexts, each mode of discourse 'takes centre stage as the organising paradigm or retreats to the status of a repertoire that provides discursive elements but that does not dictate the overarching form or structure'. Elements from the three repertoires were 'combined and recombined, used in articulation with or against one another, and deployed with varying degrees of intentionality' (Frankenberg, 1993: 140).

The essentialist repertoire became particularly evident in discussions about interracial sexual relationships. Frankenberg found that some women thought of such relationships as deviant, as crossing fixed boundaries. Interracial couples were often considered to be marginal, betwixt and between accepted social categories. This applied even more strongly to their children who might be described as 'outcasts' (Frankenberg, 1993: 95). Frankenberg interprets this as deriving from a view that sees identity as biologically ascribed, even if the women speaking made no direct reference to blood, genes or biology and, indeed, seemed to be talking in terms of cultural belonging. It was in the women's references to children as 'half and half' or someone as 'part Spanish' that the genealogical discourse came through (Frankenberg, 1993: 96–7). In fact Frankenberg overloads her data somewhat by equating essentialist discourse with biologising idioms. Essentialism does not necessarily rely on ideas about biology. Her interviewees never seem to mention biology as such and, as far as one can tell, she did not ask them directly about their ideas on such matters as blood, genes or biology. A genealogical discourse certainly emerges in talk about 'mixed' children, but it also seems probable that, in this discourse, notions of social and physical inheritance are inextricably intertwined. One interviewee, for example, talked of a Japanese American girl who, she says, was seen as an 'outcast' by 'both cultures'. She continued:

> You see a Black and a white couple together and they have a child and you know the whites'll say 'ugh' and the Blacks'll say the same. As a matter of fact, I used to work for a couple – he was Black, she was white. They had kids, but by previous marriages. They didn't make their own and I thought, 'That's great!' (Frankenberg, 1993: 95)

For Frankenberg this illustrates a biological discourse as the hidden reality underlying the apparently cultural idiom. It seems certain the woman is thinking in essentialist terms, but the connections she sees as linking child to parents seem to be genealogical in the broadest sense: involving interwoven connections of blood and culture.

A third set of evidence comes from a small pilot study I did in the city of Cali, Colombia, in 1998.[1] I admit that I am introducing complications by using Latin American material in a context that, until now, has been mainly focused on 'Euro-American' – or 'Western' – ideas about kinship and race. As Bouquet (1993) argues, even within Europe the theories of kinship typical of British anthropology do not easily characterise Portuguese kinship. But, given the paucity of empirical material on this theme, I will present a few comments simply by way of illustration. The significance of the comments these people make about *sangre* (blood) should not be assumed: in the Latin American context, with its complex ideologies of *mestizaje* (mixture) between 'races', notions of blood are generally imbued with ambivalent and varied notions of mixture and purity.[2] I do not want to go into these complexities here, but simply to show that, among the small number of people I interviewed – mostly black people – there were common ideas about certain traits 'being in the blood', but also that such ideas were not always highly determinist. They seemed to refer to essences, but essences that were not automatically fixed and permanent.

One young black man, a low-income dweller, rap artist and local cultural activist, seemed to adhere to an environmentalist perspective. He said that a black person would take on the traits of whichever particular region of Colombia s/he grew up in. He continued:

I say this: that in Africa the drums have sounded so much and for so long that the people have assimilated it into themselves [*la gente lo ha asimilado en sí*]. It's something ... The drum, the sound, the music are indivisible from the African man. I believe more in that than in saying that we have a special body, or X type blood – I don't believe in those things. I believe more that we are part of the drum, of *la rumba* [partying][3] and vice versa. The drum is an instrument for man to communicate with God. But equally we are the instrument of God for him to communicate with everything. So I say there is a link between the divine, the way of seeing the world, the forms of *la rumba* and the human being. So I think that the closest one gets to that reality is on the African side. I think that this instrument, the drum, makes a hell of a difference in the universe, because of its acoustics, its form. So, if a person has, for 2,000 years, been listening to a drum – boom, boom, boom, always that beat – something has to happen in the body, in his mentality, in his rhythmic way of being, of moving.

This man specifically distances himself from a reductively genetic or biological discourse, but he nevertheless retains a naturalised perspective, which is also biological in a broader sense of referring to the organic body. He takes an environmentalist line, but sees the environment (and indeed God) as instilling a naturalised character. In relation to a question about 'natural rhythm', he added:

For me the problem is not one of the kind of body one has, one's height, the colour of one's eyes, the colour of one's hair, what creed one believes in. Instead, [it is a question of] the power of [being able to] experience it, feel it, do it.

Here, he implicitly rejects a simplistic association between black people and 'natural rhythm', but he has also himself created a strong argument for something approaching such an association: the history and environment of African people – and by implication their descendants in the Americas – have ingrained a certain 'power' into their bodies and minds.

Another black man, this time involved with folkloric dance, also began with remarks that indicated a simple environmentalist idea. He recounted how his mother and father had played instruments and danced with him and his brother (also involved in folkloric dance groups) when they were young and said: 'So all that was being transmitted to us and that's why we're like we are.' However, his experience at a school where the mainly white, middle-class students listened to rock on Walkmans and did not bother with dancing prompted him to say of the students: 'They are very lifeless, very slow. You can't see that style in them, that charisma. They're like sticks.' And he added: 'I think it's in the blood, in the descent.' He admitted that whites could learn to dance well, but retained reservations:

They have the same capacity, but they don't do it the same way we do it. They try to do it the best they can, but you can't see that impetus, that desire, that force that one has oneself who has lived all that stuff.

He added: 'There are some [white] people who get it [the rhythm] because of the milieu in which they live. But they don't do it the same.' On the one hand, then, 'living' provided the desire and force; on the other, even sharing a lived experience was not enough to bring whites and blacks to the same level.

Talking about his own *sangre*, he said:

It's more alive. That enthusiasm, that power, the conviction of knowing that one can do the things that come to one. I can't explain why, when I hear the boom-boom-boom of a drum, I run out to have a look. There's a certain something [*un no sé qué*][4] which grabs me and pulls me; it calls me as if by telepathy: 'Come, because this is yours.'

He then commented on 'people from the coast' – which in Colombia is a common euphemism for black people, but literally refers to the Atlantic and Pacific coastal regions where a lot of people of African descent live. He said 'they have a certain something for getting into folklore [i.e. folkloric music and dance], I don't know if it's the blood or the tradition'. When I asked him to comment further on this 'blood', he added: 'It's like ties which bind me to the skins [i.e., the drum skins], to noise, to folklore.' I asked whether such ties were linked to heredity in anyway and he responded: 'Of course, it is one's African heritage, it comes from one's descent.' When I asked him if *sangre* was the same thing as genes, he said 'Yes, sure', but he seemed less than certain of his ground, nervous that he might be quizzed on technical matters he knew little about.

Like the previous man's comments, this response shows an eclectic movement between ideas of blood and environment or tradition. Blood certainly figures large and sometimes it is explicitly linked to heredity and genealogy and even, when pressed, to genes. But at other times 'blood' is a way of talking about his innermost being, what he is deep down as an individual and this is also a result of having 'lived' certain experiences. Certainly this discourse is very naturalising in the sense that blood is part of the organism, something bodily, mysterious and uncontrollable, but it is not clearly genetic and there is also some uncertainty about where that 'something' comes from: 'I don't know if it's the blood or the tradition.'

The evidence presented from New Zealand and Colombia (and implicitly the US) suggests that the trope of 'blood' is a common one in talk about race. It suggests that a simple shift to 'cultural racism' is far from evident in general, even if in most public arenas in the Western world – and I include Latin America for this purpose – it is no longer usual practice to talk about race in terms of biology, blood and genes. The Colombian material is suggestive that, as in kinship, tropes of blood are often ambiguous, coexisting uncertainly with other tropes about tradition and the environment, but it is not much more than a suggestion. Material from Euro-American, or Euro-Australasian, contexts is very sparse so an extended analysis or comparison is not possible. Nevertheless it is worth arguing that this racialising, natu-ralising discourse indicates that the process of naturalisation, the references to 'blood' – and even genes – need to be approached with an open mind, without assuming such discourse is easily assimilated to taken-for-granted academic notions of fixed, biological essences.

RACE AND GENETIC ESSENTIALISM

While 'blood' may be a common trope in everyday talk about race, recent research on the use of a biological idiom in racial discourse maintains that, far from a cultural idiom of race achieving a blanket dominance nowadays, a genetic discourse is gaining new prominence. This research focuses on the genetic idiom and on the idea that genetic determinism is on the increase, largely due to the growing public profile of genetics. While this is a necessary and valid focus, it pre-emptively restricts the field of study. Once again, too many assumptions are being made about the nature of racialised discourse and the references it makes to human nature, biology and genetics. Let me give two examples.[5]

Nelkin and Lindee (1995b) argue that, from about 1990, there has been an increasing use of deterministic genetic imagery to sustain ideas of racial and gender difference among humans, even if at the same time molecular biology has shown that in genetic terms humans are fundamentally the same. This genetic essentialism has recently overturned the public consensus, dominant since the 1950s, that nurture was more important than nature. They make this argument first with respect to ideas about gender. They argue that genetic differences first captured the public imagination (which they assess mainly through media representations) with stories about sociobiology in the 1970s. By the 1980s such stories became more common and less contested – although this seems to contradict the previous claim that a preference for cultural explanations of difference dominated until the 1990s.

When they come to race, Nelkin and Lindee do not follow a clear historical argument, but focus on the publications of the race-and-IQ psychologists such as Jensen, Eysenck and Herrnstein, spanning 30 years from 1969, and on some media and text representations from the 1980s and 1990s. There is no way to assess the claim that geneticised notions of racial difference have become more common in the 1990s because no systematic before-and-after comparison is made. There is also some looseness about their idea of what constitutes a reference to genetics. They note, for example, that political discourse in the US often uses code words such as 'welfare mothers' or 'urban underclass' which are recognised to refer above all to African Americans. These code words, say Nelkin and Lindee (1995b: 397) 'foster biological gen-eralisations'. But is a coded reference to African Americans necessarily a 'biological' generalisation? And, if so, is it therefore a genetic one? 'Genetic language' is also said to appear in sports broadcasting and some examples given do clearly refer to genetics. But others are not clear. A baseball manager's reference to black players' supposed 'lack of [the] necessities' vital for team management may be genetic language, or it may not (Nelkin and Lindee, 1995b: 398). It is, without doubt, racist, but that is only partly the issue here. The issue is – what *kind* of racism are we dealing with?

The conclusion that 'In the 1990s, race theorists are more and more willing to publicly express their views on genetic differences between blacks and whites' (Nelkin and Lindee, 1995b: 398) is thus not very convincing. The authors do show that some people in academic psychology, politics and popular media use genetic arguments in a highly determinist way to account for supposed 'racial' differences, but they do not present a distinct historical trend in this tendency. On the other hand, on the basis of a systematic study of the press, Condit (1999a: 196) claims that 'linkages among race, crime and heredity were not as direct and overt [in the period 1980–95] as in the previous era [1956–76]'. It is also worth bearing in mind Tapper's work on the pathologisation of blacks by the US medical establishment (Tapper, 1995, 1997). He shows that very deterministic links between black people and sickle cell anaemia were made by US doctors over a period from 1900 into the 1950s: the presence or absence of the genetic discourse which was harnessed to these endeavours in the 1950s seems to have made little difference to the level of determinism.

A similar problem of assuming too much about geneticisation underlies Simpson's analysis of ethnicity and essentialism in a context of new genetic technologies (Simpson, 2000). He describes the Icelandic human genome project, aimed at mapping the genes of most of the national population, and speculates on the results of this endeavour: 'If they so wish, Icelanders can imagine themselves as part of a unique genetic community, essentially the same in their differences' (Simpson, 2000: 5). The problem is that there is little way of knowing what changes are being introduced by the genetic idiom, apart from the fact that 'genes' form part of the talk. Simpson (2000: 5) acknowledges that discourses already exist which 'portray Icelanders as guardians of a unique heritage'. Granted, the popularisation of genetic idioms will surely give new ways of imagining ethnicity – and this is really Simpson's main point. But there is also an implied argument that these new ways will be more determinist and this is more difficult to sustain because it is clear that plenty of determinist ideologies have been purveyed in the past without the use of a specifically *genetic* idiom: vaguer notions such as 'blood' can be just as effective. On the other hand, as Condit argues (1999a), genetic idioms are not always as deterministic as critics think.

VARIED DISCOURSES OF RACE AND BIOLOGY

In keeping with my argument about the ambiguity of the nature–culture divide in discourses about race (and kinship) and against the idea that racial discourse is simply moving in the direction of greater geneticisation and, specifically, greater genetic essentialism, I explore here some discourses about race that are certainly naturalising, may be biologising, but are not automatically geneticising or highly determinist. That does not necessarily make them non-racist or a good way of talking about race, but it is nevertheless important to appreciate their character. We need to grasp the multifaceted and flexible character of naturalisation.

Twine's study of white mothers of African-descent children in Britain shows complex notions of relatedness at work (Twine, 2000). She shows that these white mothers are often assumed by black people not to have the skills and experience necessary to guide their children through a racist environment. In contrast, black mothers are thought to automatically possess these skills – and this is despite the fact that such mothers recognise that their own parents, often Caribbean immigrants, had not always been useful in advising them about racism in Britain. People often describe the connection a black mother has with the experiences of her children as 'empathy'; whereas white mothers are more likely only to feel 'sympathy'. Much of the language used to explain this empathy is environmentalist: the black mother has *lived* racism while the white woman has not (e.g., Twine, 2000: 90), yet the automatic assumption of empathy – and the automatic assumption of white maternal lack of empathy, despite the acknowledgement that white mothers of mixed race children by black fathers themselves experience considerable racism – also suggests to me a rather naturalised relatedness. Indeed Twine (2000: 104) says, 'all black mothers were believed to possess maternal competence *by virtue of belonging to the same race as their children*' (emphasis added). A typical ambiguity of the action of nature and nurture is evident. Twine (2000: 104) states:

> While some white mothers expressed concerns that racial difference and racism were strong enough to disrupt the maternal bond with their children, others expressed the belief that the mother–child bond transcends race, so their children's experience of being labelled racially 'other' would not threaten that primary intimacy.

Twine does not discuss issues of naturalisation here, but they surely arise. The maternal bond is established by intimacy, but also by ideas about biology; the threat to the maternal bond is from the experience of racism, but also, perhaps, from ideas about racial similarily constituting some natural relatedness or 'empathy'. The dividing line between biology and lived experience is vague, to say the least. Indeed it is not clear that 'biology' as such – let alone genes – are at issue, since they are never mentioned. The reason *why* black mothers have empathy is located in a vague area, somewhere between experience and an unspecified natural relatedness. These are, in one sense, essentialist idioms, but the essence involved seems rather vague and unspecified, at times 'impervious' to social context (to use Omi and Winant's phrase (1994: 181, n. 6)), yet at other times not.

Something similar can be gleaned from Ragoné's discussion of transracial surrogacy arrangements (Ragoné, 1998, 2000). She mentions that most surrogates and commissioning couples played down any racial difference between them, stating that this would make no difference one way or another. But one African American gestational surrogate said her mother was happy she was not carrying a black child because she, the mother, thought that the surrogate would want to keep a black child: 'racial resemblance raises certain questions for her [the surrogate] about relatedness even when there is no genetic tie' (Ragoné, 1998: 126). In many of the studies of adoption and surrogacy discussed earlier, physical resemblance between parents and children was often a major point of concern: such resemblance was taken to be the sign of a biological link and the lack of it was often troubling for parents whose child was not or was only partially genetically related. (In keeping with my overall argument, however, 'resemblance' could be construed in flexible ways. Thus the fathers of boys born of sperm donation, once their son was old enough to display gestures and mannerisms similar to their own, might speculate on whether the child was 'actually' theirs.)[6] In the transracial surrogacy case, although the means or kind of relatedness that might exist between the black surrogate and a black baby is not specified, it is clearly a naturalised link. There is perhaps a suggestion of a link of 'blood' or biology, but there is also a suggestion that it is simply 'natural' for a mother to feel a greater bond with a baby of her own 'race'. This is a naturalising argument which – although sociobiologists would doubtless invoke genes as the cause of this – does not rely directly on notions of blood, biology or genes.

Surrogacy also furnishes a rather different example of a non-genetic, biological idiom of blood. Teman (2000: 16–17) observes that the 1996 Israeli law regarding surrogacy arrangements was formed through a dialogue between the Orthodox Rabbinical Establishment and secular officials of the state. The law allows surrogacy agreement only between Israeli citizens, in order to prevent non-Israeli couples obtaining children born of an Israeli surrogate or a non-Israeli woman gestating an Israeli child. The commissioning couple and the surrogate mother must also be of the same religion (see also Kahn, 2000: 142–3). A Jewish baby must be gestated in a Jewish womb to ensure that the baby is entirely Jewish: 'Jewish babies are only born from Jewish wombs' (Kahn, 2000: 173). Jewish identity is passed down through the maternal line, but this 'line' is understood – at least by the orthodox Jews and rabbis that reportedly ensured these measures became law – to include not just genetics, but the 'blood' that circulates between mother and child during gestation. Indeed this is so much the case for some rabbis that, according to Kahn (2000: 131), they permit the use of non-Jewish donor ova for Jewish women who cannot use their own eggs: the Jewishness of the carrying mother (which is mandatory) is enough to ensure the Jewishness of the child. Other rabbis, however, see the child's identity as more strongly determined by the genetic line and require the child of a non-Jewish ovum to be converted. Kahn (2000: 165) sees this emphasis on gestation and parturition as the key elements in creating Jewish children as a specifically Jewish 'counterdiscourse' that 'stands in direct opposition to dominant Euro-American beliefs that biogenetic material is the ultimate determinant ... of kinship'. As might be expected, I see rather more continuity between these Jewish beliefs and their Euro-American counterparts.

Teman (personal communication) also reports that some orthodox Jewish commissioning couples worry that their surrogate does not observe the necessary rituals, such as fasting on Yom Kippur or going to take ritual baths of purification. That is, they want the surrogate to be 'kosher', so that her womb is kosher and thus also the child. Teman observes further that couples who hire surrogates may be sensitive to the differences of skin colour that exist among Jews in Israel. If such couples are light-skinned, they may fear that a dark-skinned surrogate will cause the baby to come out darker; one couple even feared their baby might emerge 'looking Yemenite' because the surrogate's boyfriend was Yemenite.[7] (There are strong hints here of a belief in telegony.)

Like the comments by Hartouni (1997) and Thompson (forthcoming) on the importance of gestation in establishing kinship links, discussed in Chapter 4, this Israeli example suggests that racial (or racialised religious) identities can involve an idiom of 'blood' understood as something natural and biological without there being a discourse of genetic linkage at all and with a fairly performative concept of biology being involved.[8]

A different set of examples concerns three representations of race which have been the subject of critical commentary. I refer to the coffee-table book, *The Family of Man*, critiqued by Haraway (1997: 243); the PR material of the clothing company Benetton, critiqued by Lury (2000) and Castañeda (forthcoming; see also Back and Quaade, 1993); and the special issue of *Time* magazine which featured a computer-generated mixed race woman – 'the new face of America' – critiqued by Haraway (1997: 259–64), Hammond (1997) and Castañeda (forthcoming).

The Family of Man was published in 1955 at a time when, Haraway argues, the 'new physical anthropology' was also establishing a post-war consensus about the basic genetic similarity of humans, visible also in the UNESCO declarations about race made in 1950 and 1951 (see also Haraway, 1989: ch. 8). It was a photo album showing different peoples from all over the world engaged in the same activities – first courtship, marriage, pregnancy, labour, babyhood and parenting; then working, playing, fighting, ageing and death. The message was one of unity in diversity, of a universal humanity underlying cultural variation.

The Benetton material, produced in their advertisements and their magazine, *Colors*, often focuses on race. It displays people of many different racialised appearances together and also plays with racial identity: one woman is shown made up with cosmetics as a black, a white and an oriental woman; Queen Elizabeth is shown as a black woman, the Pope as an oriental man. The message is that racial identity is appearance, it is superficial, like clothing, and above all it is a matter of (consumer) choice. There is no significant difference under the skin.

Time magazine produced a special issue in 1993 on immigration into the US. As part of this, a computer morphing programme was employed to 'mix' 14 images of faces – seven women and seven men of Middle Eastern, Italian, African, Vietnamese, Anglo-Saxon, Chinese and Hispanic origin. The result, displayed on the front cover, was a new 'Eve'. Inside, the original fourteen photos were reproduced along with the morphed results of all the possible combinations between them.

These three sets of representations are all critiqued, by the various authors cited above, because, in presenting and celebrating diversity and hybridity, they either gloss over the real racism and racial inequalities that lie behind this diversity and/or they reinstate the basic familiar categories of difference that they seem to be making light of. Haraway (1997: 243) says that for all the emphasis on difference in *The Family of Man*, there is a 'grammar of indifference, of the multiplication of sameness'. *Time*'s Eve, or SimEve as Haraway calls her, is similarly said to be 'smoothly homogenised' (Haraway, 1997: 262). Castañeda (forthcoming) notes of the 14 parents of Eve that the categories into which they fall 'are evacuated of complicated histories and politics of culture, geography, and nation that they might otherwise signify'. Hammond (1997: 118) comments that, in the 'technophilic reproduction' that is employed in producing Eve, 'stereotypical racial typologies remain in place'. Of Benetton's material, Castañeda (forthcoming) also argues that 'race is evacuated as a signifier of specific histories linked to contemporary social, political, and cultural worlds'. Lury (2000) argues that race is dematerialised and subjected to a cultural, not a biological, essentialism. Race is reduced to choice, itself represented as a natural thing, and context is erased as problems of power, money and race are overwhelmed by diversity and consumer choice.

I have no quibble as such with these critiques which seem to me incisive and absolutely right. I am interested, however, in the contrast these representations make to the story of increasing genetic essentialism. All these representations use naturalising and biologising visual idioms, without referring directly or even at all to genetics. Lury (2000: 148) argues that 'the novel productivity of the [Benetton] images is missed if it is argued that racial difference is *naturalised* here, if by that is meant that race is presented as an unchanging and eternal biological essence'. I would agree that *if* naturalisation is understood only in this extremely limited way, then the concept is not appropriate. But why limit it in this way? By abandoning ideas of naturalisation and moving instead to cultural essentialism, Lury surely diminishes the fact that all these images rely completely on visual clues of biology – not biology understood as genetics and even less as something related to 'an unchanging and eternal essence', but biology nevertheless. The visual clues may well suggest something about essences, but it is not necessary to assume eternal or unchanging essences: 'Euro-American racial thinking related the visual markers of race to the *protean* hidden properties of different human kinds' (Stoler, 1995: 205, emphasis added).

Likewise *The Family of Man* and *Time*'s Eve convey naturalised messages about race through visual cues of racial difference. As the critics of *Time*'s Eve recognise, the technology of morphing clearly stands in for sexual reproduction and, in this case, for 'miscegenation'. Yet Haraway (1997: 263–4) says that with SimEve we are not faced with 'the naturalised typologies of Teddy Bear Patriarchy's early-twentieth-century racial discourse' and instead critiques the erasure of 'racial domination, guilt and hatred'.[9] Castañeda (forthcoming) similarly contends:

This form of racialisation does not consist, then, in the establishment of a hierarchy for domination based on biologised or even culturalised racial difference. Its violence – its racism – consists instead in the evacuation of histories of domination and resistance (and of all those events and ways of living that cannot be captured in those two terms), accomplished through morphing as a specific kind of technological (and heterosexual) reproduction.

The semantic load attached to these cues is one of a perverted anodyne disingenuous universality, which erases the history and contemporary realities of racialised political and economic hierarchies. It is important to emphasise as well, however, that there *is* a powerfully naturalising, biologising discourse at work here – we just need a broader idea of what naturalisation and biology mean. In this case, biology includes the superficial physical features that are cues for racial identity. These physical cues may be manipulable, through surgery, cosmetics, clothing or morphing, but that doesn't deny their status as natural. The physical cues at issue here are, of course, not any old traits of appearance but are the ones assumed to be linked to global geographies of difference and assumed to be heritable – that is, they are *racial* cues. These cues thus evoke another layer of naturalised meanings – often understood as deeper and more real (Wade, 1993b) – but they do not depend on these for their naturalising and biologising effect.

CONCLUSION

My purpose in this chapter has been to explore the terrain of naturalising discourses. My technique has admittedly been that of suggestion rather than the systematic marshalling of ethnographic evidence: that, it seems, is a job for the future. I have tried to indicate that we need a broader view of what naturalisation consists of: it may entail genetics but it may not; it may entail biology, but biology itself has to be seen as entailing more than 'unchanging and eternal essences'. I have given some brief illustrations of what I consider may be legitimately viewed as naturalising discourses in order to show some of the variety involved. These indicate that the boundaries of naturalisation are not clear; there is an ambiguous line separating the way people talk of cultural and natural facts.

Once this is appreciated, it gives us new insights into the shifts that are said to have occurred from biological racism to cultural racism with, it may be said, a very recent trend back towards a geneticised discourse of race. Certainly these shifts are observable in some sense. The 1950s did constitute an important break away from a biological discourse of race towards a cultural one *in certain public spheres*; there is a geneticised discourse of race, *in certain circles*, which may have been growing from the 1990s although it is a little early to tell. But these phenomena are not the whole picture. Rather they represent different ways in which long-standing ideas and uncertainties about permanence and change, about similarity and difference, about what makes a person what they are, have been worked out. It is clear that naturalising idioms remain important in cultural racism and I hope that the material above has shed some light, albeit preliminary, on what such idioms imply and entail.

What are the implications of this argument for understanding racism? I am arguing that naturalising and essentialising discourses of race are more flexible than has previously been recognised. It might be objected, with good reason, that the practices and discourses of racism are frequently highly inflexible, imposing authoritative versions of racial identity, seen as an immutable character. In practice, it could be said, people may equivocate between nature and culture in particular cases of reckoning about racialised personhood, but these are only ripples on the surface of a deeper sea of collective representations of race as permanent, along with associated practices of discrimination and symbolic and physical violence. It is indeed indisputable that, in a given social context, powerful discourses of racism can impose authoritative versions of racial identity which prejudice some people and favour others. There is a real and very powerful sense in which racial discourses can and do fix.

However, it is important to see more deeply how those discourses work. They do not work just by evoking a simple unchanging and eternal essentialism, based on narrow versions of biology and genetics, although they may very well include these elements. I cite once more Stoler's comments (see Chapter 2) that 'racial essentialism is not, as we have often assumed, about a *fixed* notion of essence' (Stoler, 1997a: 104) and that a 'notion of essence does not necessarily rest on immovable parts but on the strategic inclusion of different attributes, of a changing constellation of features and a changing weighting of them' (Stoler, 1997b: 200). It is precisely this strategic inclusion – or strategic naturalisation or strategic interdigitation of the natural and cultural (see Chapter 4) – that gives racism its chameleon powers. Racism can and does fix, but the flexibility of essentialism means that it can fix in opportunist ways that colonise the realm of nature in varied ways. Opening up the notion of naturalisation, beyond genetics and reductionist notions of biology, allows us to see the variability of a naturalising discourse and how it can be harnessed to projects of racism in different ways. For example, the insistence of Israeli law on the purity of surrogacy arrangements and the fears of some Israeli couples that their surrogate's dark skin will affect their baby are both instances of racism: both depend on naturalising arguments that go well beyond genetics and narrow definitions of unchanging biological essence. Or again, an apparently cultural discourse of racism that, for example in the UK, refers to the 'bad smell' of Asian food can also be seen as a naturalising idiom when it is appreciated that food is understood as an important aspect of what makes people who they are: it is an environmentalist argument that sees the body as acquiring *relatively* ingrained characters and tastes through lived experience. In this example, some might argue that racist discourse has simply shifted from 'biology' to 'culture'; others might note that a naturalising idiom is still involved in this culturalist discourse, without giving us much idea of what that idiom is and how it works. I argue that it is clear that a naturalising discourse is indeed being deployed and, moreover, that we need to pay attention to its content, its environmentalist character and indeed its biological idiom – as long as biology is understood as being more than just a matter of genetics and unchanging essences. In Chapter 2 I cited Hall who observed the paradox of the 'overwhelming power of the racial binary to *fix*' and the fact that the binary system of power thus established was also '*at the same time* ... troubled and subverted by ambivalence and disavowal' (Hall, 1996a: 27). This paradox is at least in part explained if we grasp the flexible nature of racial essentialism.

On the other hand, appreciating this flexibility also opens up avenues of challenge, contestation and destabilisation. If, in practice, many people think about personhood, how people come to be what they are and how they are related to each other in ways that see 'natural' connections as flexible and changeable, then racist appropriations of naturalisations that try to fix them are always less than certain, always open to reinterpretation. Such destabilisations may pale before the virulence of some racist discourses and practices, but they are vital nonetheless. One way to contest racist naturalisations is to contend that 'nature' has nothing to do with what people are, and that it is all a matter of 'culture' or 'society'. Another way is to argue that 'nature' is a more flexible domain than is commonly thought and that, especially when it comes to human nature, it is itself a cultural process, rather than a domain opposed to 'culture'. The evidence presented in this and the preceding chapter seem to indicate that many people in the West already think along these lines, despite their deployment of nature–culture dualisms.

6.   EMBODYING RACIALISED NATURES

In Chapter 1 I noted that definitions of race tend to focus on history (race is a discourse that emerged with the European 'Discoveries') and/or on reference to the physical human body. The latter part of the delimitation of what constitutes the field of race has two related components: a) the physical appearance or phenotype; b) the notion of heredity or genealogy. The two are clearly linked in that the relevant aspects of physical appearance are some of the ones that are, or are thought to be, inherited. In the last three chapters I have been concentrating mainly on the notions of heredity, 'blood', genealogy, biogenetic substance and the 'natural' relatedness that is thought to connect people to each other, particularly their forebears and their offspring. My argument has been that the naturalising discourses that are woven with these notions need to be explored with care and that they manifest a tension between fixity and fixability which is generally lost from view when they are simply characterised as naturalising, biologising or geneticising and as therefore invoking permanent essences.

In this chapter I focus on the racialised physical body or phenotype. I argue that, while racial discourse is indeed characterised by a reference to physical bodily appearance, this realm of reference also needs to be explored in more detail. It is often assumed that, by virtue of being naturalising or biologising, such a reference is also highly determinist, implying ineradicableness and permanence. I think that this takes too much for granted. There may be high levels of determinism involved, but there may not. Social studies specialists have tended to assume that, because 'biology' is at issue, we are at once located in the realms of 'biological racism'. Because, for them, race is a social construction, any reference to biology, such as aspects of physical appearance, is automatically consigned to the false consciousness of racist lay belief – where it remains unexamined. I argue, first, that this misrepresents biology – both as a discipline and a domain of phenomena. Biology is fundamentally about processes and development, about the relationship of the organism to its environment. It is wrong therefore to automatically assign determinist meanings to biological discourse. Biology does include the study of human nature, but this is not a study of something fixed. It is in human nature to grow old, but ageing is hardly a matter of fixity. There may be an underlying pattern to how humans age, but that pattern is not fixed. We need therefore to see bodies, including racialised bodies, as developing, changing entities.

I argue, second, that racialised discourses and experiences shape the body over time. This shaping may create ingrained characteristics in individuals and aggregates of individuals – a tendency to high blood pressure among African American men in the US, for example. In that sense, experience, as it is congealed in the body, is given a certain fixity. A body's lifetime of formation cannot be reversed or radically altered with ease. Yet that process of formation is also, by definition, open to intervention and alteration. Biology has to be seen as a socially mediated set of processes.

Now this is primarily a critique at an analytic level, a call to social science disciplines for a change to the way biology is understood. It may be objected that this does not get to grips with the determinist ways in which many people *think about* biology in its relation to race. However, I suggest that the material adduced in Chapter 5 illustrates that people outside academic circles may have a more flexible understanding of biology than is often assumed to be the case. Simple determinist connections may indeed be made, but they may not be. This is a question for empirical analysis, not assumption. Thus when people refer to racialised bodies and their assumed characteristics – speed, rhythm, smell, awkwardness, sexual continence; even skin colour and hair texture – it is a question for ethnographic investigation exactly how these traits are conceived to be constituted and reproduced. Even if such traits are said to be 'in the blood', it would be worth asking to what extent 'blood' is thought to be formed by, for example, food and climate, rather than assuming it equates with 'genes' (although even then, as we have seen, the meaning of the gene is hardly simple). I admit that this thesis is somewhat speculative and the lack of ethnographic investigation about such matters in relation to race makes the idea difficult to substantiate in a systematic way, but in the interests of exploring what tends to be taken for granted and given the examples adduced in the previous chapters which indicate people's flexible concept of biology, I believe it is worth putting the thesis forward.

BIOLOGY AND DETERMINISM

There is some justification for the view that the discipline of biology can include a rather determinist view of human beings. Ingold (2000b) launches a broadside against the 'selectionists' – including sociobiologists, evolutionary psychologists and gene-culture co-evolutionists – many of whom come from within biology or biological anthropology (see also Ingold, 1990, 2000a). These people adopt versions of neo-Darwinism and they have in common

a belief that everything from the architecture of the mind to manifold and ever-changing patterns of human behaviour can be attributed to designs or programmes that have been assembled from elements of intergenerationally transmissible information, through a process of variation under selection analogous, if not identical, to that which is supposed to bring about the evolution of organic forms. (Ingold, 2000b: 1)

The 'elements' to which Ingold refers are primarily genes, but he specifies a broader term in order to include cultural 'memes', a concept coined by some selectionists to denote 'elements' of learned behaviour which are said to act in the same way as a genetically controlled phenotypical trait: that is, to the extent that they influence reproductive fitness in a given environment, they are subject to selective pressures. The inclusion of memes and concepts of gene-culture co-evolution (in which the interactive evolution of genes and 'bits' of culture is the focus) immediately takes such selectionism away from a simple genetic determinism, but, for Ingold, there is no doubt that these sociobiological and evolutionary psychological approaches retain a determinist view of humans. If human behaviour is not determined solely by genes, it is still determined by 'designs or programmes' assembled from 'elements' that are installed in the individual either through genetic trans-mission or socialisation. Ingold's view is that 'persons come into being as centres of intentionality and awareness within fields of social relationships' (Ingold, 2000b: 1). From Ingold's phenomenological perspective, cultural form is not the result of determinations by genetic or cognitive blueprints, but is generated by the movements of humans in their practical engagement with the components of their surroundings (Ingold, 1995: 77).

Nevertheless if we are assessing the extent to which the discipline of biology is pervaded by a biologically, and especially genetically, determinist discourse, then the admission of cultural 'elements' – even if very simplistic from the perspective of an anthropological view of culture as process rather than blueprint – certainly distances it from such determinism. Hinde (1991) complains that the biology that Ingold (1990) criticises is only sociobiology which looks simply at functional and evolutionary questions in explaining the characteristics of an organism; other biologists also look at proximate causes located in the immediate environment and at developmental processes. In addition, says Hinde, some of the recent biology which does look at processual developments, sees the individual and the environment as mutually constitutive. Hinde still insists that there are things which are basic human propensities, acquired during evolution. These, however, depend on various influences for their realisation. He uses the example of fear of snakes (Hinde, 1987). Children are not automatically afraid of snakes, but they seem to acquire that fear very easily. To explain this, Hinde looks at wild vervet monkeys who always fear snakes; vervet monkeys reared in the laboratory do not. However, laboratory-reared monkeys who witness wild ones displaying fear of snakes soon acquire the same fear. Crucially this only happens if the fear is directed at a snake; witnessing a monkey trained to show fear of flowers does not create fear of flowers. Hinde's argument is then that, in many human cultures, displays of fear towards snakes are commonplace, not only in the presence of a real snake, but also around rep-resentations of them. This intertwines with a genetic predisposition to acquire the fear of snakes and may even end up creating phobias about snakes (which are much more common than phobias about things, such as guns and cars, which are more liable to kill people in most contexts today). Whatever one may think of such an explanation, it is not a simple form of genetic reductionism.

The need to be alive to the variation within the discipline of biology and genetics, is reinforced by recalling some of the material presented in Chapter 3. Keller (1995: 15–16) notes how German biologists were less keen on adopting the increasingly determinist discourse of 'gene action' that was taking over British and US biology. She also notes that this discourse itself began to wane and become markedly less determinist after the mid 1980s as molecular biology adopted a discourse derived from complex cybernetic systems theory. This was prefigured by the emergence of the sub-discipline of developmental biology in the 1960s which took over existing interests in embryology and organic growth (Keller, 1995: 25–6). In fact from 1980 'developmental biology became one of the, if not the, prime research areas of the biological sciences' and the effect of 'this shift in research priorities has been to radically subvert the dogma of gene action' (Keller, 1995: 111). This variety within biology needs to be held against the idea that 'genetic essentialism' is a univalent trend (Nelkin and Lindee, 1995a) or that 'in contemporary biology the centre is taken by genetic discourse' (Gilbert, 1995). The 'gene fetishism' that Haraway (1997: 141) identifies is certainly evident in the pervasive reference to genes in popular science and media, but, as Condit (1999a) argues, this is not a simple trend and is written and read in a variety of ways.

Within the discipline of biology there are currents that depart very substantially from simple genetic reductionism and biological determinism. In their introduction to a recent volume, *Building a Biocultural Synthesis*, Goodman and Leatherman (1998: 25) outline their agenda for a 'new biocultural anthropology' that is completely opposed to what they call the 'biosocial perspective' based on sociobiology and evolutionary psychology. This new approach socialises biology and bridges the divide between biology and cultural studies by seeing how human biology is constituted through social processes. Ingold (2000a: 379) takes this agenda further when he argues that cultural differences '*are themselves biological*' because 'they emerge in the process of development of the human organism in its environment'. Culture, in this view, is not a superstratum of learned behaviour that lies atop the substratum of genetically endowed human biology; instead culture and nature are mutually constituting. I explore below what this might mean in practice in relation to racialised bodies.

This discussion only scratches the surface of these issues, but my point is simply to suggest that social scientists need to think twice about assuming that to talk about biology is automatically to talk about genetics or about fixity and permanence. I am aware that this is obvious enough to many social scientists already, but when the issue of race rears its head, stereotyped views of biology can emerge which conflate popular and scientific views of biology and associate both with simple determinism.

EMBODYING RACE

If biological phenomena are inherently processual and not necessarily reducible to simple determinations, this should not blind us to the fact that certain biological phenomena take on a relatively ingrained character. By the same token, such ingrainedness should not blind us to the fact that the process of ingraining is just that – a process in which social and biological factors intertwine in complex ways. There is both a measure of permanence and instability, of fixity and fixability. I want to look, albeit briefly, at some processes in which race is literally embodied, that is, the experience of being a person with a given racial identity shapes the physical body in particular ways.

There is a good deal of literature on the body and embodiment which it is not my purpose to review here.[1] Csordas (1990, 1994) remarks that most anthropology of the body focuses on it as an object or a symbol, rather than as the 'existential ground of culture', the thing through which people live their lives. Similarly Butler (1993) voices a concern with the common notion that the body is a socially constructed entity, perceived in culturally specific ways and shaped by culturally specific processes. She fears this undermines the body as a material entity which, although it is a product of construction, also constrains construction. For Butler, although bodies are created through performance, this does not evacuate the materiality of the body because performance is a 'discursive mode by which ontological effects are installed' (Butler, cited in Gilroy, 1995: 17). A similar concern was voiced earlier by Turner (1984), in his critique of Foucault's view of the body as a product of discourse, and it has been developed more recently by Shilling (1993; see also Moore, 1994a: ch. 4; Turner, 1994).

Shilling shows that taking bodies seriously as both social and biological entities is not as recent an enterprise as Butler's critique might suggest. His discussion of work by Norbert Elias, Pierre Bourdieu and Robert Connell indicates this (Shilling, 1993: chs 5, 6, 7). Building on these three scholars, Shilling's own approach tries to steer a course between a) naturalistic accounts of the body which are grounded in biological essentialism – he invokes a fixed determinist biology and essence – and posit an unchanging natural body; and b) social constructionist approaches, particularly evident in post-structuralist work, which see the body as thoroughly constituted by representations, but which make the body itself disappear as a biological phenomenon (Shilling, 1991, 1993). He adopts a dialectical approach which sees the body as an unfinished project which is a 'material object located in nature, but subject to social change', which is 'not just constructed by social relationships' but also enters 'into the *construction* of these relationships' and the significance of which is 'both facilitated and limited by the *historical development* of cultural, political and economic factors' (Shilling, 1991: 664).

In the literature on the body there is little on racialised embodiment. There is a large amount of work on the representation of black bodies which describes and analyses what can be called a dominant Western discourse – often focusing on black masculinity and femininity – and this is certainly relevant as establishing the representational context in which many black men and women experience their daily lives.[2] Related to this is some work on the personal experience of living in a racialised body – usually a black body – for example, Frantz Fanon's famous work.[3] Shilling makes a few passing comments on race and racism, but they are limited. He notes, for example, that while Bourdieu explores the class dimensions of what he calls physical capital, he ignores racism. In Bourdieu's analysis class difference is reflected and reproduced through the body's physical capital, that is, the symbolic value attached to certain bodily traits and manners which can be cultivated by the investment of time and money (e.g., learning to play tennis or walk a particular way). This physical capital is used in strategies aimed at consolidating or changing one's position, and that of others, in the class system. Shilling notes that UK and US racism means that the significance attached to skin colour affects the ability of black people to 'produce sym-bolically valued bodily forms' (Shilling, 1993: 148). This brief remark not only oversimplifies the complex and ambivalent values attached to blackness in these societies, it also keeps the analysis at a superficial level – literally skin deep. I am more concerned with how racialised experience enters the body itself, shaping bodily constitution, technique, movements, diseases and powers.[4]

Martin's work on women's experience of menstruation, childbirth and menopause sheds some light on racialised dimensions of embodiment. She outlines a dominant medicalised discourse about these female bodily processes and then traces how different women (black, white, middle-class, working-class) experience them and how they relate to the dominant discourse (Martin, 1989). She comments on different rates for black and white women of morbidity and mortality in relation to pregnancy and birth. She also notes that medical staff often saw black women as problematic in a variety of ways. Perhaps not surprisingly, half of her black working-class interviewees reported bad birth experiences in hospital compared to none of her white working-class respondents. But Martin has very little on if or how black and white women's bodies developed in different ways as a result of their varying social locations and experiences.

One interesting example of processes of racialised embodiment is a review of recent research on African American participation in sport in the US (L. Harrison, 1995). Harrison explores answers to the question of why black men are over-represented in sports such as basketball and American football. He suggests that it is because blacks and whites in the US acquire different 'self-schemata' which are 'cognitive generalisations about the self that originate from past experiences and shape and direct cognitive processing of self-relevant information' (L. Harrison, 1995: 9). Jargon aside, this boils down to a cognitive design or programme located in the mind which shapes behaviour and perception. Like Ingold (1986, 1995, 2000a), I am not happy with the cognitivist notion of programmes installed in the mind which are simply put into execution by the body, but if we bracket this part of the account, there is still something useful to be gained from it. Harrison argues that people acquire their 'self-schemata' from a variety of sources – the media, valued role models, the expectations others have of them. They also acquire them from direct experience of, or rather experience *in*, the environment – an environment they themselves constitute. Harrison cites a study of basketball playing which compared inner-city basketball courts, mainly played on by black men, and 'non-city' courts, mainly the territory of white men. The inner-city courts had large numbers of players competing for valuable court time. Winners stayed on court, so skills in dribbling, shooting and passing were highly selected for and the better players got the most practice in a highly competitive game environment. In contrast, non-city players often faced the problem of getting enough people to make up a game; these players often practised in contexts rather free from the pressures of a competitive game, and they could often practise skills on their own. Harrison glosses all this as the acquisition of 'schemata', things located in the mind, but if we dispense with the Cartesian mind–body dualism that this invokes and recognise that bodily skills such as these become literally incorporated into the body – even if we posit that the site of this literal incorporation is the neuronal circuits of the brain[5] – we can see that the people learning and growing up in these different environments over periods of many years in some sense develop different bodies, that is, bodies with different skills. In Ingold's terms, 'the differences we call cultural are indeed biological' – an argument that, he continues, 'carries no racist connotations whatever' once biology is seen as a cultural process and culture as a biological one, mutually constituting each other as people inhabit the world (Ingold 2000a: 391).

The phrase that comes to mind in relation to this example is 'second nature'. One practises something until it becomes second nature. Many basketball skills have to become second nature in order for them to be effective; they have to be executed 'without thinking'. It is worth making a brief detour to examine the term as it seems to occupy precisely the ambiguous space between nature and culture that is a central theme in this book. The term has been used for centuries.[6] It was developed as a theoretical concept principally by scholars of the Frankfurt School of critical theory for whom it meant 'nature transformed by human agency and renaturalised as everyday life' and an 'ideologically effective renaturalisation of the social order' (Franklin, Lury and Stacey, 2000: 22, 51). For Adorno, second nature was to be seen 'not as biology but as history that is congealed into nature' (R.M. Young, 1995: ch. 3). For the Frankfurt School scholars, second nature was a kind of imprisonment, a form of reified alienation typical of industrial capitalism. Franklin, Lury and Stacey (2000: 21–6) develop the concept further to mean nature assisted by culture which then also uses nature as an endorsement, grounding cultural processes in claims to naturalness.

This is very relevant to my concerns with the body in the sense that the skills or characteristics that are acquired as second nature may very well be seen as simply 'natural' in the sense of innate, permanent and ineradicable. They may also be seen as 'natural' to a whole class of people, such as 'blacks' or 'whites'. Such ideas may also form part of hierarchies of social relationships and even be marshalled into the economic reifications of industrial capitalism (as in ideas of whites as more able to take on supervisory jobs than blacks). Yet there is something too easy about conflating 'second naturing' with naturalisation *tout court* seen, as usual, as creating permanence. Not all naturalisations invoke indelibility and second naturalisations do so rather less. Crucially, in the common-sense use of the term, the word 'second' is not without meaning: it marks the difference between something seen as 'truly natural' and something seen as acquired yet acting as if it were natural. In this sense, second naturing is precisely *not* an 'ideologically effective' renaturalisation, because its 'as-if' character is explicitly recognised. Something is created which is 'as good as' nature, for practical purposes – and it is exactly *practical purposes* which matter here – yet that something is recognised as having been acquired through practice.

This gives a picture of the natural and the cultural in a horizontal relationship of interchangeability, each being 'as good as' the other. This is rather different from a vertical model which sees the natural as basic, primary, rooted in nature and reflecting the way things must be, the way they 'really are', while culture sits on top of nature as a post hoc artifice which for all its elaboration cannot erase the mark of its natural foundation. Of course processes of naturalisation can and do invoke the vertical model, but my argument is that they do not always do so (even if most social scientists assume that they do). Models of nature–culture relationships are not confined to the vertical model and processes of naturalisation can include processes of creating second natures.

A second example of racialised embodiment – that is, a process of embodiment that is characteristic of humans in general, but that takes on racial dimensions in particular historical contexts – comes from medical anthropology. Oths (1999), for example, finds that black women in southern US prenatal clinics received medical care that was, as far as she could tell from records and observation, identical to that received by white women. These whites were, on average, less well educated than the black women and were higher risk pregnancies on such measures as use of tobacco, alcohol and drugs. Yet the black women tended to have lower-weight babies (who then suffered the health problems that tend to go with low birth weight). Oths concludes that racism might have a role to play. Its impact is not to be found in the clinical encounter, as Oths was not able to detect it there, despite the racist stereotyping evident in the talk of white doctors and nurses behind the scenes, as it were. Instead, she proposes that it impacts gradually and subtly on the lives of black women in ways that affects their overall health. However, the exact mechanism of impact remains unclear.

Dressler, working in a similar field, is more specific. He notes that it has long been known that black men in the Caribbean and the US tend to suffer from higher blood pressure than white men, even when various intervening variables, such as tobacco use, diet and socioeconomic status, are controlled (Dressler, 1996). In Africa black men do not generally have higher blood pressure than white Americans, so it is not possible to argue for a simple genetic determination. Instead, Dressler argues that African Americans in the US, besides being disadvantaged economically, also suffer more frustration and anger at not being able to fully achieve the kinds of goals they and others expect of US men. This leads to hypertension, not just as a temporary reaction, but, over long periods of time, as a chronic condition.

In later research Dressler develops a model of 'cultural consonance' (Dressler, Balieiro and Dos Santos, 1999; Dressler, Bindon and Neggers, 1998; see also Dressler, 1999) which specifies the degree to which individuals, in their own lives, manage to meet the criteria which are widely agreed within their local context to define a preferred lifestyle. Comparing southern Brazil and the southern US, he finds that darker skin colour is related to higher blood pressure and higher cultural consonance is related to lower blood pressure. When colour and cultural consonance are put together, it reveals that the highest blood pressures, both in Brazil and in the US, are found among the darker-skinned blacks with the lowest cultural consonance. Blacks of the same skin colour with high cultural consonance have lower blood pressures even than Brazilian whites or light-skinned African Americans with the same level of cultural consonance. Although Dressler does not explain this latter finding in any detail, his overall conclusion is that 'the meaning of skin colour can change, depending on the degree to which an individual lives the prototypical lifestyle encoded in a local cultural model' (Dressler, 1999: 7).

One may have reservations about the rather mechanical nature of Dressler's 'cultural models' (based in the Brazilian case on participation in consumer culture as an indicator of a successful lifestyle), but the overall argument is compelling. People's lived experience is gradually incorporated into their bodies as somatic characteristics. That experience is not as simple as being poor or deprived, it is also about how one reacts to that situation in a local cultural context.

This material raises uncomfortable issues. It seems to lead back to 'a biologically-fixed, essentialised conception of racial identity' (Hall, 1996a: 21). But it is vital to realise that the biology that is referred to here is *not fixed*. These biocultural processes are, in principle, ongoing, open to intervention and change; in short, they are fixable. If predictable and consistent patterns emerge – such as a trend to higher blood pressure among African American men – then this is because of consistent patterns in the cultural context not simply because 'biology' itself is involved. What is needed here is an appreciation of the difficult tension between permanence and change: social processes become congealed into the body to create forms that are not immediately changeable; yet in principle such forms are changeable because they are themselves in process.

This balance is not necessarily so far removed from realms normally seen as completely social. Tyler (2000), for example, discusses whites' discourse about race in the Midlands region of England. One young person told how her father was racist and how he would never change: he would die a racist. His racism had become ingrained, it was second nature to him, he could not change. Tyler (2000: 147–58) reports that racist attitudes are seen as things that may be passed on to children, but the mechanism is unpredictable: a racist family environment might engender racism in the children; or the youngsters might see such parental beliefs as old-fashioned (not to say immoral), something belonging to the older generation and out of kilter with the current times. The discourse used here of ingrainedness, nature and the passing on of family traits is not phrased in terms of biology or of blood. It could be seen as a naturalising argument in the sense that it invokes the father's character as a natural entity. The point is that, without any reference to biology, the same problems of fixity and fixability are being discussed. Once we get away from a notion of biology as totally opposed to the social, on the other side of the fence, as it were, we can see how the two realms of discourse may converge and interpenetrate.

CONCLUSION

In understanding race, social science might do well to be open-minded about biology. I have argued in previous chapters that it is too often taken for granted that we know what is involved in naturalisation, essentialisation, biologisation and geneticisation. In this chapter I have been suggesting that some social scientists are already exploring how racial identity and biology can intertwine as processes, rather than in a putatively one-way determinist relationship. This is a slightly different line of argument from that in my previous chapters. In these I was arguing that a variety of people – some of them intellectuals, others 'ordinary' people thinking about genetics, kinship and NRTs – had rather more nuanced and complex ideas about nature and culture, biology and genetics and blood and nurture than was suggested by the pictures painted of these ideas in the social science literature. In this chapter I have been arguing that social scientists should also take a closer look at biology itself, as studied by specialists.

The next question is that of the extent to which the flexible biocultural processes I have been describing are nevertheless *seen* as explicable in terms of a determinist and essentialising, perhaps genetic, biology by various observers. Supporting the idea that we are witnessing a trend towards genetic essentialism, Koenig and Marshall (1999) argue that in biomedical research, there is a tendency to use existing racial labels and categories, reifying them as supposed biological communities and making easy links between specific illnesses and the genetic profiles supposedly typical of such communities. In fact, they show that it is in the press releases and other popular reporting about such research that the easy links are made, while the relevant articles in the specialist journals give much weaker grounds for assuming such simple connections. Rapp (1999: 216) also notes that, when she began her study of amniocentesis in the early 1980s, press stories about genetics were relatively infrequent and that 'by now, there is a newspaper or television report each week of a genetic "base" for a dramatically expanding list of traits'.

This is an interesting, and worrying, argument. But, as I have argued at some length, the trend towards ever greater genetic essentialism is not all it seems (see Condit, 1999a, 1999b; see also Chapters 4 and 5). Rapp (1999: 216) also notes that, of the reports that come out on the genetic basis for traits, 'some are substantiated, but many remain in dispute'. What is needed is ethnographic research on how various people see the matter. It may well be that in the context of illness, people who may be undergoing genetic counselling and talking to doctors are likely to adopt some quite determinist and geneticised accounts of illness. Lock's account of genetic counselling for breast cancer suggests this (Lock, 1998), although Rapp's work on the genetic counselling surrounding amniocentesis suggests that this is not necessarily the case (Rapp, 1999; see Chapter 4, above). When talking about sporting skills or a sense of rhythm, a rather different picture may also emerge, as I argued in Chapter 5.

'Ordinary' people may well have ideas about blood, human nature and biology that involve the complex interpenetration of concepts of nature and nurture, determinism and ongoing performative constitution. If this is so, then not only should we, as social scientists, spend more time exploring these ideas, but we should also take a more flexible view of biology itself as a realm of human and socially mediated processes. In terms of understanding racial identities, this opens the way to seeing that such identities may involve biological dimensions that have nothing to do with genetic determinations and fixed essences but rather with the body as an ongoing process. This, in turn, may help us to appreciate how racial identities are formed, their significance and the power of racism to shape people's bodies and lives.

CODA

It is not my purpose here to summarise the arguments I have already made. I hope these are by now clear. Instead I will reflect on an opposition that has occupied me in the past and which I think can be illuminated by the ideas I have put forward in this book.

In the historical and social science literature on race in the Americas, it is not uncommon to find a contrast being made between North America and Latin America in terms of the racial formations and types of racism said to characterise each region. I have commented on this matter before (Wade, 1993a, 1993b, 1997), but I think the lessons to be learned from the contrast are valuable enough to make it worth examining again. Very briefly, Latin America, usually in the guise of Brazil, was said by some to be a 'racial democracy', compared to the North American (usually in practice the southern US) system of formal racial segregation. If other commentators denied that a 'racial democracy' existed in Brazil, they still might say that Brazil was basically a class society in which racial identities played a minor role, while, in contrast, race was a primary social classification and criterion of status in the class society of the US. Later, more thorough challenges to the myth of racial democracy revealed the extent of racial discrimination in Brazil, while social protest movements by Afro-Brazilians also put a severe dent in such a mythology.[1]

In a recent article I suggested that one of the dimensions of this contrast was an opposition between the idea that in the US, concepts of race were connected to a 'deep' biology of the 'blood', while in Brazil (and by extension in other areas of Latin America), race was a superficial matter of mere phenotype or physical appearance (Wade, 1993b). That is, in the US racial identity was generally assigned according to ideas about ancestry and what this contributed to an individual's blood (or genes), such that anyone with 'one drop' of 'black blood' would be classified as a black person, whatever his or her physical appearance. In contrast, in Brazil racial identity was seen as more fluid: a person's physical appearance (especially skin colour, hair type and facial features) was a primary clue, but the same physique would be classified in different ways by different observers or by the same observer in different circumstances. The person's apparent class status, for example, would make a difference to racial labelling. Racial identity was thus also more superficial: it was only one of the things that defined social status; class factors were equally if not more important. I suggested in that article that this contrast between the deep and the superficial was misleading in that it seemed to suggest that 'real' racism existed only in the US, while the racism that existed in Brazil, being tied to a flexible and superficial level of appearance alone, was merely a pale version of the real thing (cf. Ferreira da Silva, 1998). I argued that, instead of working with this underlying contrast, each type of racism and racial formation should be examined in its own right to see how it operated. This was also my own goal in examining race in Colombia (Wade, 1993a).

The arguments made in this book reinforce this point. There is a strong sense in which scholarly thought about racism and race, explicitly or implicitly, uses the US and northern Europe in the late nineteenth and early twentieth centuries as a kind of benchmark. These places, during this period, are held to be the apogee of racism. I do not of course deny that racial and racist ideologies were very fully developed in these places during this time: it was of this time that Robert Knox could say 'race [was] everything' (see Chapter 3). But I see no reason to therefore assess every form of racism in relation to this type as if it were the common standard. This leads to a narrow definition of ideas of race and ideologies of racism only in terms of their invocation of determinist biology, unchanging (biological) essences, naturalisations understood as biological and permanently fixing. I showed in Chapter 3 that even during this turn of the century period in northern Europe and the US, determinism and fixity were not quite the simple phenomena that they have often been taken to be. And, outside of this particular historical context, notions of biology, blood, nature and nurture have proven to be rather varied and complex. Of course ideas of permanence and fixity, unchanging essences and determinist biology can and do appear in a variety of ideas about race and can underwrite racism in many contexts. But there is no need to assume that they do so or to take such notions as human nature, blood and biology for granted.

A recent example of the persistence of this underlying contrast between biology and culture and the way it is deployed when talking about racism in Latin America is De la Cadena's excellent book on Peru, *Indigenous Mestizos* (2000). De la Cadena in no way denies the power of racism in Peru and avoids making simplistic comparisons with the US. However, she sees Peru, from about 1920, as an example of 'racism without race' (De la Cadena, 2000: 4). From that time, references to 'biology' were generally replaced by references to 'spirit', 'soul' or culture when Peruvians talked of differences between whites, mestizos and indigenous people. Racism is thus defined as 'the discriminatory practices that derive from the belief in the unquestionable intellectual and moral superiority of one group of Peruvians over the rest' (De la Cadena, 2000: 4). Since this way of thinking does not resort to 'racial terminology', it is presumably rather difficult to distinguish it from a discourse of class, but De la Cadena does not explore this. In effect, we 'know' that race is at issue, because of the evident continuities between the culturalist discourse post 1920 and the more biological discourse that preceded it: 'Race [after 1920] was still silently invoked, as immanent cultural tradition' (De la Cadena, 2000: 141). The word 'immanent' also gives us a clue. We again 'know' that race is (silently) at issue here, because the culture (or spirit or soul) that forms part of the discourse is implied or said to be innate.

De la Cadena's analysis is rich and persuasive, yet I cannot help but wonder if her account of 'racism without race' reveals all it could. Of course one must take her word that, from 1920, intellectuals in Cuzco dispensed with the biologically determinist concept of race, as it existed in intellectual circles more widely at that time. This is not at issue. But it seems clear that the 'racialised notions of culture' to which she refers were used to 'naturalise social differences' (De la Cadena, 2000: 140–1). Is it not possible that we are missing something by not exploring ideas about human nature, blood, heritage? To some extent, these issues can be addressed by looking at how Peruvians saw culture as a natural, innate, heritable entity; but one wonders if De la Cadena is not taking the intellectuals too literally at their word when, dispensing as they did with biology, conceived in terms of an early-twentieth-century deterministic racial typology, she also dispenses with biology conceived in a broader way to include ideas about human nature, procreation, blood and bodies. For example, De la Cadena explains how 'notions of racial purity' resurfaced in the 1950s, in the context of the Indigenous Women's Beauty Contest. The rules for this contest required entrants to supply proof of 'racial purity' and 'indigenous lineage'. And, despite the fact that bodily attributes were, after 1920, generally not seen as important in defining status, the rules also specified certain physical attributes the candidates had to have, deemed to be characteristic of authentic indigenous women (De la Cadena, 2000: 178). The resurfacing of this discourse about bodies and heritage is not really explained by De la Cadena, although there is perhaps a tacit suggestion that it is motivated by the intersection of race and gender. If, however, we unpick the boundary between biology and culture and wonder whether ideas about biology, in a broad sense, really did disappear after 1920 and whether ideas about bodies, heritage, blood and culture were not, perhaps, subject to the strategic inter-digitation of processes of naturalisation and socialisation, then the resurfacing of this type of discourse seems to make rather more sense.

In sum, identifying Peruvian forms of racism as basically cultural – an argument that could be, and often is, extended to the rest of Latin America, even when the role of superficial physical appearance is also recognised – may be restricting the analysis unnecessarily and reinforcing an analytic divide between North American and Latin American forms of racism in terms of the presence or absence of biologising and, more broadly, naturalising idioms. There are of course important differences between Latin American and North American forms of racism and racial identifications and these differences involve the varied ways in which ideas about biology, blood and natural connections are deployed. I am reluctant, however, to reduce this to a simple opposition between 'biological' and 'cultural' forms of racism.

In putting together the arguments that make up this book, I have not been able to use as much ethnographic material as I would have liked. I have spent substantial sections of the book discussing kinship and then reading across from kinship to race. (Although this strategy was not only aimed at engaging a greater variety of ethnographic literature: as I have said at various moments, I think it has been important to try to link these two domains, generally held separate in anthropology.) The question, which I raised briefly in Chapter 5, is then whether the lack of ethnographic material about ideas of biology, blood, human nature and nurture in the domain of racial identifications reflects the unimportance of such ideas for most people in the West or the blind spots of the investigators who have studied the matter. My hunch is that the latter plays a major role. Questions of biology, essence and nature figure frequently in definitions and analyses of race, but often only in name. They are figures brought in to re-establish boundaries, limits and domains that are already taken for granted. They are rarely subject to intensive ethnographic exploration in their own right. This seems to be a job for the future and I hope that the material deployed in this book acts as a stimulus to further enquiry.

NOTES

CHAPTER 1

1. For overviews of the US literature on race at this time, see Banks (1996: ch. 3), Banton (1987: ch. 4), Hannerz (1980), Lal (1986, 1990). Examples of anthropological work on race in Latin America include Harris (1974) and Wagley (1952), both of which emerged from the UNESCO sponsored studies of race relations in Brazil (see Wade 1997: 51–7); the work of Whitten (1981, 1986 [1974]) on Ecuador also deals directly with racial classifications and racism.
2. See the May 1998 issue of the *Newsletter* for a full list.
3. See the AAA website: <www.ameranthassn.org/racepp.htm>.
4. See especially F. Harrison (1995, 1998) and B. Williams (1989) for overviews. See also Baker (1998), Banks (1996), Brodkin (2000), Cowlishaw (2000), Domínguez (1986), Frankenberg (1993), Gregory and Sanjek (1994), Lewis (2000), Modood and Werbner (1997), Mukhopadhyay and Moses (1997), Ragoné and Twine (2000), Rahier (1999), Reynolds and Lieberman (1996), Shanklin (1994), Streicker (1995, 1997), Twine (1998), Wade (1993a, 2000), Werbner and Anwar (1991), Werbner and Modood (1997), Whitten and Torres (1998), B. Williams (1991, 1995, 1996b).
5. The Collins Dictionary defines phenotype as 'the physical constitution of an organism as determined by the interaction of its genetic constitution and the environment' – which is rather more inclusive than just physical appearance.
6. See the special issue of the *Bulletin of Latin American Research*, vol. 17, no. 2, 'Race and ethnicity in the Andes', edited by Mary Weismantel. See also De la Cadena (2000), Wade (1997).
7. See, among others, Anthias and Yuval-Davis (1992: 2), Balibar (1991b: 56), Banks (1996: 54, 99), Banton (1983: 77), Cashmore and Troyna (1990: 31, 44), Dikötter (1992: ix), Harrison (1995: 65; 1998: 613), Jenkins (1997: 24), Miles (1989: 79), Omi and Winant (1994: 55), Rex (1986: 21), Shanklin (1994: 105), Smedley (1998: 694), Wieviorka (1995: 120).
8. On 'racial' ideas about the Irish and Jews see Hirschfeld (1996: 44–8), Shanklin (1994), Smedley (1993). On *limpieza de sangre*, see Mörner (1967). On Chinese ideas about race, see Dikötter (1992, 1996, 1997).
9. Frost (1990) notes that colour of skin was linked more to gender – a dark complexion was a masculine trait in medieval Europe – than to geographical origin.
10. The Chain of Being refers to the theory, current in Western thought from the ancient Roman period through the seventeenth century, that all existing forms in the universe were arranged in a permanent, unilineal hierarchy, with God at the top and the lowliest forms of existence at the bottom (Hodgen, 1964; Lovejoy, 1964).

CHAPTER 2

1. Useful overviews which focus on issues of race and social stratification include Anthias and Yuval-Davis (1992: ch. 3), Cashmore and Troyna (1990), Miles (1989, 1993), Omi and Winant (1994), Rex (1986), Rex and Mason (1986), Solomos (1989).

2. See the literature cited in Note 1.
3. For general discussions of the interweaving of ideas of race and nation (which often include a discussion of gender and sexuality), see, among others, Anthias and Yuval-Davis (1992: ch. 2), Balibar and Wallerstein (1991), Brah (1996), Foucault (1998; see also Stoler, 1995), Miles (1989: ch. 4; 1993: ch. 2), Williams (1989, 1995, 1996a). See also, for example, Gilroy (1987) on Britain, Mosse (1985: ch. 7) on Europe, Stepan (1991) on Latin America generally, Wade (1993a) on Colombia, Wetherell and Potter (1992) on New Zealand, Williams (1991, 1996c) on Guyana, Whitten (1986 [1974]) on Ecuador. See Wade (1997: ch. 5) for an overview of the literature on Latin America. On the unmarked nature of whiteness in the US, see Frankenberg (1993). On multiculturalism, see Modood and Werbner (1997), and Werbner and Modood (1997). On the conditional and exoticising inclusion of blacks in Colombia, see Wade (1999a, 2000).
4. Some of the literature cited in Note 3 is relevant here. See also, among others, Brodkin (2000), Fanon (1986: chs 2, 3), Gilman (1986), Haraway (1997: ch. 6), hooks (1991), Linke (1997, 1999), Lury (2000), Martinez-Alier (1974), McClintock (1993, 1995), Moore (1994a: ch. 3), Mosse (1985), Parker *et al.* (1992), Ragoné and Twine (2000), Smith (1996), Stoler (1995), Williams (1996a), R.J. Young (1995), Yuval-Davis and Anthias (1989), Zack (1997).
5. See the literature cited in the previous note.
6. See, for example, Barker, Hulme and Iversen (1994), Donald and Rattansi (1992), Frankenberg (1993), Gates (1986), Goldberg (1993: ch. 7), Hall (1992a), Haraway (1997: ch. 6), Hyatt and Nettleford (1995), Lipsitz (1994), Low (1996), Lury (2000), Moore (1997), Nederveen Pieterse (1992), Read (1996), Wade (2000), Wetherell and Potter (1992), Winant (1993).
7. See Hall (1996b, 1996c).
8. See Giddens (1987: ch. 4). See also Ebert (1995), Ulin (1991). Some currents in Cultural Studies have been criticised in this way (Lave *et al.*, 1992). Foucauldian approaches to, for example, the body have also been challenged for losing a grasp on the materiality of the body (Butler, 1993; Comaroff and Comaroff, 1992: 40; Shilling, 1993; Turner, 1994).
9. See Chapter 6 for a discussion and references.
10. See, for example, Butler (1993), Shilling (1993), Turner (1994); see also Ebert (1995).
11. See Chapter 6. In the 1950s, Fanon made some comments about this (Fanon, 1986: 110). More recently, Alcoff (1999) and Johnson (1993) have addressed the issue from the vantage point of phenomenological philosophy. On the performance of racial identities – which involves a notion of embodiment – see Rahier (1999) and Ugwu (1995). See also Werbner (1997) on the performative role of violence in racism.
12. Hall refers to Bhabha's Preface to a new edition of Fanon's *Black Skin, White Masks* (Fanon, 1986).
13. There is some ambiguity here caused by the cycle of reflexivity which connects academic practice to the non-academic world: it is not exactly clear whether identities have become central to people in the world in general, in which case they become important to academics who study people; or whether the concept of identity has become increasingly central within the internal critiques and developments of academic discourse itself, in which case the idea might then affect (some) non-academic people. Both processes occur of course and influence each other, but the exact balance is unclear.
14. See Amos and Parmar (1984), hooks (1981), Knowles and Mercer (1992), Landry and MacLean (1993: ch. 9).
15. See, for example, two studies which use this phrase as a title: Community Relations Commission (1976) and Watson (1977). For a critique of this approach see Lawrence (1982: 122–32).
16. See, for example, Mac an Ghaill (1992), Tizard and Phoenix (1993).

17. For example, in their study of mixed race children – which is strictly speaking different from the issue of children of migrants torn between 'parental' and 'host society' cultures, but which raises the same questions – Tizard and Phoenix found that a fair number of their sample said they valued their mixed race identity because it allowed them to 'bridge both black and white cultures' (1993: 164).

18. There is a big literature on race and IQ. For an overall guide, see Gould (1981), Jones (1997: 197–9) Kohn (1995: ch. 5). For more detailed material, see Eysenck (1971), Flynn (1980), Herrnstein and Murray (1994), Jensen (1969), Mogdil and Mogdil (1986: chs 7, 8; 1987: chs 11, 12). See also the special supplement of *Current Anthropology*, 'The eternal triangle: race, class and IQ. Reviews on The Bell Curve: intelligence and class structure in American life', vol. 37: S143-S181, 1996.

19. See also *Ethos*, vol. 25, no. 1, which has a special topic section on 'The Conceptual Politics of Race' with an article by Hirschfeld, five critical commentaries which mainly disagree with Hirschfeld, and a reply by him. See also Toren (1993).

CHAPTER 3

1. On this sketch of Western, or Euro-American, views of nature and culture in humans, see Edwards (2000: 27–30), Ingold (1986: 160–1, 358; 1990; 2000a: ch. 21), Ingold *et al.* (1996), Richards (1998), Schneider (1980, 1984), Strathern (1992a: 2–3, 125;1992b: 18–19), Toren (1993). See also Haraway (1991: 11, 133–4; 1997: 102).

2. See, e.g., Hodgen (1964), Jordan (1977), Stepan (1982), Stocking (1982), Todorov (1993: ch. 2).

3. See, e.g., Glacken (1967: 109, 256, 590), Greene (1959: ch. 8; 1984: ch. 12), Jordanova (1987: 5), Lubinsky (1993), Richards (1989), Ritvo (1997: 120–9), Spary (1996), Theunissen (1994).

4. See Stepan (1982: ch. 5; 1991), Kevles (1995), Paul (1995), Cowan (1985).

5. See also Alonso (1994) who discusses tropes of natural substance and kinship in relation to ideas about the nation and ethnicity; and Keyes (1976) who makes connections between kinship and ethnicity.

6. See Glacken (1967), Jahoda (1992), Jordanova (1986a), Lovejoy (1948: 69–77), Lovejoy and Boas (1965: 11–22, 446–56), Soper (1995), Strathern (1992a), Trigg (1988), Williams (1988: 219–24).

7. This 'epigenetic' view, according to which the differentiated embryo developed from amorphous beginnings, was engaged in a shifting debate with 'preformationism', also popular during the seventeenth and eighteenth centuries, according to which the embryo's structured form was already given, whether by the female ovum (the ovist view) or by the male sperm (the spermist or animalculist view). See Gasking (1967), Mayr (1982: 106, 645), Stubbe (1972: ch. 5). Preformationists of both varieties held that the final form of the new organism could be influenced by the ovum, in the case of spermists, or the sperm, in the case of ovists, so that offspring could resemble both mother and father. These naturalists also held that the embryo's nourishment – which included the ovum or the sperm – would affect its final form (Gasking 1967: 72, 122).

8. By 'racialism' Todorov (1993: 91–4) means something quite specific (and characteristic of the nineteenth and early twentieth centuries), viz., a theorised ideology that 'races' exist, that physical type and collective character correlate, that individual character is determined by the collective, that some races are inferior to others and that the world should be organised accordingly.

9. For example, in 1874 Galton published *English Men of Science: Their Nature and Nurture*.

10. See also Smedley (1993).

CHAPTER 4

1. See also Turney (1998: 218–19) who cites Nelkin and Lindee (1995a) to the effect that the gene has become a powerful cultural icon, but does not explicitly argue that genetic essentialism is on the increase.
2. Cytoplasm: the living contents of a cell contained within the cell membrane but excluding the nucleus, which contains the DNA.
3. This is an influence to which Van Dijck pays a good deal of attention (1998: 92–6), but which Condit barely mentions (1999a: 290, n. 1), asserting that Van Dijck is over-privileging the impact of a single author.
4. On challenging ideas of 'nature', see also Cronon (1995), Franklin, Lury and Stacey (2000), Haraway (1991, 1997), Van Dijck (1998).
5. Restrictions of space mean that I can not discuss this material in detail. Both authors explore the nature of biology in kinship in ways highly relevant to my argument. Weston contends that gay and lesbian families are a challenge to the whole idea of biology and procreative sexual intercourse as the foundation of kinship in the US. Hayden argues that lesbian mothers do employ notions of biology, but in a specific way that disperses biology, makes it more elastic and robs it of a single self-evident meaning.
6. See also Domínguez (1986: ch. 3) who shows that in nineteenth- and twentieth-century Louisiana, questions of racial identity inflected the way in which birth ties were seen. Although the illegitimate child of an interracial union might try to activate claims on his or her white father's resources, such claims were widely denied, putting into question the enduring and solidary nature of the tie.
7. Hayden (1995: 45) also refers to this passage and claims that Schneider saw choice of relatives as a central element in his model. This seems to me overindulgent towards Schneider.
8. However, rather than interpreting this as evidence of ambiguity and vagueness about the division between the social and the biological, Strathern (personal communication) prefers to think in terms of the choices people make in emphasising different elements. This is close to what Thompson (forthcoming) calls 'strategic naturalisation'.
9. I wonder if this is why Schneider and others after him use the term 'biogenetic', although neither he nor most others make it clear why they do use this term – as opposed to simply 'genetic'. However, Schneider (1980: 23) is clearly thinking of genetics as he says that Americans think that mother and father contribute 'the same kinds and amounts' of biogenetic substance to a child.
10. Naturally I am making very broad generalisations here. There would doubtless be a good deal of variation in 'lay belief' by class, region, age, religion, ethnic/racial identity and so on. Nevertheless I follow anthropological studies of the kind cited here that generalise about American or English or Euro-American kinship patterns. See, however, Bouquet (1993) on the specifically English character of some constructions of kinship and the difficulties of generalising from these to a Portuguese context.
11. See Banton (1987: 26–7) whose mention of Pearson's thesis drew my attention to it; see also Ritvo (1997: 107–10).
12. See also Weston (forthcoming). Titmuss (1973: 120, 128) records that in the late 1960s two US states still had laws requiring the racial segregation of blood in blood banks; the same was true of South Africa where not only the blood, but also all records about blood and blood donor premises were racially labelled and segregated into four categories.

CHAPTER 5

1. I am grateful to the University of Manchester for funding the fieldwork that included this study.

2. For more detail, see Hale (1996), Smith (1997), Twine (1998), Wade (1993a), Whitten and Torres (1998).

3. *Rumba* is in its original sense a type of Afro-Cuban urban dance that emerged in Havana in the late nineteenth century and became stylised as a global popular music from about the 1920s. In Colombia today the term is used to refer to a party involving music and dance.

4. *Un no sé qué* literally means 'an I don't know what', i.e. *un je ne sais quoi*.

5. See also Balibar (1991a: 26), Condit (1999a: 141–4, 196–7), Duster (1996), Haraway (1997: ch. 6). Like Nelkin and Lindee (1995b), Duster focuses on the race and IQ debate as a case study in growing genetic determinism. Haraway, wisely in my view, makes no claims about whether determinism is growing or declining, but simply traces the changing tropes for race in the twentieth century as employed in science and popular science: 'race' (1900–30), 'population' (1940s to 1970s) and 'genome' (1975–90s). Balibar notes that, within the mainly culturalist neo-racism, there is room for the 'return of the biological theme' in the form of sociobiological arguments about the natural evolutionary propensity of humans to be xenophobic and ethnocentric and also in the form of a discourse that, as foreshadowed in Foucault's analysis of nineteenth-century Europe, mixes biology and culture in its focus on the external regulation of people's reproduction, health and performance.

6. See Ragoné (1998: 126) who cites a study on sperm donation by Snowden, Mitchell and Snowden (1983).

7. I am grateful to Elly Teman for emailing me her findings on the racialised aspects of surrogacy and also giving me access to her Masters thesis.

8. See also Weston (forthcoming) who explores the racial and class meanings surrounding blood transfusion in the US. She looks at the fear and anxiety depicted in a 1950s fictional account of a direct, arm-to-arm white–black transfusion – which, once accomplished, nevertheless created a diffuse kinship between the participants and their families. She then compares this to the images surrounding a 1997 campaign to collect blood for the widow of Malcolm X after she was badly burned: the wide and cross-racial response to the campaign was optimistically said to transcend racial divisions. In both cases, blood was thought to create some kind of relatedness. On the symbolism attached to blood, see also Linke (1999), Titmuss (1973) and Vialles (1994).

9. 'Teddy Bear Patriarchy' is Haraway's shorthand here for ideologies current in the early twentieth century of clear racial and gender hierarchies, underpinned by a typological science of race (see Haraway, 1989: ch. 3).

CHAPTER 6

1. See Shilling (1993) and Turner (1984) for general accounts of approaches to the body. See also Feder (1989).

2. For example: Andrews (1996), Honour (1989), hooks (1992), Low (1996), Nederveen Pieterse (1992), Page (1997), Read (1996), Rony (1996), Shilling (1993: 55–9).

3. See Fanon (1986). See also Alcoff (1999) and Johnson (1993). There is a good deal of social psychology literature in the US on black people's perceptions of their bodies, usually with an emphasis on perceived attractiveness and self-esteem in relation to skin colour and weight: see, for example, Bond and Cash (1992), Harris (1995) and Makkar and Strube (1995).

4. Weismantel (2001) takes up the theme of racialised bodies being formed through metabolic processes of biology, using Andean ethnography to sustain her argument.

5. Eric Kandel, a neurobiologist, arguing the current view in molecular biology that environment and learning influence the chemical processes by which genes express

themselves in phenotype, states: 'There can be no changes in behaviour that are not reflected in the nervous system and no persistent changes in the nervous system that are not reflected in structural changes [in the brain] on some level of resolution.' He goes on: 'Since each of us is brought up in a somewhat different environment, exposed to different combinations of stimuli, and we develop motor skills in different ways, each brain is modified in unique ways' (Kandel, 1998).

6. According to R.M. Young (1995: ch. 3) Democritus 'opposed Aristotle's belief that the qualification to rule was determined at birth, by nature. Democritus argued that it was informed by education, which constituted a "second nature"'.

CODA

1. There is a large literature on these themes. See Wade (1997) for a brief account and references. See also Hanchard (1999), Reichmann (1999), Winant (1992).

REFERENCES

Alcoff, Linda Martín (1996) Philosophy and racial identity. *Radical Philosophy* 75: 5–14.
—— (1999) Toward a phenomenology of racial embodiment. *Radical Philosophy* 95: 15–26.
Alexander, Claire E. (1996) *The art of being black: the creation of black British youth identities* (Oxford: Oxford University Press).
Alonso, Ana María (1994) The politics of space, time and substance: state formation, nationalism, and ethnicity. *Annual Review of Anthropology* 23: 379–405.
Amit-Talai, Vered and Caroline Knowles (eds) (1996) *Re-situating identities: the politics of race, ethnicity and culture* (Ontario: Broadview Press).
Amos, V. and P. Parmar (1984) Challenging imperial feminism. *Feminist Review* 17: 3–19.
Andrews, David L. (1996) The fact(s) of Michael Jordan's blackness: excavating a floating racial signifier. *Sociology of Sport Journal* 13: 125–58.
Anthias, Floya and Nira Yuval-Davis (1992) *Racialized boundaries: race, nation, gender, colour and class and the anti-racist struggle* (London: Routledge).
Appiah, Kwame Anthony and Henry Louis Gates, Jr (1995) *Identities* (Chicago: University of Chicago Press).
Back, Les and Vibeka Quaade (1993) Dream utopias, nightmare realities; imaging race and culture within the world of Benetton advertising. *Third Text* 22: 65–80.
Baker, Lee D. (1998) *From savage to Negro: anthropology and the construction of race* (Berkeley: University of California Press).
Balibar, Etienne (1991a) Is there a 'neo-racism'? In *Race, nation and class: ambiguous identities*, by Etienne Balibar and Immanuel Wallerstein, pp. 17–28 (London: Verso).
—— (1991b) Racism and nationalism. In *Race, nation and class: ambiguous identities*, by Etienne Balibar and Immanuel Wallerstein, pp. 37–67 (London: Verso).
Balibar, Etienne and Immanuel Wallerstein (1991) *Race, nation and class: ambiguous identities* (London: Verso).
Banks, Marcus (1996) *Ethnicity: anthropological constructions* (London: Routledge).
Banton, Michael (1983) *Racial and ethnic competition* (Cambridge: Cambridge University Press).
—— (1987) *Racial theories* (Cambridge: Cambridge Univeristy Press).
—— (1991) The race relations problematic. *British Journal of Sociology* 42(1): 115–30.
Barker, Anthony (1978) *The African link: British attitudes toward the Negro in the era of the Atlantic slave trade* (London: Frank Cass).
Barker, Francis, Peter Hulme and Margaret Iversen (eds) (1994) *Colonial discourse/post-colonial theory* (Manchester: Manchester University Press).
Barker, Martin (1981) *The new racism: Conservatives and the ideology of the tribe* (London: Junction Books).
Barth, Frederick (ed.) (1969) *Ethnic groups and boundaries: the social organisation of culture difference* (London: Allen and Unwin).
Blauner, Bob (1989) *Black lives, white lives: three decades of race relations in America* (Berkeley: University of California Press).

Bond, Selena and Thomas F. Cash (1992) Black beauty: skin colour and body images among African-American college women. *Journal of Applied Social Psychology* 22(11): 874–88.

Bouquet, Mary (1993) *Reclaiming English kinship: Portuguese refractions of British kinship theory* (Manchester: Manchester University Press).

Bourdieu, Pierre (1977) *Outline of a theory of practice* (Cambridge: Cambridge University Press).

Brah, Avtar (1996) *Cartographies of diaspora: contesting identities* (London: Routledge).

Brodkin, Karen (2000) Global capitalism: what's race got to do with it? *American Ethnologist* 27(2): 237–56.

Butler, Judith (1990) *Gender trouble: feminism and the subversion of identity* (London: Routledge).

—— (1993) *Bodies that matter: on the discursive limits of 'sex'* (London: Routledge).

—— (1996) Sexual inversions. In *Feminist interpretations of Michel Foucault*, edited by Susan J. Hekman, pp. 59–76 (Philadelphia: University of Pennsylvania Press).

Carsten, Janet (2000a) Introduction: cultures of relatedness. In *Cultures of relatedness: new approaches to the study of kinship*, edited by Janet Carsten, pp. 1–36 (Cambridge: Cambridge University Press).

—— (2000b) 'Knowing where you've come from': ruptures and continuities of time and kinship in narratives of adoption reunions. *Journal of the Royal Anthropological Institute* 6(4): 687–703.

Cashmore, Ernest and Barry Troyna (eds) (1982) *Black youth in crisis* (London: Allen and Unwin).

—— (1990) *Introduction to race relations.* 2nd edn (London: Falmer Press).

Castañeda Claudia (Forthcoming) Incorporating the trans-national adoptee. In *Imagining adoption*, edited by Marianne Novy (Ann Arbor: University of Michigan Press).

Collingwood, R.G. (1945) *The idea of nature* (Oxford: Clarendon Press).

Comaroff, John and Jean Comaroff (1992) *Ethnography and the historical imagination* (Boulder: Westview Press).

Community Relations Commission (1976) *Between two cultures: a study of relationships between generations in the Asian community in Britain* (London: Community Relations Commission).

Condit, Celeste Michelle (1999a) *The meanings of the gene: public debates about human heredity* (Madison: University of Wisconsin Press).

—— (1999b) How the public understands genetics: non-deterministic and non-discriminatory interpretations of the blueprint metaphor. *Public Understanding of Science* 8: 169–80.

Cowan, Ruth Schwartz (1985) *Sir Francis Galton and the study of heredity in the nineteenth century* (n.p.: Garland).

Cowlishaw, Gillian K. (2000) Censoring race in 'post-colonial' anthropology. *Critique of Anthropology* 20(2): 101–23.

Cox, Oliver C. (1948) *Caste, class and race: a study of social dynamics* (New York: Doubleday).

Cronon, William (ed.) (1995) *Uncommon ground: toward re-inventing nature* (New York: W.W. Norton).

Cross, Malcolm and Michael Keith (1993) Racism and the postmodern city. In *Racism, the city, and the state*, edited by M. Cross and M. Keith, pp. 1–30 (London: Routledge).

Csordas, Thomas (1990) Embodiment as a paradigm for anthropology. *Ethos* 18(1): 5–47.

—— (ed.) (1994) *Embodiment and experience: the existential ground of culture and the self* (Cambridge: Cambridge University Press).

Davison, Charlie (1997) Everyday ideas of inheritance and health in Britain. In *Culture, kinship and genes: towards cross-cultural genetics*, edited by Angus Clarke and Evelyn Parsons, pp. 167–74 (London and New York: Macmillan and St. Martin's Press).

De la Cadena, Marisol (2000) *Indigenous mestizos: the politics of race and culture in Cuzco, 1919–1991* (Durham: Duke University Press).

Dikötter, Frank (1992) *The discourse of race in modern China* (Stanford: Stanford University Press).

—— (1996) Culture, 'race' and nation: the formation of national identity in twentieth-century China. *Contemporary China: The Consequences of Change*, special issue of *Journal of International Affairs* 49(2): 590–645.

—— (ed.) (1997) *The construction of racial identities in China and Japan: historical and contemporary perspectives* (London: C. Hurst).

Domínguez, Virginia R. (1986) *White by definition: social classification in Creole Louisiana* (New Brunswick: Rutgers University Press).

—— (1997) The racialist politics of concepts, or is it the racialist concepts of politics? *Ethos* 25(1): 93–100.

Donald, James and Ali Rattansi (eds) (1992) *'Race', culture and difference* (London and Milton Keynes: Sage and Open University Press).

Dressler, William W. (1996) Hypertension in the African American community: social, cultural, and psychological factors. *Seminars in Nephrology* 16(2): 71–82.

—— (1999) Culture, skin colour and arterial blood pressure. Paper given in the panel 'Performing Race in the Crisis of the Medical Moment', 98th Annual Meeting of the American Anthropological Association, 17–21 November 1999.

Dressler, William W., Mauro Balieiro and Jose Ernesto Dos Santos (1999) Culture, skin color and arterial blood pressure in Brazil. *American Journal of Human Biology* 11: 49–59.

Dressler, William W., James R. Bindon and Yasmin R. Neggers (1998) Culture, socioeconomic status and coronary disease risk factors in an African American community. *Journal of Behavioural Medicine* 21: 527–44.

Duster, Troy (1996) The prism of heritability and the sociology of knowledge. In *Naked science: anthropological inquiry into boundaries, power and knowledge*, edited by Laura Nader, pp. 119–30 (London: Routledge).

Ebert, Teresa (1995) *Ludic feminism and after: postmodernism, desire, and labor in late capitalism* (Ann Arbor: University of Michigan Press).

Edwards, Jeanette (2000) *Born and bred: idioms of kinship and new reproductive technologies in England* (Oxford: Oxford University Press).

Edwards, Jeanette and Marilyn Strathern (2000) Including our own. In *Cultures of relatedness: new approaches to the study of kinship*, edited by Janet Carsten, pp. 149–66 (Cambridge: Cambridge University Press).

Edwards, Jeanette *et al.* (1993) *Technologies of procreation: kinship in the age of assisted conception* (Manchester: Manchester University Press).

Epstein, A.L. (1978) *Ethos and identity* (London: Tavistock).

Escobar, Arturo and Sonia E. Alvarez (eds) (1992) *The making of social movements in Latin America: identity, strategy, and democracy* (Boulder: Westview Press).

Eysenck, Hans (1971) *Race, intelligence and education* (London: Temple Smith).

Fanon, Frantz (1986) *Black skin, white masks* (London: Pluto Press).

Fausto-Sterling, Anne (1985) *Myths of gender: biological theories about women and men* (New York: Basic Books).

—— (2000) *Sexing the body: gender politics and the construction of sexuality* (New York: Basic Books).

Feder, Michel (with Ramone Naddaff and Nadia Tazi) (eds) (1989) *Fragments for a history of human body.* 3 vols (New York: Zone).

Ferreira da Silva, Denise (1998) Facts of blackness: Brazil is not (quite) the United States ... and racial politics in Brazil? *Social Identities* 4(2): 201–34.

Flynn, J. (1980) *Race, IQ and Jensen* (London: Routledge and Kegan Paul).

Foucault, Michel (1998) *The will to knowledge. The history of sexuality: Volume 1*, translated by Robert Hurley (London: Penguin Books).

Frankenberg, Ruth (1993) *White women, race matters: the social construction of whiteness* (London: Routledge).

Franklin, Sarah (1997) *Embodied progress: a cultural account of assisted conception* (London: Routledge).

—— (2000) Life itself: global nature and the genetic imaginary. In *Global nature, global culture*, by Sarah Franklin, Celia Lury and Jackie Stacey, pp. 188–227 (London: Sage).

Franklin, Sarah, Celia Lury and Jackie Stacey (2000) *Global nature, global culture* (London: Sage).

Franklin, Sarah and Susan McKinnon (eds) (Forthcoming) *Relative values: new directions in kinship studies* (Durham: Duke University Press).

Franklin, Sarah and Helena Ragoné (eds) (1998) *Reproducing reproduction: kinship, power, and technological innovation* (Philadelphia: University of Pennsylvania Press).

Friedman, Jonathan (1994) *Cultural identity and global process* (London: Sage).

Frost, Peter (1990) Fair women, dark men: the forgotten roots of colour prejudice. *History of European Ideas* 12: 669–79.

Fuss, Diana (1989) *Essentially speaking: feminism, nature and difference* (London: Routledge).

Gailey, Christine Ward (2000) Ideologies of motherhood and kinship in US adoption. In *Ideologies and technologies of motherhood: race, class, sexuality, nationalism*, edited by Helena Ragoné and France Winddance Twine, pp. 11–55 (London: Routledge).

Gasking, Elizabeth (1967) *Investigations into generation, 1651–1828* (London: Hutchinson).

Gates, Henry Louis, Jr (ed.) (1986) *'Race', writing and difference* (Chicago: University of Chicago Press).

Giddens, Anthony (1987) *Social theory and modern society* (Cambridge: Polity Press).

Gilbert, Scott F. (1995) Resurrecting the body: has postmodernism had any effect on biology? *Science in Context* 8(4): 563–77.

Gilman, Sander (1986) Black bodies, whites bodies: toward an iconography of female sexuality in late nineteenth-century art, medicine, and literature. In *'Race', writing and difference*, edited by Henry Louis Gates, Jr, pp. 223–61 (Chicago: University of Chicago Press).

Gilroy, Paul (1982) Steppin' out of Babylon: race, class and autonomy. In *The empire strikes back, race and racism in 70s Britain*, edited by the Centre for Contemporary Cultural Studies, Birmingham University (London: Hutchinson and CCCS).

—— (1987) *'There ain't no black in the Union Jack': the cultural politics of race and nation* (London: Hutchinson).

—— (1995) 'To be real': the dissident forms of black expressive culture. In *Let's get it on: the politics of black performance*, edited by Catherine Ugwu, pp. 12–33 (London and Seattle: Institute of Contemporary Arts and Bay Press).

Glacken, Clarence J. (1967) *Traces on the Rhodian shore: nature and culture in Western thought from ancient times to the end of the eighteenth century* (Berkeley: University of California Press).

Goldberg, David (1993) *Racist culture: philosophy and the politics of meaning* (Oxford: Blackwell).

Goodman, Alan H. and Thomas L. Leatherman (eds) (1998) Traversing the chasm between biology and culture: an introduction. In *Building a new biocultural synthesis: political-economic perspectives on human biology*, edited by Alan H. Goodman and Thomas L. Leatherman, pp. 3–42 (Ann Arbor: University of Michigan Press).

Gould, Stephen J. (1981) *The mismeasure of man* (New York: W.W. Norton).

Greene, John C. (1959) *The death of Adam: evolution and its impact on Western thought* (Ames: Iowa State University Press).

—— (1984) *American science in the age of Jefferson* (Ames: Iowa State University Press).

—— (1989) Afterword. In *History, humanity and evolution: essays for John C. Greene*, edited by James R. Moore, pp. 403–13 (Cambridge: Cambridge University Press).

Gregory, Steven and Roger Sanjek (eds) (1994) *Race* (New Brunswick: Rutgers University Press).

Guillaumin, Colette (1995) *Racism, sexism, power and ideology* (London: Routledge).

Hale, Charles R. (ed.) (1996) Mestizaje. Special issue of *Journal of Latin American Anthropology* 2(1).

Hall, Stuart (1980) Race, articulation and societies structured in dominance. In *Sociological theories: race and colonialism*, edited by UNESCO (Paris: UNESCO).

—— (1991) Old and new identities, old and new ethnicities. In *Culture, globalization and the world system*, edited by Anthony D. King, pp. 41–68 (London: Macmillan).

—— (1992a) Identity and the black photographic image. *Ten.8* 2(3). Special issue, *Critical decade: black British photography in the 80s*, pp. 24–31.

—— (1992b) The question of cultural identity. In *Modernity and its futures*, edited by S. Hall, D. Held and T. McGrew, pp. 273–326 (Cambridge: Polity Press).

—— (1996a) The after-life of Frantz Fanon. Why Fanon? Why now? Why *Black Skin, White Masks?* In *The fact of blackness: Frantz Fanon and visual representation*, edited by Alan Read, pp. 12–37 (London: Institute of Contemporary Arts).

—— (1996b) Gramsci's relevance for the study of race and ethnicity. In *Stuart Hall: critical dialogues in cultural studies*, edited by David Morley and Kuan-Hsing Chen, pp. 411–40 (London: Routledge).

—— (1996c) The problem of ideology: marxism without guarantees. In *Stuart Hall: critical dialogues in cultural studies*, edited by David Morley and Kuan-Hsing Chen, pp. 25–46 (London: Routledge).

Hall, Stuart and Paul du Gay (eds) (1996) *Questions of cultural identity* (London: Sage).

Hammond, Evelyn M. (1997) New technologies of race. In *Processed lives: gender and technology in everyday life*, edited by Jennifer Terry and Melodie Calvert, pp. 108–21 (London: Routledge).

Hanchard, Michael (ed.) (1999) *Racial politics in contemporary Brazil* (Durham: Duke University Press).

Hannerz, Ulf (1980) *Exploring the city: inquiries toward an urban anthropology* (New York: Columbia University Press).

Haraway, Donna (1989) *Primate visions: gender, race and nature in the world of modern science* (London: Routledge).

—— (1991) *Simians, cyborgs and women: the re-invention of nature* (London: Free Association Books).

—— (1997) *Modest_Witness@Second_Millennium.FemaleMan©_Meets_Oncomouse, Feminism and Technoscience* (London: Routledge).

Harris, Marvin (1974) *Patterns of race in the Americas* (New York: Norton Library).

Harris, Shanette M. (1995) Family, self, and sociocultural contributions to body-image attitudes of African-American women. *Psychology of Women Quarterly* 19: 129–45.

Harrison, Faye V. (1992) The Du Boisian legacy in anthropology. *Critique of Anthropology* 12(3): 239–60.

—— (1995) The persistent power of race in the cultural and political economy of racism. *Annual Review of Anthropology* 24: 47–74.

—— (1998) Introduction: expanding the discourse on race. *American Anthropologist* 100(3): 609–31.

Harrison, Ira E. and Faye V. Harrison (eds) (1999) *African American pioneers in anthropology* (Urbana: University of Illinois Press).

Harrison, Louis, Jr (1995) African Americans: race as a self-schema affecting physical activity choices. *Quest* 47: 7–18.

Hartouni, Valerie (1997) *Cultural conceptions: on reproductive technologies and the remaking of life* (Minneapolis: University of Minnesota Press).

Hayden, Corinne P. (1995) Gender, genetics and generation: reformulating biology in lesbian kinship. *Cultural Anthropology* 10(1): 41–63.

Herrnstein, Robert and Charles Murray (1994) *The Bell curve: intelligence and class structure in American life* (New York: Free Press).

Hinde, Robert (1987) *Individuals, relationships and culture: links between ethology and the social sciences* (Cambridge: Cambridge University Press).

—— (1991) A biologist looks at anthropology. *Man* 26(4): 583–608.

Hirschfeld, Lawrence A. (1996) *Race in the making: cognition, culture and the child's construction of human kinds* (Cambridge, Mass.: MIT Press).

—— (1997) The conceptual politics of race: lessons from our children. *Ethos* 25(1): 63–92.

Hodgen, Margaret T. (1964) *Early anthropology in the sixteenth and seventeenth centuries* (Philadelphia: University of Pennsylvania Press).

Hollinger, David A. (1997) The disciplines and the identity debates, 1970–1995. *Daedalus* 126(1): 333–51.

Honour, Hugh (1989) *The image of the black in Western art.* Vol 4, *From the American Revolution to World War I.* Part 2, *Black models and white myths* (Houston: Menil Foundation).

hooks, bell (1981) *Ain't I a woman? Black women and feminism* (London: Pluto Press).

—— (1991) *Yearning: race, gender and cultural politics* (London: Turnaround).

—— (1992) *Black looks: race and representation* (Boston: South End Press).

Howell, Signe (Forthcoming) Self-conscious kinship: some contested values in transnational adoption. In *Relative values: new directions in kinship studies,* edited by Sarah Franklin and Susan McKinnon (Durham: Duke University Press).

Huet, Marie-Hélène (1993) *Monstrous imagination* (Cambridge, Mass.: Harvard University Press).

Hughes, Diane (1997) Racist thinking and thinking about race: what children know but don't say. *Ethos* 25(1): 117–25.

Hutnyk, John (1996) Adorno at Womad: South Asian crossovers and the limits of hybridity-talk. In *Debating cultural hybridity: multi-cultural identities and the politics of anti-racism,* edited by Pnina Werbner and Tariq Modood, pp. 106–36 (London: Zed Books).

Hyatt, Vera Lawrence and Rex Nettleford (eds) (1995) *Race, discourse and the origin of the Americas: a new world view* (Washington: Smithsonian Institution Press).

Ingold, Tim (1986) *Evolution and social life* (Cambridge: Cambridge University Press).

—— (1990) An anthropologist looks at biology. *Man* 25(2): 208–29.

—— (1995) Building, dwelling, living: how animals and people make themselves at home in the world. In *Shifting contexts: transformations in anthropological knowledge,* edited by Marilyn Strathern, pp. 57–80 (London: Routledge).

—— (2000a) *The perception of the environment: essays in livelihood, dwelling and skill* (London: Routledge).

—— (2000b) The poverty of selectionism. *Anthropology Today* 16(3): 1–2.

Ingold, Tim, Marilyn Strathern, John Peel, Christina Toren and Jonathan Spencer (1996) The concept of society is obsolete. In *Key debates in anthropology,* edited by Tim Ingold, pp. 55–98 (London: Routledge).

Jahoda, Gustav (1992) *Crossroads between culture and mind: continuities and change in theories of human nature* (Cambridge, Mass.: Harvard University Press).

Jardine, Nicholas (1996) *Naturphilosophie* and the kingdoms of nature. In *Cultures of natural history,* edited by N. Jardine, J.A. Secord and E.C. Spary, pp. 230–45 (Cambridge: Cambridge University Press).

Jenkins, Richard (1997) *Rethinking ethnicity: arguments and explorations* (London: Sage).

Jensen, Arthur (1969) How much can we boost IQ and scholastic achievement? *Harvard Educational Review* 39(1): 1–123.

Johnson, Charles (1993) A phenomenology of the black body. *Michigan Quarterly Review* 32(4): 599–614.

Jones, Simon (1988) *Black culture, white youth: the reggae tradition from JA to UK* (Basingstoke: Macmillan Education).

Jones, Steve (1997) *In the blood: God, genes and destiny* (London: Flamingo).

Jordan, Winthrop (1977) *White over black: American attitudes toward the Negro, 1550–1812* (New York: W.W. Norton).

Jordanova, Ludmilla (1984) *Lamarck* (Oxford: Oxford University Press).

—— (ed.) (1986a) *Languages of nature: critical essays on science and literature* (London: Free Association Books).

—— (1986b) Introduction. In *Languages of nature: critical essays on science and literature*, edited by Ludmilla Jordanova, pp. 15–47 (London: Free Association Books).

—— (1986c) Naturalizing the family: literature and the bio-medical sciences in the late eighteenth century. In *Languages of nature: critical essays on science and literature*, edited by Ludmilla Jordanova, pp. 86–116 (London: Free Association Books).

—— (1987) *Sexual visions: images of gender in science and medicine between the eighteenth and twentieth centuries* (London: Harvester Wheatsheaf).

Kahn, Susan Martha (2000) *Reproducing Jews: a cultural account of assisted conception in Israel* (Durham: Duke University Press).

Kandel, Eric R. (1998) A new intellectual framework for psychiatry. *American Journal of Psychiatry* 155(4): 457–69.

Keller, Evelyn Fox (1995) *Refiguring life: metaphors of twentieth-century biology* (New York: Columbia University Press).

Kevles, Daniel J. (1995) *In the name of eugenics: genetics and the uses of human heredity*. 2nd edn (Cambridge, Mass.: Harvard University Press).

Keyes, Charles (1976) Towards a new formulation of the concept of ethnic group. *Ethnicity* 3: 202–13.

Knowles, Caroline and Sharmila Mercer (1992) Feminism and antiracism: an exploration of the political possibilities. In *'Race', culture difference*, edited by James Donald and Ali Rattansi, pp. 104–26 (London: Sage).

Knox, Robert (1850) *The races of men: a fragment* (London: Henry Renshaw).

Koenig, Barbara A. and Patricia A. Marshall (1999) Deploying 'race', 'ethnicity' and 'culture' in the new molecular medicine. Paper given in the panel 'Performing Race in the Crisis of the Medical Moment', 98th Annual Meeting of the American Anthropological Association, 17–21 November 1999.

Kohn, Marek (1995) *The race gallery: the return of racial science* (London: Jonathan Cape).

Kulick, Don (1998) *Travesti: sex, gender, and culture among Brazilian transgendered prostitutes* (Chicago: University of Chicago Press).

Lal, Barbara Ballis (1986) The 'Chicago School' of American sociology, symbolic interactionism and race relations theory. In *Theories of race and ethnic relations*, edited by John Rex and David Mason, pp. 280–98 (Cambridge: Cambridge University Press).

—— (1990) *The romance of culture in an urban civilization: Robert E. Park on race and ethnic relations in cities* (London: Routledge).

Lambek, Michael and Andrew Strathern (1998) *Bodies and persons: comparative perspectives from Africa and Melanesia* (Cambridge: Cambridge University Press).

Landry, Donna and Gerald MacLean (1993) *Materialist feminisms* (Oxford: Blackwell).

Laqueur, Thomas (1990) *Making sex: body and gender from the Greeks to Freud* (Cambridge, Mass.: Harvard University Press).

Larson, James L. (1979) Vital forces: regulative principles or constitutive agents: a strategy in German physiology, 1786–1802. *Isis* 70: 235–49.

Latour, Bruno (1993) *We have never been modern*, translated by Catherine Porter (London: Harvester Wheatsheaf).

Lave, Jean, P. Duguid, N. Fernandez, E. Axel (1992) Coming of age in Birmingham: cultural studies and conceptions of subjectivity. *Annual Review of Anthropology* 21: 257–82.

Lawrence, Errol (1982) In the abundance of water the fool is thirsty: sociology and black 'pathology'. In *The empire strikes back: race and racism in 70s Britain*, edited by Centre for Contemporary Cultural Studies, Birmingham University pp. 95–142 (London: Hutchinson and CCCS).

Lewis, Laura A. (2000) Blacks, black Indians, Afromexicans: the dynamics of race, nation, and identity in a Mexican *moreno* community (Guerrero). *American Ethnologist* 27(4): 898–926.

Lieberman, Leonard and Larry T. Reynolds (1996) Race: the deconstruction of a scientific concept. In _Race and other misadventures: essays in honor of Ashley Montagu in his ninetieth year_, edited by L.T. Reynolds and L. Lieberman, pp. 142–73 (Dix Hills, N.Y.: General Hall Inc.).

Linke, Uli (1997) Gendered difference, violent imagination: blood, race, nation. _American Anthropologist_ 99 (3): 559–73.

—— (1999) _Blood and nation: the European aesthetics of race_ (Philadelphia: University of Pennsylvania Press).

Lipsitz, George (1994) _Dangerous crossroads: popular music, postmodernism and the poetics of place_ (London: Verso).

Lock, Margaret (1998) Breast cancer: reading the omens. _Anthropology Today_ 14(4): 7–16.

Loizos, Peter and Patrick Heady (eds) (1999) _Conceiving persons: ethnographies of procreation, fertility and growth_ (London: Athlone).

Lovejoy, Arthur (1948) _Essays in the history of ideas_ (Baltimore: Johns Hopkins University Press).

—— (1964) _The great chain of being: a study in the history of an idea_. 2nd edn (Cambridge, Mass.: Harvard University Press).

Lovejoy, Arthur and George Boas (1965) _Primitivism and related ideas in antiquity_. 2nd edn (New York: Octagon Books).

Low, Gail Ching-Liang (1996) _White skins/black masks: representation and colonialism_ (London: Routledge).

Lubinsky, Mark S. (1993) Degenerate heredity: the history of a doctrine in medicine and biology. _Perspectives in Biology and Medicine_ 37(1): 74–90.

Lury, Celia (2000) The united colours of diversity: essential and inessential culture. In _Global nature, global culture_, by Sarah Franklin, Celia Lury and Jackie Stacey, pp. 146–87 (London: Sage).

Mac an Ghaill, Máirtín (1992) Coming of age in 1980s England: reconceptualizing black students' schooling experience. In _Racism and education: structures and strategies_, edited by Dawn Gill, Barbara Mayor and Maud Blair, pp. 42–58 (London: Sage).

MacCormack, Carol and Marilyn Strathern (eds) (1980) _Nature, culture and gender_ (Cambridge: Cambridge University Press).

Makkar, Jalmeen K. and Michael J. Strube (1995) Black women's self-perceptions of attractiveness following exposure to white versus black beauty standards: the moderating role of racial identity and self-esteem. _Journal of Applied Social Psychology_ 25(17): 1547–66.

Marable, Manning (1995) _Beyond black and white_ (London: Verso).

Martin, Emily (1989) _The woman in the body_ (Milton Keynes: Open University Press).

Martinez-Alier, Verena (1974) _Marriage, colour and class in nineteenth-century Cuba_ (Cambridge: Cambridge University Press).

Mayr, Ernst (1982) _The growth of biological thought: diversity, evolution and inheritance_ (Cambridge, Mass.: The Belknap Press of Harvard University Press).

McClintock, Anne (1993) Family feuds: gender, nationalism and the family. _Feminist Review_ 44: 61–80.

—— (1995) _Imperial leather: race, gender and sexuality in the colonial contest_ (London: Routledge).

Meek, Ronald (1976) _Social science and the ignoble savage_ (Cambridge: Cambridge University Press).

Miles, Robert (1989) _Racism_ (London: Routledge).

—— (1993) _Racism after 'race relations'_ (London: Routledge).

Modell, Judith (1986) In search: the purported biological basis of parenthood. _American Ethnologist_ 13(4): 646–61.

—— (1994) _Kinship with strangers: adoption and interpretation of kinship in America_ (Berkeley: University of California Press).

Modood, Tariq and Pnina Werbner (eds) (1997) _The politics of multiculturalism in the new Europe: racism, identity and community_ (London: Zed Books).

Mogdil, Sohan and Celia Mogdil (eds) (1986) *Hans Eysenck: consensus and controversy* (London: Falmer Press).

—— (eds) (1987) *Arthur Jensen: consensus and controversy* (London: Falmer Press).

Moore, Henrietta (1994a) *A passion for difference* (Cambridge: Polity Press).

—— (1994b) Understanding sex and gender. In *Companion encyclopaedia of anthropology: humanity, culture and social life*, edited by Tim Ingold, pp. 813–30 (London: Routledge).

Moore, Robin (1997) *Nationalizing blackness: afrocubanismo and artistic revolution in Havana, 1920–1940* (Pittsburgh: University of Pittsburgh Press).

Mörner, Magnus (1967) *Race mixture in the history of Latin America* (Boston: Little Brown).

Mosse, George (1985) *Nationalism and sexuality: respectability and abnormal sexuality in modern Europe* (New York: Howard Fertig).

Mukhopadhyay, Carol C. and Yolanda T. Moses (1997) Reestablishing 'race' in anthropological discourse *American Anthropolgist* 99(3): 517–33.

Nederveen Pieterse, Jan (1992) *White on black: images of Africa and blacks in Western popular culture* (New Haven: Yale University Press).

Nelkin, Dorothy and Susan Lindee (1995a) *The DNA mystique: the gene as cultural icon* (New York: W.H. Freeman).

—— (1995b) The media-ted gene: stories of race and gender. In *Deviant bodies: critical perspectives on science and popular culture*, edited by Jennifer Terry and Jacqueline Urla, pp. 387–402 (Bloomington: Indiana University Press).

Omi, Michael and Howard Winant (1994) *Racial formation in the United States: from the 1960s to the 1990s*. 2nd edn (London: Routledge).

Oths, Kathryn S. (1999) Who's who in southern pre-natal clinics. Paper given in the panel 'Performing Race in the Crisis of the Medical Moment', 98th Annual Meeting of the American Anthropological Association, 17–21 November 1999.

Page, Helán E. (1997) 'Black male' imagery and media containment of African American men. *American Anthropologist* 99(1): 99–111.

Parker, Andrew, *et al.* (eds) (1992) *Nationalisms and sexualities* (London: Routledge).

Paul, Diane B. (1995) *Controlling human heredity: 1865 to the present* (Atlantic Highlands, N.J.: Humanities Press).

Pearson, Veronica (1972) Telegony: a study of this belief and its continued existence. Unpublished MSc dissertation, University of Bristol.

Pilkington, A.E. (1986) Nature as ethical norm in the Enlightenment. In *Languages of nature: critical essays on science and literature*, edited by Ludmilla Jordanova, pp. 51–85 (London: Free Association Books).

Popkin, Richard H. (1973) The philosophical basis of eighteenth-century racism. In *Racism in the eighteenth century*, edited by Harold E. Pagliaro, pp. 245–62 (Cleveland: The Press of Case Western Reserve University).

Rabinow, Paul (1992) Artificiality and the enlightenment: from sociobiology to biosociality. In *Incorporations*, edited by J. Crary and S. Kwinter, pp. 234–52 (New York: Zone).

Ragoné, Helena (1994) *Surrogate motherhood: conception in the heart* (Boulder: Westview Press).

—— (1996) Chasing the blood tie: surrogate mothers, adoptive mothers and fathers. *American Ethnologist* 23(2): 352–65.

—— (1998) Incontestable motivations. In *Reproducing reproduction: kinship, power, and technological innovation*, edited by Sarah Franklin and Helena Ragoné, pp. 118–31 (Philadelphia: University of Pennsylvania Press).

—— (2000) Of likeness and difference: how race is being transfigured by gestational surrogacy. In *Ideologies and technologies of motherhood: race, class, sexuality, nationalism*, edited by Helena Ragoné and France Winddance Twine, pp. 56–75 (London: Routledge).

Ragoné, Helena and France Winddance Twine (eds) (2000) *Ideologies and technologies of motherhood: race, class, sexuality, nationalism* (London: Routledge).

Rahier, Jean M. (1999) *Representations of blackness and the performance of identities* (Westport, Conn.: Greenwood Press).

Rapp, Rayna (1999) *Testing women, testing the fetus: the social impact of amniocentesis in America* (London: Routledge).

Read, Alan (ed.) (1996) *The fact of blackness: Frantz Fanon and visual representation* (London: Institute of Contemporary Arts).

Reichmann, Rebecca (ed.) (1999) *Race in contemporary Brazil: from indifference to inequality* (Philadelphia: University of Pennsylvania Press).

Rex, John (1986) *Race and ethnicity* (Milton Keynes: Open University Press).

Rex, John and David Mason (eds) (1986) *Theories of race and ethnic relations* (Cambridge: Cambridge University Press).

Reynolds, Larry T. and Leonard Lieberman (eds) (1996) *Race and other misadventures: essays in honor of Ashley Montagu in his ninetieth year* (Dix Hills, N.Y.: General Hall Inc.).

Richards, Evelleen (1989) Huxley and woman's place in science: the 'woman question' and the control of Victorian anthropology. In *History, humanity and evolution: essays for John C. Greene*, edited by James R. Moore, pp. 253–84 (Cambridge: Cambridge University Press).

Richards, Martin (1997) It runs in the family: lay knowledge about inheritance. In *Culture, kinship and genes: towards cross-cultural genetics*, edited by Angus Clarke and Evelyn Parsons, pp. 175–94 (London and New York: Macmillan and St. Martin's Press).

—— (1998) The meeting of nature and nurture and the development of children: some conclusions. In *Biosocial perspectives on children*, edited by Catherine Panter-Brick, pp. 131–46 (Cambridge: Cambridge University Press).

Ritvo, Harriet (1997) *The platypus and the mermaid and other figments of the classifying imagination* (Cambridge, Mass.: Harvard University Press).

Rony, Fatimah Tobing (1996) *The third eye: race, cinema, and ethnographic spectacle* (Durham: Duke University Press).

Schneider, David (1972) What is kinship all about? In *Kinship studies in the Morgan centennial year*, edited by Priscilla Reining, pp. 32–63 (Washington: The Anthropological Society of Washington).

—— (1977) Kinship, nationality and religion in American culture: toward a definition of kinship. In *Symbolic anthropology*, edited by J. Dolgin, D. Kemnitzer and D. Schneider, pp. 63–71 (New York: Columbia University Press).

—— (1980) *American kinship: a cultural account*. 2nd edn (Chicago: University of Chicago Press).

—— (1984) *A critique of the study of kinship* (Ann Arbor: University of Michigan Press).

Shanklin, Eugenia (1994) *Anthropology and race* (Belmont, CA: Wadsworth Publishing).

—— (1998) The profession of the color blind: sociocultural anthropology and racism in the 21st century. *American Anthropologist* 100(3): 669–79.

Shilling, Chris (1991) Educating the body: physical capital and the production of social inequalities. *Sociology* 25(4): 653–72.

—— (1993) *The body and social theory* (London: Sage).

Simpson, Bob (2000) Imagined genetic communities: ethnicity and essentialism in the twenty-first century. *Anthropology Today* 16(3): 3–6.

Sloan, Phillip R. (1973) The idea of racial degeneracy in Buffon's *Histoire Naturelle*. In *Racism in the eighteenth century*, edited by Harold E. Pagliaro, pp. 293–322 (Cleveland: The Press of Case Western Reserve University).

Smedley, Audrey (1993) *Race in North America: origin and evolution of a worldview* (Boulder: Westview Press).

—— (1998) Race and the construction of human identity. *American Anthropologist* 100(3): 690–702.

Smith, Carol A. (1996) Race/class/gender ideology in Guatemala: modern and anti-modern forms. In *Women out of place: the gender of agency and the race of nationality*, edited by Brackette Williams, pp. 50–78 (London: Routledge).

—— (1997) The symbolics of blood: *mestizaje* in the Americas. *Identities* 3(4): 495–521.

Snowden, Frank M. (1983) *Before colour prejudice: the ancient view of blacks* (Cambridge, Mass.: Harvard University Press).

Snowden, Robert, G.D. Mitchell and E.M. Snowden (1983) *Artificial reproduction: a social investigation* (London: Allen and Unwin).

Solomos, John (1986) Varieties of Marxist conceptions of 'race', class and the state: a critical analysis. In *Theories of race and ethnic relations*, edited by John Rex and David Mason (Cambridge: Cambridge University Press).

—— (1989) *Race and racism in contemporary Britain* (London: Macmillan).

Soper, Kate (1995) *What is nature? Culture, politics and the non-human* (Oxford: Blackwell).

Spary, Emma (1996) Political, natural and bodily economies. In *Cultures of natural history*, edited by N. Jardine, J.A. Secord and E.C. Spary, pp. 178–96 (Cambridge: Cambridge University Press).

Stepan, Nancy Leys (1982) *The idea of race in science: Great Britain, 1800–1960* (London: Macmillan in association with St Antony's College, Oxford).

—— (1991) *'The hour of eugenics': race, gender and nation in Latin America* (Ithaca, N.Y.: Cornell University Press).

Stevenson, Leslie (1987) *Seven theories of human nature.* 2nd edn (Oxford: Oxford University Press).

Stocking, George (1971) What's in a name? The origins of the Royal Anthropological Institute (1837–1871). *Man* 6: 369–90.

—— (1982) *Race, culture and evolution: essays on the history of anthropology.* 2nd edn (Chicago: University of Chicago Press).

Stolcke, Verena (1993) Is sex to gender as race is to ethnicity? In *Gendered anthropology*, edited by Teresa del Valle (London: Routledge).

—— (1995) Talking culture: new boundaries, new rhetorics of exclusion in Europe. *Current Anthropology* 36(1): 1–23.

Stoler, Ann Laura (1992) Sexual affronts and racial frontiers: European identities and the cultural politics of exclusion in colonial Southeast Asia. *Comparative Studies in Society and History*, 34(3): 514–51.

—— (1995) *Race and the education of desire: Foucault's 'History of Sexuality' and the colonial order of things* (Durham: Duke University Press).

—— (1997a) On political and psychological essentialisms. *Ethos* 25(1): 101–6.

—— (1997b) Racial histories and their regimes of truth. *Political Power and Social Theory* 11: 183–220.

Strathern, Marilyn (1992a) *After nature: English kinship in the late twentieth century* (Cambridge: Cambridge University Press).

—— (1992b) *Reproducing the future: anthropology, kinship and the new reproductive technologies* (Manchester: Manchester University Press).

—— (1996) Cutting the network. *Journal of the Royal Anthropological Institute* 2(3): 571–635.

Streicker, Joel (1995) Policing boundaries: race, class, and gender in Cartagena, Colombia. *American Ethnologist* 22(1): 54–74.

—— (1997) Spatial reconfigurations, imagined geographies, and social conflicts in Cartagena, Colombia. *Cultural Anthropology* 12(1): 109–28.

Stubbe, Hans (1972) *History of genetics: from prehistoric times to the rediscovery of Mendel's laws*, translated by T.R.W. Waters (Cambridge, Mass.: MIT Press).

Tapper, Melbourne (1995) Bodies: medico-racial knowledge, politics and the study of disease. *Comparative Studies in Society and History* 37: 76–93.

—— (1997) An 'anthropathology' of the 'American Negro': anthropology, genetics and the new racial science, 1940–52. *Social History of Medicine* 10(2): 263–89.

Teman, Elly (2000) Surrogate motherhood in Israel. Unpublished MSc dissertation. Department of Sociology and Anthropology, Hebrew University of Jerusalem.

Theunissen, Bert (1994) Knowledge is power: Hugo de Vries on science, heredity and social progress. *British Journal for the History of Science* 27: 291–311.

Thompson, Charis (Forthcoming) Strategic naturalizing: kinship in an infertility clinic. In *Relative values: new directions in kinship studies*, edited by Sarah Franklin and Susan McKinnon (Durham: Duke University Press).

Titmuss, Richard M. (1973) *The gift relationship: from human blood to social policy* (London: Penguin Books).

Tizard, Barbara and Ann Phoenix (1993) *Black, white or mixed race? Race and racism in the lives of young people of mixed parentage* (London: Routledge).

Todorov, Tzvetan (1993) *On human diversity: nationalism, racism and exoticism in French thought* (Cambridge, Mass.: Harvard University Press).

Toren, Christina (1993) Making history: the significance of childhood cognition for a comparative anthropology of mind. *Man* 28(3): 461–78.

Trigg, Roger (1988) *Ideas of human nature: an historical introduction* (Oxford: Blackwell).

Turner, Bryan (1984) *The body and society: explorations in social theory* (Oxford: Blackwell).

Turner, Terence (1994) Bodies and anti-bodies: flesh and fetish in contemporary social theory. In *Embodiment and experience: the existential ground of culture and the self*, edited by Thomas Csordas, pp. 27–47 (Cambridge: Cambridge University Press).

Turney, Jon (1998) *Frankenstein's footsteps: science, genetics and popular culture* (New Haven: Yale University Press).

Twine, France Winddance (1998) *Racism in a racial democracy: the maintenance of white supremacy in Brazil* (New Brunswick: Rutgers University Press).

—— (2000) Bearing blackness in Britain: the meaning of racial difference for white birth mothers of African-descent children. In *Ideologies and technologies of motherhood: race, class, sexuality, nationalism*, edited by Helena Ragoné and France Winddance Twine, pp. 76–108 (London: Routledge).

Tyler, Katharine (2000) White hegemony in Leicestershire: race, nation, place and class. Unpublished PhD dissertation, University of Manchester.

Ugwu, Catherine (ed.) (1995) *Let's get it on: the politics of black performance* (London and Seattle: Institute of Contemporary Arts and Bay Press).

Ulin, Robert (1991) Critical anthropology twenty years later: modernism and postmodernism in anthropology. *Critique of Anthropology* 11(1): 63–90.

Van den Berghe, Pierre (1981) *The ethnic phenomenon* (New York: Elsevier).

Van Dijck, José (1998) *Imagenation: popular images of genes* (London: Macmillan).

Vialles, Noëlle (1994) *From animal to edible* (Cambridge: Cambridge University Press).

Wade, Peter (1985) Race and class: the case of South American blacks. *Ethnic and Racial Studies* 8(2): 233–49.

—— (1993a) *Blackness and race mixture: the dynamics of racial identity in Colombia* (Baltimore: Johns Hopkins University Press).

—— (1993b) 'Race', nature and culture. *Man* 28(1): 1–18.

—— (1995) The cultural politics of blackness in Colombia. *American Ethnologist* 22(2): 342–58.

—— (1997) *Race and ethnicity in Latin America* (London: Pluto Press).

—— (1999a) The guardians of power: biodiversity and multiculturality in Colombia. In *The anthropology of power: empowerment and disempowerment in changing structures*, edited by Angela Cheater, pp. 73–87 (London: Routledge).

—— (1999b) Working culture: making cultural identities in Cali, Colombia. *Current Anthropology* 40(4): 449–71.

—— (2000) *Music, 'race' and nation: música tropical in Colombia* (Chicago: University of Chicago Press).

Wagley, Charles (ed.) (1952) *Race and class in rural Brazil* (Paris: UNESCO).

Watson, James Lee (ed.) (1997) *Between two cultures: migrants and minorities in Britain* (Oxford: Blackwell).

Weiner, Michael (1995) Discourses of race, nation and empire in pre-1945 Japan. *Ethnic and Racial Studies* 18(3): 433–56.

Weismantel, Mary (2001) *Cholas and pishtacos: stories of race and sex in the Andes* (Chicago: University of Chicago Press).

Werbner, Pnina (1997) Essentialising essentialism: ambivalence and multiplicity in the constructions of racism and ethnicity. In *Debating cultural hybridity: multi-cultural identities and the politics of anti-racism*, edited by Pnina Werbner and Tariq Modood, pp. 226–54 (London: Zed Books).

Werbner, Pnina and Muhammad Anwar (eds) (1991) *Black and ethnic leaderships in Britain: the cultural dimension of political action* (London: Routledge).

Werbner, Pnina and Tariq Modood (eds) (1997) *Debating cultural hybridity: multi-cultural identities and the politics of anti-racism* (London: Zed Books).

Weston, Kath (1991) *Families we choose: lesbians, gays, kinship* (New York: Columbia University Press).

—— (Forthcoming) Kinship, controversy and the sharing of substance: the race/class politics of blood transfusion. In *Relative values: new directions in kinship studies*, edited by Sarah Franklin and Susan McKinnon (Durham: Duke University Press).

Wetherell, Margaret and Jonathan Potter (1992) *Mapping the language of racism: discourse and the legitimation of power* (London: Harvester Wheatsheaf).

Whitten, Norman (1986) *Black frontiersmen: a South American case.* 2nd edn (Prospect Heights, Illinois: Waveland Press).

—— (ed.) (1981) *Cultural transformations and ethnicity in modern Ecuador* (Urbana: University of Illinois Press).

Whitten, Norman and Arlene Torres (1998) General introduction: to forge the future in the fires of the past: an interpretive essay on racism, domination, resistance, and liberation. In *Blackness in Latin America and the Caribbean: social dynamics and cultural transformations*, Vol. 1, edited by Norman Whitten and Arlene Torres, pp. 3–33 (Bloomington: Indiana University Press).

Wieviorka, Michel (1995) *The arena of racism* (London: Sage).

—— (1997) Is it so difficult to be anti-racist? In *Debating cultural hybridity: multi-cultural identities and the politics of anti-racism*, edited by Pnina Werbner and Tariq Modood, pp. 139–53 (London: Zed Books).

Williams, Brackette (1989) A class act: anthropology and the race to nation across ethnic terrain. *Annual Review of Anthropology* 18: 401–44.

—— (1991) *Stains on my name, war in my veins: Guyana and the politics of cultural struggle* (Durham: Duke University Press).

—— (1995) Classification systems revisited: kinship, caste, race and nationality as the flow of blood and the spread of rights. In *Naturalizing power: essays in feminist cultural analysis*, edited by Sylvia Yanagisako and Carol Delaney, pp. 201–36 (London: Routledge).

—— (ed.) (1996a) *Women out of place: the gender of agency and the race of nationality* (London: Routledge).

—— (1996b) Introduction: mannish women and gender after the act. In *Women out of place: the gender of agency and the race of nationality*, edited by Brackette Williams, pp. 1–33 (London: Routledge).

—— (1996c) A race of men, a class of women: nation, ethnicity, gender and domesticity among Afro-Guyanese. In *Women out of place: the gender of agency and the race of nationality*, edited by Brackette Williams, pp. 129–58 (London: Routledge).

Williams, Raymond (1988) *Keywords: a vocabulary of culture and society* (London: Fontana).

Winant, Howard (1992) Rethinking race in Brazil. *Journal of Latin American Studies* 24: 173–92.

—— (1993) Difference and inequality: postmodern racial politics in the United States. In *Racism, the city and the state*, edited by M. Cross and M. Keith (London: Routledge).

Woodward, Kathryn (ed.) (1997) *Identity and difference* (London: Sage in association with the Open University).

Yanagisako, Sylvia and Carol Delaney (eds) (1995) Naturalizing power. In *Naturalizing power: essays in feminist cultural analysis*, edited by Sylvia Yanagisako and Carol Delaney, pp. 1–22 (London: Routledge).

Young, Robert J. (1995) *Colonial desire: hybridity in theory, culture and race* (London: Routledge).

Young, Robert M. (1995) *Whatever happened to human nature?* (London: Process Press Paperback) (Available on-line at <http://human-nature.com/rmyoung/papers/paper56.html >.)

Yuval-Davis, Nira and Floya Anthias (eds) (1989) *Woman-nation-state* (New York: St. Martin's Press).

Zack, Naomi (ed.) (1997) *Race/sex: their sameness, difference and interplay* (London: Routledge).

INDEX

Note: Authors are cited if quoted or discussed in the text, but not if only cited.